KATY

Access for Success

> Making Inclusion Work for Language Learners

Pearson

Pearson Canada Inc., 26 Prince Andrew Place, North York, Ontario M3C 2H4.

ISBN 978-0-13-463271-1

1 17

Printed and bound in the United States of America

Publisher: Lise Tremblay
Marketing Manager: Barbara Mlotek
Managing Editor: Joanne Close
Developmental Editor: Cathy Fraccaro
Project Manager, Editorial: Lisa Dimson
Copy Editor: Katherine Revington
Proofreader: Linda Jenkins
Permissions Research: Rachel Irwin and Integra Publishing Services
Project Manager, Permissions: Joanne Tang
Manager, Project Management K–12: Alison Dale
Cover Design: David Cheung
Cover Photo: Marc Romanelli/Blend Images/Getty Images
Interior Design: David Cheung
Composition: Cenveo Publisher Services
Vice-President, Product Development: Mark Cobham
Director, Professional Services: Chris Allen

Pearson

Table of Contents

CHAPTER 7

CHAPTER 8

CHAPTER 9

Acknowledgements

First, we want to thank the Second Language Research Institute of Canada (L_2RIC), housed within the Faculty of Education at the University of New Brunswick, for supporting the research initiatives upon which parts of this book are built. A sincere thank you goes out to our L_2RIC colleagues and, in particular, to Dr. Joseph Dicks, director of L_2RIC, for their ongoing support and encouragement. We also gratefully acknowledge the support of the Department of Canadian Heritage, Government of Canada.

We had the privilege of working with wonderful Immersion teachers from the Anglophone West School District in New Brunswick. These teachers graciously participated in an action research project with us, and together we explored the implementation process of Universal Language Actions in L2 classrooms. Our thanks go to these individuals:

Julie Beyea	Denise Bullock	Sylvie Gagnon
Tarah Gauvin	Naomi Harvey	Sarah Jenkins
Kim Kertson	Stephanie Mackey-McCarthy	Ann Manderson
Peter Manson	Nathalie Michaud	Marie-Josée Paulin
Claudia Phillips	Rebecca Piercy	Chantal Samson
Danielle Toner	Jonathan Wilson	

A special thank you goes to Kathy Hennessey, who studied the concept of Universal Language Actions as part of her graduate work with us here at the University of New Brunswick. For sure, her research contributions have benefited and will continue to benefit second language learners.

Our research initiatives could not even have gone ahead without the unwavering support of the Anglophone West School District. Special thanks go to Dianne Kay (Director of Curriculum and Instruction), Chantale Cloutier and Amanda Desveaux (FSL subject coordinators), Shawna Allen-VanderToorn (EAL subject coordinator), and Léo-James Lévesque (former FSL subject coordinator). We greatly appreciate how they value the role research plays in continuing to move second language education forward.

Thanks also go to the teachers of Anglophone North, South, and East districts who joined in several conversations about the protocol found at the end of this book.

Finally, we would like to thank Sylvie Arseneau from the New Brunswick Department of Education and Early Childhood Development for understanding and supporting our vision for this work. Sylvie provided the support to take some of these discussions with teachers province wide, which enhanced the richness of our understandings and the quality of what we have produced.

In closing, we reaffirm our personal and professional commitments to inclusive language education. Though we are both motivated to support as many teachers and students as possible through our work, our greatest inspiration comes from two young language learners in our lives: Huxton (Katy) and Mikael (Renée). May they—and all learners—have the opportunity to explore and learn as many languages as they want!

REVIEWERS

Michelle De Abreu
Second Language Consultant
Institute for Innovation in Second Language Education
Edmonton Public Schools
Alberta

Shawna Allen-VanderToorn
Subject Coordinator
Anglophone West School District
New Brunswick

Edie Bovey
Coordinator of Curriculum and Staff Development
Algonquin and Lakeshore CDSB
Ontario

Lesley Doell
Facilitatrice et accompagnatrice pédagogique de l'immersion française
Divisional French Immersion Instructional Coach and Facilitator
Conseil scolaire Foothills
Alberta

Michael Green
French as a Second Language Teacher (Immersion and Core)
Galt Collegiate Institute
Waterloo Region District School Board
Ontario

Léo-James Lévesque
Assistant Professor
FSL Methodology Specialist and Coordinator of Field Placements
School of Education, St. Thomas University
New Brunswick

Lorraine Richard
FSL Consultant
Ontario

Caroline Roux
Mentor en littératie pour le programme d'immersion française
Yellowknife Education District 1
Northwest Territories

Introduction

Over the course of the last three decades in education, one of the most prominent guiding principles and philosophies for instruction to emerge has been inclusion. Within second language education, the term *inclusion* has never been broader than it is today. Nor has there ever been a greater need to emphasize inclusion. As teachers working with language learners, we recognize that over time our classes have become more and more diverse. Our students do not all learn a second language in the same way or at the same rate. Moreover, we are more than likely working with students with various learning needs (e.g., difficulties, specific learning disabilities, giftedness). We work with students from different cultural, educational, or language backgrounds, as well as students who have socio-affective needs. We work with "double" language learners: newcomers to the country or, perhaps, students who have heritage ties to a language, but not any knowledge of that language. All this has led us to recognize that offering professional learning opportunities about inclusion within second language education would be worthwhile. We are thankful that the publishers agreed!

We have written this book for educators working with language learners, whether or not the learners are enrolled in a specific second language program. Language learners find themselves in both our mainstream regular classes and in our second language programs. This book is designed to support language learners—that is, *all* students who are in the process of learning an additional language, whether it be their second, third, or perhaps even fourth. In other words, this book is for teachers working with *any* group of language learners.

Throughout this book, we explore different dimensions of what it means to facilitate inclusion for language learners. In our work as former classroom teachers, as teacher educators, and as researchers, we have both come to recognize that virtually all pedagogical practices and actions that pertain to facilitating an inclusive language learning environment are of benefit to all students in the class.

Access Points

We are bringing together inclusion and second language education. This book is about helping students **access** language education in a way that is consistent with their skills, experiences, needs, and goals.

What is required to make second-language learning contexts inclusive environments? In such an environment, students from various cultural, linguistic, and educational backgrounds, of different socio-economic statuses, or with a wide range of difficulties (e.g., learning disabilities, low levels of academic abilities, and behavioural challenges) can learn successfully and to the best of their abilities. We contend that access to language learning education has four different points of entry—access points, if you will. We define these points in the next section.

Access Point 1: The Foundational Knowledge of Inclusive Language Education

This book begins by considering some of the research, constructs, and philosophies that currently shape our conception of inclusion within second language education and the development of second language proficiency, in general. Since such knowledge bases can influence a teacher's beliefs and values, which, in turn, can influence actual teaching actions in the classroom, this is a logical starting point for this text.

Chapters 1 and 2 form Access Point 1.

In Access Point 1, we establish the parameters for what it means to be inclusive in language education. We also consider various contexts and expectations of language education to see how both of those dimensions may influence efforts to be inclusive in the classroom. Further, we spend some time exploring some of the myths and questions we have confronted in situations questioning the feasibility of inclusion in second language education.

Within this access point, we also look at some of the processes and expectations of language learning in general, how it differs from language acquisition, and the ways in which language development can be influenced by factors both within and beyond a teacher's direct control. We have found that having a greater understanding of what second language learning can look like can make it easier to navigate ways to support a student's efforts to develop proficiency in another language.

In Access Point 1, we aim to show the value of knowing and understanding both fundamental and specialized research and scholarly understandings of second language education. In our work thus far, we have found that an absence of these understandings has led to poor decisions about supporting inclusion within the language classroom.

Access Point 2: The Learner as a Key Player

Chapters 3 and 4 form Access Point 2.

We recognize that students play a central role in helping us facilitate inclusion within second language education. So, Access Point 2 focuses on students. Students bring with them different backgrounds and experiences to the learning process. They come to the learning situation with different mindsets and different skill sets that ultimately guide our instructional planning and delivery. We also acknowledge that language learners need to be actively involved in the learning process. We know that language learning is enhanced when learners value their role in the learning. We want to foster autonomous language learners who are capable of understanding and advocating for their own learning needs.

Access Point 3: Inclusive Pedagogies in Support of Second Language Education

Chapters 5 through 9 form Access Point 3.

Language learning becomes more accessible and the environment more inclusive when teachers deploy particular combinations of inclusive pedagogical practices. Accessing inclusive, accessible language education requires two key constructs of teaching practice: (1) Universal Language Actions and (2) differentiation and its various applications. Both have been found to facilitate language learning and allow learners to better access the target language and the curriculum.

We have often been in situations with teachers where we knew that the inclusive teaching practices we were advocating to address a specific student learning need could do more. Indeed, we were motivated to write this book because the practices or pedagogical actions we suggest to support *some* learners should be part of general classroom practices—they strongly support good language learning in general. Accessing inclusive pedagogies is crucial if every language learner is to meet his or her greatest potential.

Access Point 4: Assessment and Decision Making in Support of Inclusive Language Education

This access point is about recognizing the important role we all play, as individuals and as a collective, in supporting language learners. First, accessing inclusive second language education requires us to collect and understand information (data) about our students through good assessment practices. Good decision making that facilitates language learning for our students requires us to draw upon all our strengths as effective reflective practitioners.

Chapters 10 and 11 form Access Point 4.

Second, we recognize that we work within systems of support. It is important that, collectively, we work together to support students learning an additional language. Access to inclusive second language education is about taking the conversation within and beyond the classroom. Bringing multiple perspectives together can be incredibly beneficial for figuring out paths forward, but the process is complicated if not all stakeholders are familiar with how learning a language shapes the overall learning experience. We offer proper protocols for collecting data about our students and ideas for ongoing supports.

Closing Thoughts

We believe that access is facilitated through teacher-initiated and teacher-led actions and beliefs that are designed to open the learning experience as much as possible to as many students as possible within the class—in other words, the access allows for inclusion. Our four access points are informed by research on best practices from across the learning landscape—from general education to special education to literacy education and a few areas in between. Our job in this text will be to weave together how practices and understandings from these different sub-disciplines can be applied to support students in second-language learning settings, no matter their reason or need for studying the target language.

We hope that these four access points will help conversations about facilitating an inclusive language learning environment. We have offered them because we recognize the individual differences in all of our learning and experiences with inclusion and how those variations mean that people will want to enter such conversations in different ways. We also offer this structure as a way to demonstrate how notions of access and inclusion are multifaceted and require depth in multiple areas: (1) knowledge about the topic, (2) understanding of student needs, (3) skill with particular teaching practices, and (4) facility with conversations that require the three previous topics to be explored simultaneously.

This icon indicates that additional resources and opportunities for extended learning beyond the chapters are found on the *Access for Success* website: www.pearsoncanada.ca/afs

This resource not only describes why inclusionary approaches are needed, but also guides language teachers through the implementation process by providing specific examples as to what pedagogical actions and differentiation look like for language learners. This resource further explains favourable conditions needed for learners to succeed within second language classrooms and asks teachers to reflect on their own inclusionary teaching practices.

The need to promote second-language learning contexts as inclusive environments persists. In such environments, students of different backgrounds and experiences can maximize their talents and interests, work through challenges, and find success. We hope you find inspiration and ideas for how to make this possible in your own classrooms.

Katy Renée

The Foundational Knowledge of Inclusive Language Education

Throughout this book, we will be working at the intersection of inclusion and second language education. There are various dimensions to this intersection, and our aim is to review research, examine values and theories, and highlight teaching actions that facilitate inclusion within second language education. Exploring inclusion within second language education means that we, as teachers, provide access to learning a second language and foster continued access throughout the learning process.

We use the phrase *second language education* throughout this book. For us, it refers to events that happen in a classroom setting to help students develop proficiency in another language. We use the term *second language development* to refer to the process and experience of expanding knowledge and skill in the target language. When using terms such as *second language teaching* and *second language learning*, we are aiming to draw attention to a particular side of the education process, that is, what the teacher does in the setting versus what the student is expected to do. Figure AP 1.1 illustrates this.

Figure AP 1.1: Second Language Education

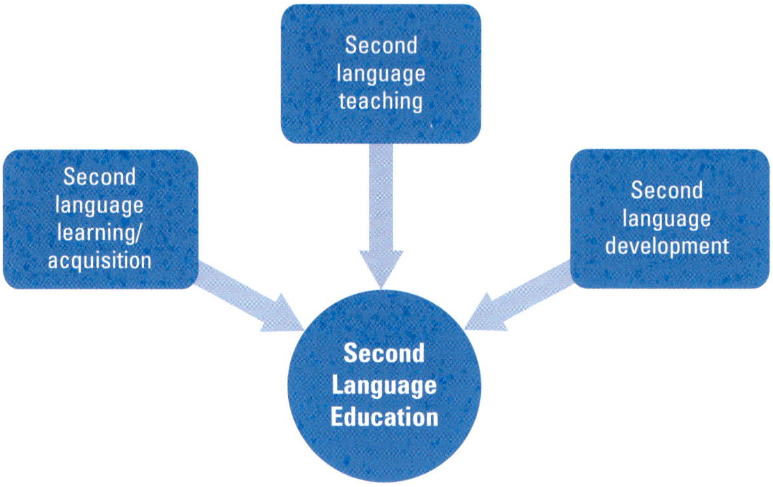

For a glossary of some of the terms used in this book, see the *Access for Success* website.

Here in Access Point 1, we focus on the knowledge bases that shape how we interpret and act on the ideas of inclusion and second language education. In Chapter 1, we take a closer look at inclusion and some of the ways it starts to intersect with second language experiences; in Chapter 2, we discuss how second language proficiency is developed and influenced.

Expanding Knowledge, Dispelling Myths: A Closer Look at Inclusion in Second Language Contexts

We have probably all had the experience of planning a dinner party for a group of friends, selecting a restaurant to host a family celebration, or planning an event. More than likely, we have had to negotiate some aspect of the planning process to ensure that the dinner party, restaurant, or venue could address certain needs within the group, including these:

- dietary needs: Do some guests have food allergies or intolerances? What about food preferences—hot, spicy, or mild? Do some guests have food philosophies that need consideration, perhaps veganism or a championship of locally sourced foods?
- seating plans and arrangements: Do we need to replace a few chairs with high chairs? Do certain people need to sit next to each other? Are there some people who should not sit near each other?
- accessibility or mobility needs: Can all guests navigate stairs? How far is the parking area from where the event is being held? Does any parking arrangement need to be set up in advance?
- religious or personal beliefs: Can alcohol be served? What food should not be served?

Sometimes, this process can be managed quickly. Other times, there may be ongoing negotiation with the guests, the hosts, or the restaurant/venue to ensure that needs are met. And on some occasions, a total change of plans may be required. (Potluck, anyone?)

Sometimes, unexpected needs arise that require us to make speedy adjustments—having to add another chair because someone decided to bring an unexpected guest, for example.

Regardless of the situation, there has, it is hoped, been some affability to these exchanges. After all, the end goal is to ensure that everyone at the event has a lovely time and positive experience within a safe eating environment. In other words, we all want everyone to feel included.

When we replace the needs mentioned above with *learning* needs, the idea of inclusion becomes suddenly more complex and, often, more emotionally charged. Perhaps more so than any other dimension of modern education, inclusion has come to be both an expectation and an ideal, something that can simultaneously excite us and vex us.

Over the course of this chapter, and throughout the rest of this book, we explore different dimensions of what it means to facilitate inclusion for language learners. In this chapter, our focus is on the notion of inclusion itself and how it shapes the experience of learning another language.

We subscribe to Valle and Connor's (2010) idea that, for inclusion to be realized, it needs deliberate attention:

> Inclusion needs tending. It is not something we put in place structurally, then sit back and hope for the best. It is not about a particular teacher's practice or a particular child. It is about everyone working consciously and collaboratively toward the common goal of nurturing a vibrant inclusive community. And achieving that goal requires shared leadership that routinely and thoughtfully takes stock of how actively its inclusive community pursues and enacts new knowledge and innovative practice. (p. 207)

Thus, as we present concepts, misconceptions, and myths with respect to inclusion for second language learners, be prepared to take stock consciously and collaboratively with us. We hope that the research we present in this chapter inspires meaningful conversations and in-depth reflection for making our classrooms vibrant inclusive communities for our language learners.

In this chapter, we consider the following issues:

- the understanding of inclusion that guides this book
- language contexts, programs, and some of the learners therein
- the state of inclusion in second language contexts
- myths about second language education that, at times, hinder our ability to make informed decisions about language programs and how to support and counsel language learners

Inclusion—Guiding Principles and Baseline Understandings

The concept of inclusion was initially positioned as an alternative to the practice of mainstreaming students with special education needs. Under the paradigm of mainstreaming, this student population had to earn the right to participate in and engage with the general education classroom through behavioural and academic milestones. Inclusion was about affording students with special needs the immediate right to be a part of the regular education curriculum (Valle & Connor, 2010).

At present, the term *inclusion* encompasses additional learner groups that have traditionally been excluded or marginalized from the dominant education discourse; these include LGBTQ people, English as a second language students, and ethnic or racial minority groups. Although our understandings of inclusion have evolved to include more learner groups, we still have to grapple with questions about what inclusion looks like in practice. So, let's consider this question: Has inclusion occurred when individuals have been granted access to a particular environment or opportunity, or is inclusion something that is realized when, upon entry into that environment or opportunity, new members are able to gain something from the experience? For us, inclusion must be more than just giving access to the setting: **inclusion has to be about ensuring that the access leads to some form of success**.

Inclusive education has brought with it an overall shift in the paradigm that had been previously applied to difference, disability, and difficulty within the classroom context. Inclusion has aimed to shift focus to the assets and skills that individuals bring with them to the learning experience, to view the disability, difference, or disorder as a dynamic trait within the individual that can be addressed through appropriate supports and resources within the classroom (Valle & Connor, 2010).

The antecedent of inclusion has been referred to as the *medical model* in that it has viewed disability, difference, or disorder as a deficit within the individual that has limiting consequences on the person's potential to achieve. Any resources and supports that can be offered to the student are thought to be likely limited in their scope or impact (Valle & Connor, 2010). Another notable difference between the inclusive paradigm and the medical model is that "regular" education teachers (including language teachers) have a deep and rich pedagogy that has inherent elements that respond to the needs of all learners. In other words, in the inclusive paradigm, it does not take a specialized skill set to address learners' needs. Rather, it takes an awareness of how the knowledge and skills we, as teachers, already possess can be best leveraged to support all learners' needs. Figure 1.1 summarizes the differences between the medical model and the inclusive education paradigm.

Figure 1.1: Medical Model Versus Inclusive Education Paradigm

The Medical Model of Disability, Difference, or Disorder	The Paradigm of Inclusive Education
• Deficit oriented (e.g., focused on what the student can't do) • Views student disability, disorder, or difference as something that is inherent and fixed; it cannot be addressed through support • Maintains that struggling learners should be in a special education experience • Views students in two groups: able and disabled • Sees the student as the driving force of the context: student deficits are the biggest influence on the learning experience	• Focused or based on strengths • Views student disability, disorder, or difference as something that is responsive to appropriate support • Believes that regular educators have the skills and knowledge to support student needs • Views students as a collective group • Sees the teacher as the driving force of the context: the biggest influence is what the teacher does (or does not do) to support learners

As a final note in this section, we acknowledge that two of the major challenges that exist in implementing the ideals of the inclusive paradigm are the teacher knowledge base of learning needs and challenges and the supports they require. For teacher credentialing in Canada (and in some parts of the United States), it is not a requirement to have taken coursework focused on diverse learning needs and how to respond to them in the classroom (Mady & Arnett, 2015). Thus, many teachers begin their careers without the information they need to fully respond to the inclusive education mandates. To some degree, this perpetuates the ideas of the medical model, since the omission of such coursework implies that diverse learner needs are someone else's responsibility. We call on teacher education programs and teacher licensure bodies to address this glaring oversight—and we urge school districts and larger offices of education to push for this change.

Second Language Education and the Good Language Learner

In this book, we are largely framing our inquiry to explore second language education, which refers to both the teaching and learning sides of the classroom experience. In a lot of what we do in this text, we are focused on the teaching actions that support student learning, but we acknowledge that students are active agents in the learning experience. (For more information, see Chapter 4.) Overall, we are interested in the totality of learning contexts in which students gain proficiency in another language, even if that language is not their second language—but instead their third or fourth. We are, however, keeping the practice in the field of referring to this as *second language education*.

The field of second language education has its own layers of complexity. From program type to the timing of when learners begin their study of another language, and from the nature of the language they are studying to the expectations of how they are to use the target language in the classroom and beyond, there are many dimensions that influence the process of building proficiency in another language. In this section, we focus on a certain thread of research and inquiry in second language education: that of the **good language learner**. We believe that this construct needs to be confronted as we explore how to make language learning an inclusive experience.

Over many decades, second language education has featured notable narratives and inquiries of what made for good language learners (e.g., Lightbown & Spada, 2013; Naiman, Frölich, Stern & Todesco, 1996; Rubin & Thompson, 1994). These texts have sought to capture and convey which learner traits, skills, or even "inherent abilities" made students excel in language learning. They have often been (implicitly) structured on the premise that students who have these particular qualities should have access to the learning experience and that students who lack these qualities should be viewed as questionable, unlikely-to-succeed participants. In other words, the traditional (and arguably outdated) notion of good language learners described language learners as having fixed personalities, approaches to learning, and motivations (Norton & Toohey, 2011). More recent understandings of second language learners include the understanding that their identities are fluid, context dependent, and context producing. As Naiman et al. (1996) explain, "the successful or good language learner, with predetermined overall characteristics, does not exist. There are many ways of learning a language successfully ... existing stereotypes do not apply" (p. ix).

Anecdotally, we can report that within discussions among practitioners, there is still a notable undercurrent that accepts the premise that some students are meant to study a language or should study a language and some students should not. This premise is founded on a belief that some learners cannot learn the language or achieve a certain level of proficiency, or will at least have a lot of difficulty doing so. Based on where we are with our own understandings and expertise on the topic of inclusive language education, we see this ongoing interest in the good language learner as one possible reason for the concerns about making language education an inclusive experience. In its place, we encourage a reframing of the idea—a move away from the belief that there are good and not-so-good language learners, toward the idea that all students can become good language learners with explicit and appropriate support.

Inclusion for Language Learners

The notion of inclusion is broader than it ever has been before. In this book, we are primarily focusing on the inclusion of students in language education, and so we will spend a few paragraphs looking at what exactly we mean by this.

Let's first consider language learner populations. Who are we interested in?

- We are interested in the educational experiences of students who need additional supports to work through some aspects of learning the target language, with interpreting or expressing it. These difficulties may not always be present. It is possible that some students may need additional support to master a particular learning goal and support is given as needs arise. At other times, students may need ongoing support to work through the curricular goals because of persistent learning challenges.
- We are also interested in supporting the experiences of students who are navigating multiple languages simultaneously (e.g., an overall school language and another language in a school or extracurricular program, as well as a different home language). We refer to such students as *allophones*, a term created in the Canadian French–speaking world to refer to individuals whose first language is neither French nor English.
- Finally, we are interested in supporting the language education experiences of students who have heritage ties to a language but may have varied day-to-day access to those languages. Some of these students are from Indigenous communities, working to learn their ancestral language. Other heritage language learners include students who have language rights to the target language, most typically found for students with heritage ties to French and who are enrolled in French language schools (even if they do not speak French at home). Finally, there are programs (in or out of traditional schools) where students can learn the languages their families have brought with them to Canada.

Language education can occur in various school settings, each with its own contextual features that shape the learning experience. In many settings, several different types of second language education could be happening at once. Let's consider different scenarios that highlight our need to consider more inclusive pedagogies for various language learning contexts. Below are the kinds of language education and program configurations that could be identifiable in any given school.

Scenario 1

This high school is in an English-speaking area and is considered an English first language school. It offers French immersion, bringing into the same classes students who are in the early and late French immersion programs. The school also offers various types of language classes, where the language of study is learned in a special period of the school day. For example, there are

- mandatory English language classes for recently arrived newcomers to Canada
- mandatory French language classes for learners who are not in the French immersion program (e.g., Core French, Post-Intensive French)
- optional Spanish language classes (considered international language classes) for students who are choosing to add another language
- various content-area classes (e.g., math, science) that allophones with lower proficiency in English attend. (In these cases, allophones are mixed with English first language students, and the extent to which these students' language needs are supported varies.)

In language education, the term *submersion* is used to describe language learning settings in which the language learners are not provided with explicit support to help grow their skills in the language or navigate the content in the target language. Submersion is meant to convey the opposite of what happens in an immersion classroom.

Scenario 2

This elementary school offers a French immersion program in an area that has a large bilingual English–French population. Within the immersion program, there are three key groups of students:

- students who speak English at home
- students who speak French at home
- allophone students who speak another language at home

Because of the language use patterns in the outside community, the French immersion classroom has morphed somewhat into a French/English immersion classroom. To better include allophones, the teacher has built in time during the day for them to teach their classmates some words in their home languages. The school also offers a Core French program for students not enrolled in the French immersion program. The Core French program has similar groups of students as those in French immersion.

Scenario 3

This French language school is in an area of Canada with a small population of native francophones (*français en milieu minoritaire*), but a growing population of students who have the right to attend French language schools because a parent or grandparent has status as a native francophone.

The area is also attracting the attention of some newcomers to Canada who may or may not be from French-speaking parts of the world. In this French language school, there are essentially four groups of students:

- francophone students who speak predominantly French at home
- bilingual students who speak both French and English at home (*familles hexogames*)
- students with heritage ties to French but who do not use French at home
- newcomers to Canada who may or may not have previous ties to French but now have possible access to French outside of the home

Scenario 4

In this large city, both a large First Nations Cree population and a large Chinese population are present. The local school for the First Nations community offers a Cree immersion program for students enrolled there. The local public schools offer class periods (at middle school and high school) to study the Indigenous language, as well as the Mandarin language. Mandarin is featured in many local events. There are also programs for studying French (immersion and core), but since French study is not compulsory, the programs are quite small.

Scenario 5

What context(s) for language learning are in *your* school?

Types of Second Language Programs

As is evident by these scenarios, there are various program models for second language education. These models differ with respect to the amount of time the students spend in the language, the targeted language learning outcomes, and the pedagogy used to deliver the program. Some program names reflect more interest in how the learning experience is organized, while other program names refer to the kind of language the students access within the programs.

Immersion Programs

Immersion programs offer students the opportunity to learn subjects such as sciences, language arts, and mathematics within a rich language environment. For example, students learn to speak, read, and write in French in their language arts classes, and they also develop second language proficiency through the learning of subjects in that target language (Lambert & Tucker, 1972). Many models exist to offer students options as to when they can begin an immersion program (early, late, middle). Immersion programs are designed to offer language choices that are different from the language of the broader school community. Here are a few examples of immersion programs:

- English-speaking (anglophone) students learning French in Canada
- Spanish-speaking students learning English and English-speaking students learning Spanish in the United States
- First Nations children learning Cree as a way to maintain, preserve, or recapture the language. (This scenario describes a heritage language program, too.)

Students enrolled in immersion programs spend a considerable part of their day exposed to the target language, so immersion teachers use specialized second language pedagogy to support the learning of the target language and subject areas.

Bilingual programs (or partial immersion programs) are sometimes grouped in this type of language program. Within bilingual programs, either teachers or students (or both) use two different languages over the course of the school day. Usually, both languages being used in class are also used in the immediate community around the school.

It should be noted that different immersion programs exist to meet different outcomes and language objectives.

"X" Language Programs

In "X" language programs, students learn a second language as a subject. Here, we see examples of programs named for either how the instruction is organized (e.g., core versus intensive) or what the language context of the program is (e.g., heritage or foreign language). Within this category, we find, among others, Core French or English programs (LeBlanc, 1990), Intensive French (Netten & Germain, 2004) or English programs, and single classes to teach Indigenous languages or other languages from around the world.

Core programs in either English or French range from 20 to 90 minutes a day (often depending on whether they are at the elementary or secondary level) (LeBlanc, 1990). In these classes, students typically learn to communicate about various topics in the target language, such as weather and food preferences, and to express likes, dislikes, and opinions.

In a few districts (including in Ontario), there is the unique Extended French program, which is sometimes described as a middle ground between Core French and French immersion. Students have a class focused on French language, but they also take a few electives in French.

Intensive programs are typically used to instruct students in languages other than the language of school. They offer a two-part structure. First, there is an intensive period of five to six months during a particular grade (usually Grade 5, 6, or 7) in school in which students receive a concentrated language education all day, every day to give them a jump-start with the target language. After that point, students get one or two class periods a week for the rest of that academic year and any subsequent years of language study in which they continue to develop their skills in the language (Netten & Germain, 2005).

Heritage language programs allow students to study a language they have access to or knowledge of through family ties. A heritage language program can either be structured as an immersion or as a core experience.

Foreign/international language programs are contexts in which the students learn a language not accessible in the broader society, even though some speakers of that language or even a small community of speakers of the language may be in the area. Examples include studying German in Canada or studying Arabic in the United States.

These language programs generally offer a lesser amount of instructional time in the target language as compared to immersion programs. Again, it should be noted that different "X" language programs exist to meet different outcomes and objectives.

The State of Inclusion Within Second Language Programs

In terms of inclusion within second language programs, most studies have focused on immersion and Core French programs. With regard to immersion, the program is no longer as strongly anchored to the premise of being a language program for academically elite students as it once was. The original intention of the French immersion program was to make a learning experience relevant for a variety of learners (Lambert & Tucker, 1972), and today we recognize that the face of immersion education is becoming increasingly diverse. Students are entering immersion programs with particular learning needs (learning difficulties or giftedness), with diverse backgrounds and cultures, or with different home literacy experiences.

Efforts are being made across the country from various ministries of education to advocate for the inclusion of students with exceptionalities and different backgrounds in immersion programs (Bourgoin, 2014). There is still evidence of the debate as to whether French immersion programs should be for all students (for a review of this literature and summary of this debate, see Mannavarayan, 2003); there is also evidence of teacher resistance to providing support to students with identified disabilities (Mady & Arnett, 2009; Wise 2011). However, there are increasing expectations and efforts to make French immersion programs more inclusive (e.g., Genesee, 2013) and evidence of how specific supports can be of benefit to students in the program (e.g., see Genesee, 2007a; LeBouthillier, 2013; Wise & Chen, 2010).

To a lesser extent, there has been some consideration of inclusion within Core French and Intensive French programs, even though those programs combine to serve more students than French immersion. Arnett (2003, 2010) found through case study research that teaching actions that were used to respond to specific learner needs—in other words, accommodations—were consistent with teaching actions that, in general, were recommended to support learning another language. Some of these teaching actions included repetition, strong use of the target language in the classroom, and use of gestures and visuals to help convey meaning. Further, Arnett (2008) found that students were aware of teacher supports that were extended in class to help foster understanding, particularly for students with identified learning needs, and that those efforts motivated the students further. Joy and Murphy (2012) lay out a case for how inclusive teaching can become a reality of Intensive French programs by exploring an activity system used in eight particular classrooms, but apart from that, there has been limited exploration in intensive programs.

Inclusion and Allophones

Language programs and mainstream classes are becoming increasingly diverse, in part because of the greater numbers of newcomers to Canada who do not speak English or French. Until the 1980s, most immigrants to Canada came from the British Commonwealth and did not face a language barrier in accessing Canadian society. Today, the majority of newcomers enter Canada speaking a language other than French or English as their home language (Mady, 2007b). Students from such families learn either French or English in school because it is the language of instruction. We often refer to these learners as *allophones*, and we use this term throughout the book.

It should be noted that, because federal funding designed to support language development for allophones is limited, school districts are tasked to find additional funds to provide the needed language education (Arnett, 2014). In districts with large populations of allophones, such language education is an easier budget priority to set, while a smaller district with a handful of allophones may struggle to do the same. These structural influences mean that instructional time for the study of the allophones' new school language could be limited to any one of the following situations: (1) after-school support one day a week for a few weeks of the year, (2) a regularized class time during the day until the students reach a certain skill level with the school language, or (3) a program for jump-starting the school language before students transition into content classes. These variations can exist within a district, which means that allophones may be unevenly supported as they navigate Canadian education.

Each school district has its own processes for bringing allophone students into the school community. These processes typically include some form of evaluation of their proficiency in the target language of the school. In some cases, the evaluations are a point of information; in other cases, they help inform decisions about the kinds of language support that will be offered to the student.

Some of you may be teaching allophones as part of a second language program (core, immersion) or as part of the mainstream program (allophones in English schools or French schools). As for allophones enrolled in second language programs, Mady (2007a, 2007b, 2013a, 2013b) has found that, when given the opportunity to study in French second language programs (e.g., Core French), allophones outperform their classroom peers. Bourgoin and Dicks (in press) have found similar results in French immersion. This study tracked students' French and English reading development, in particular.

The Universal Language Actions and differentiation practices detailed in Chapters 5 through 9 provide concrete ways to support such allophone learners.

In many cases, allophones learn an additional language in school (the school language) without being in a specific second language program. In such cases, we often use the term *English as an additional language* (EAL) or, in the case of French schools, *French as an additional language* (FAL). EAL or FAL learners are enrolled in the school's regular program and are learning subjects such as mathematics, sciences, and language arts as second language learners. These are more submersion settings. Allophones are enrolled in content classes (e.g., math, science) without any form of specialized support for their limited proficiency. In other words, they are placed in the classroom with little or no support of their language skills—a common reality for many allophone students in content classrooms. Submersion language learning situations are sometimes referred to as the "sink-or-swim" approach (e.g., Wright, 2015).

Genesee (1991) reminds us that all teachers are really second language teachers. The various disciplines each have their own linguistic demands and traditions, but because most students in those classes have proficiency in the language of the school used to teach those classes, picking up and developing skill with these more specialized languages is easier to do. Yet, students who are learning the language of school while in these content classes are in need of support that allows them to access the language in a manner consistent with their current proficiency.

> Refugee students are an important sub-population within the allophone population. While we have been writing this book, Canada has been welcoming and helping to resettle refugees affected by the war in Syria. These students may have additional needs, particularly of a psycho-social or emotional nature, as they transition into the classroom, and these needs will create more pressures for teachers to manage. Chapter 3 will address some of these concerns, but it is also important to acknowledge that a teacher is just one part of the team of supportive people some of these students may need to navigate education in Canada.

Other Important and Distinct Language Learner Groups

Some language learners fall within different categories than the ones listed above. They are not enrolled in language learning programs, nor are they in submersion settings.

French Language Right Holders

In many places in Canada (mostly in francophone communities outside Quebec), there are children who have heritage ties to French through a parent or grandparent. These children are described as French language right holders (*ayants droit*). This group of language learners is very diverse with respect to their language identities and backgrounds. Some are raised bilingually (often the result of one parent being French and the other English), some are from francophone-only homes, while others may not have much contact with the French language before coming to school. More often than not, the language of the community is English, which means that outside the home, students may be exposed to very little French (*French en milieu minoritaire*).

French language right students, irrespective of their language backgrounds, are legally able to enroll in the francophone education system. The need for differentiation and pedagogical adaptations in such educational settings is great because of students' varying linguistic abilities. In any given class, you will have students who are beginning their French language schooling with limited to no knowledge of French and are alongside students who have been raised in the language since birth.

In such situations, we have a pedagogical scenario similar to the one in which newcomers to a country or region are enrolled in a school where they do not know the language of schooling. A big part of students' identity in this learner group is tied to language learning and bilingualism. For this student population, the school language experience in a francophone school is viewed as being a part of their identity development.

Communities with Indigenous Languages

Indigenous students of their ancestral languages are heritage language learners. Though most of these language programs occur within the communities of the Indigenous populations, they represent an important facet of heritage language education.

The expansion of English and French across Canada came at the expense of Indigenous languages, a loss exacerbated further by three key forces. First, there were the residential schools in the early 20th century that supplanted the ancestral languages with English in the lives of the children in many Indigenous communities. Next, when the residential schools were closed and the majority of the students were enrolled in local public schools (most of which were anglophone), ancestral languages were further minimized (Bear Nicholas, 2009). Finally, in the 1970s, when the National Indian Brotherhood (1972) wrote a position paper against the Canadian government's promotion of political assimilation of Indigenous communities, linguistic assimilation actually accelerated (Bear Nicholas, 2009). The programs that resulted from this policy conflict led to new generations of Indigenous teachers being prepared in teacher education programs to teach in English, rather than in the ancestral languages. Skutnabb-Kangas (2000) has pointed out that such efforts foster linguistic genocide. Bear Nicholas (2009) points out that many Indigenous families have thus come to believe that ancestral languages are not of value in the current landscape of Canada and have overwhelmingly chosen to educate their children in English or French.

For many decades, though, there has been a growing effort to revive these ancestral languages, using, in many cases, the immersion program model (Bear Nicholas, 2009; Grenoble & Whaley, 2006; Richards & Burnaby, 2008). The challenges facing these programs are many; they include there being fewer available speakers of the language, limited or non-existent educational materials, and negative perceptions of the value of reviving the languages. Although it is hard to overcome generations of linguistic genocide, these language programs are slowly and steadily gaining in popularity.

Other Heritage Languages

Some cities and regions of Canada with large allophone populations that share a particular language reach a point where interest in further study of that language creates two types of language learning scenarios.

First, evening and weekend programs are offered to help these heritage speakers continue to develop their proficiency in that language. Some children take these classes to communicate with grandparents, as their parents have opted to raise the children in the language of the larger community, and some children take these classes to simply further their understanding of the language at a written level.

Second, some school districts have been able to turn high interest in particular heritage languages into larger school-based programs open to students with and without heritage ties to the languages. For example, in Alberta, there are several bilingual programs for languages such as Ukrainian, Chinese, and Arabic; these programs deploy a pedagogy like you would see in an immersion classroom, but they may mix students who have heritage and non-heritage access to the language.

Tackling Pervasive Myths About Second Language Learning

Dr. Joseph Dicks, director of the Second Language Research Institute of Canada at the University of New Brunswick, has done a lot of work and professional development with teachers about popular myths of language learning and language education.

Dr. Dicks posits that part of the challenge facing language learners is related to myths and misunderstandings about how students come to develop proficiency in a second language. These false perceptions include ideas about who can or should study other languages, what it is like for the learner to manage multiple languages, when to begin to study the language, and how learning another language influences (or not) the student's first language. Many of the myths have the same underlying message: *only certain students will be successful with learning a language and so, we should limit the opportunity to study to those students*. Other myths generally question the value of second language study or promote the idea that second language learning is easy, which has led to overly high expectations of programs, teachers, and especially students.

When we hold on to these myths and misconceptions, it stands to reason that any decisions we make about opportunities to access language education or practices that make the language more accessible will be misguided and unfounded. Before we discuss the myths in greater detail, let's consider that common underlying message, bearing in mind that we all have different skills, abilities, interests, and potential and will have different degrees of success in any pursuit.

Thus, with a nod to the work of Dr. Dicks in this area, in this section we will explore some of the common myths that can impede sound decision making about providing access to language learning and practices that make language learning accessible.

Defining *Being Bilingual*

Reflect for a moment on the following question:

- How would you define *being bilingual*?

We are reflecting on this question, in part, because many of the myths we tackle below are embedded in notions related to the ability of language programs to create bilingual speakers or to learners' capacity to attain bilingual status. Programs and individual capacity are indeed two of the most important factors in this discussion, but our own understandings of bilingualism can foster even more in-depth conversations with respect to persistent myths about second language education.

According to Colin Baker (2011), it is important to not arbitrarily create "cut-off points about who is bilingual or not ..." (p. 6). Definitions can be ambiguous and categorizing who is bilingual can be politically motivated. Definitions can also be too inclusive, or perhaps too exclusive, whereas some who may have certain competencies are not recognized. Rather, Baker suggests that we focus on language ability: "a portrait of the everyday use of the two languages by individuals" (p. 7). Bilingualism exists on a continuum. Some individuals may have partial competencies in the second language, and these competencies should and need to be recognized and valued. Some may be more competent in using the target language in certain contexts (e.g., socially, in the workplace, at home) or with certain individuals. Too tightly defined definitions of bilingualism can lead to comparisons and opens the door to questions such as these: Who is judged proficient, competent, or fluent? And who is doing the judging? (Baker, 2011).

With the adoption of the Common European Framework of Reference (CEFR), we have moved toward recognizing and valuing partial competencies as well as full competencies. We are seeing a reorientation of what it means to be bilingual (Council of Ministers of Education of Canada, 2010;

Piccardo, 2014). We acknowledge the influence of the CEFR on current Canadian thinking about the construct of being bilingual and see its potential for promoting inclusivity in language teaching.

Myth 1: Learners Should Focus on First Language Literacy Skills Before Learning a Second Language

The Myth in a Real-Life Context

In 2009, the province of New Brunswick decided to change the entry point to its early French immersion program from Grade 1 to Grade 3, in large part out of concern that students need to have a better command of literacy in their first language before starting to learn a second language.

At the time of writing this book, the New Brunswick government announced that it is rescinding this decision, made by a previous government. Early French immersion returns to Grade 1 beginning in fall 2017, citing research in the field of second language acquisition.

It is a commonly held belief that learning a second language should take place only once students have a firm grasp on their first language literacy skills for fear of putting at risk their normal ability to read and write. As Genesee (2007b) noted, second language programs such as immersion "have raised a number of educational and research questions because they contradict the commonsense notion that initial reading and writing skills should be taught in a language that students already know" (p. 1).

What Does the Research Say?

Research has consistently shown that although immersion students may initially lag behind their unilingual peers in the development of English language skills, they rapidly catch up once English instruction is reintroduced in the upper elementary grades (Genesee, 2007a; Swain & Lapkin, 1982; Wiss, 1987). When provincial English literacy data were analyzed, elementary immersion students were found to be either at par or outperforming their English counterparts as long as they had been exposed to some English literacy instruction beforehand (Genesee, 2007b; Turnbull, Lapkin, & Hart, 2001).

Findings have suggested that earlier formal instruction in English bears little weight in terms of increased English-language reading proficiency. "Immersion students who receive more native language instruction do not achieve higher levels of proficiency in the native language in the long run than immersion students who receive less exposure to the native language" (Genesee, Paradis, & Crago, 2004, p. 177). In other words, students who are reintroduced to English literacy instruction in Grade 3 or 4 are at no greater disadvantage than students receiving English instruction starting in Grade 1 or 2 because literacy skills learned in one language can be transferred to another (Genesee & Jared, 2008).

Throughout this section, then, there has been an embedded consideration of the starting point of language study. Several studies have considered differences between learner outcomes depending on the point at which students began French immersion—either within the first four years of elementary school (K to 3; early) or after (Grades 4 to 7; late). Early French immersion students have been found to reach a higher level of oral competency in French (oral fluency and use of spontaneous language) than those who start later (e.g., Dicks, 1995; McVey, Bonyun, Dicks, & Dionne, 1990; Turnbull, Lapkin, Hart, & Swain, 1998). As for reading and writing skills, results are comparable irrespective of the time students entered the immersion programs (Dicks, 1995; Genessee, 1998; Turnbull et al., 1998). Dicks and Kristmanson (2008) also posit that early French immersion is "the least likely to be affected by academic ability and therefore the most inclusive of immersion programs" (p. 16).

Myth 2: Second Language Programs May Not Be Suitable for Learners with Low Academic Ability and Learners from Lower Socio-economic Backgrounds

The Myth in a Real-Life Context

This year, Jessa's parents were made aware that her progress in the second language was less than that of her peers. Her oral and reading development skills, although progressing, were of concern to her teacher. Jessa's parents work, are anglophone, and have a limited income. Providing tutoring supports outside school is not an option for them. Her parents wonder whether learning a second language is more appropriate for students who are academically stronger and who have parents with the means to provide outside help in the target language.

While the suitability of second language programs for students with limited first language abilities has been called into question, so has the suitability of second language programs for students with low levels of academic ability or for learners from lower socio-economic backgrounds. With respect to socio-economic status (SES), research was conducted because "students from families with low SES are usually at risk for failure or poor achievement in schools for reasons that are not fully understood" (Genesee, Paradis, & Crago, 2004, p. 181).

What Does the Research Say?

Research conducted in language immersion settings revealed that students with low academic ability are at no greater disadvantage when enrolled in French immersion both in terms of their English language development and overall academic achievement (Cummins, 1983; Genesee, 1992, 2007b). Findings revealed that "the below average students in immersion scored at the same level as the below average students in the L1 program ... in other words, the below average students in immersion were not disadvantaged ... as a result of participation in immersion" (Genesee, Paradis, & Crago, 2004, p. 179). Students with lower academic abilities would face the same academic challenges if they were enrolled in the English program. However, when enrolled in second language programs, they benefited from gaining proficiency in the second language.

On the issue of suitability of second language programs for students with low SES, findings are similar. Second language immersion students from low SES were at no greater risk for learning difficulties because of their enrolment in the program. This learner group fared just as well as comparable groups of students enrolled in English-only programs.

Myth 3: Second Language Programs May Not Be Suitable for Learners with Learning Difficulties or Learning Disabilities

The Myth in a Real-Life Context

Before this year, Bobby had been receiving extra literacy support, both in English and in French. Again this year, both his English and French teachers noticed that Bobby was experiencing reading difficulties. Although he has improved since starting an in-class intervention program, he is still not reading at grade level. Bobby's English teacher is concerned with the development of Bobby's first-language literacy skills and believes that Bobby cannot manage learning two languages at once.

The Myth in a Real-Life Context

Liza has a history of behavioural issues, and her prior academic performance has been marginal. Her mother is aware of Liza's academic and behavioural issues, and she is not sure if studying another language makes sense. She has also had comments from other parents of students in Liza's class who are frustrated with Liza's outbursts. A friend suggested to her that Liza be transferred back into the English programs.

We use the term *learning difficulties* in the broadest possible sense for this book; for us, these students have challenges working in their first language to the point that it influences their learning experience. These challenges can be the consequence of a formally diagnosed learning disability that is related to language or any other type of special education need that has an influence on the development and use of language. This latter group of needs can include general speech or language impairments and challenges with executive function, memory, or attention that shape how language is perceived, processed, and expressed. For us, this group includes students who have been formally diagnosed with a learning disability (e.g., dyslexia, dysgraphia) and students who have general challenges with learning (e.g., processing disorders) or challenges with attention.

What Does the Research Say?

Though the first Canadian French immersion programs were deliberately designed to recruit students with a wide range of learning needs (Lambert & Tucker, 1972), as the study of learning disabilities began to be developed in the 1970s, questions emerged as to whether students who had difficulties decoding and expressing in their first language should remain in French immersion. Due to two research studies (Trites & Price, 1976, 1977), which have since been largely questioned on methodological grounds within the broader field (e.g., Bruck, 1978, 1982; Cummins, 1983; Wiss, 1987), the seed was planted within language education in Canada—particularly for French second language programs—that students who had challenges navigating the first language should either transfer out of or be excluded from these learning experiences. Since then, it has been a challenge to dissuade popular thinking that such a practice is valid, as evidenced in other research we have both done (Arnett, 2013a; Bourgoin, 2016).

So, what does the research say? When comparing immersion students with language disabilities or impairments to students in the English-only program, Bruck (1982) found that learners with language disabilities in both programs needed more time than typically developing students to attain basic literacy and academic skills. We would expect this, given their learning needs. Bruck concluded that immersion learners with language disabilities developed "linguistic, cognitive, and academic skills at a rate similar to that at which they would develop were they placed in an all-English classroom" (cited in Genesee, 1992, p. 205). Similarly, researchers Paradis, Crago, Genesee, and Rice (2003) conducted a study of bilingual students with specific language impairments and found that "instead of demonstrating that bilingualism impedes language acquisition under conditions of impairment, the children showed that they had the ability to learn two languages despite their impairment" (p. 125). Similar findings have been noted with respect to learners with reading difficulties: second language learners are no more greatly disadvantaged than their English counterparts with similar reading difficulties (Bournot-Trites, 2008; Genesee, 2007a; MacCourbrey, Wade-Woolley, Klinger, & Kirby, 2004).

For students who have learning difficulties or other specialized learning needs, increasing evidence has demonstrated that the learning needs, in and of themselves, do not create barriers to developing proficiency in another language (Arnett, 2010; Bourgoin & Dicks, 2013; LeBouthillier, 2013; Paradis, Genesee, & Crago, 2011). While these students may require specialized support—just as a student with a physical disability may require specialized support in a physical education classroom—the students' needs are not cause alone to exclude them from the learning environment. The strategies that are typically recommended to support a student who has a specialized learning need like a learning disability are highly consistent with the methods and teaching practices that support effective second language learning (Arnett, 2003, 2008, 2010).

Myth 4: Learners Learning Multiple Languages at Once Are at Risk

The Myth in a Real-Life Context

Nir moved to Canada from Nepal, arriving in an English-speaking area where she could join an immersion program at Grade 6—which is when she is starting school. There is a global expectation that all students study another language. The immersion program is for Chinese, which interests Nir. Nir has some English, but not enough skill in the language for the content classes she will need to take in English. She speaks Nepali at home and has a good working knowledge of Hindi, due to her love of Bollywood films. When she is enrolled at the school, there is some discussion (sparked by the resettlement support person) as to whether Nir should focus only on English and not study Chinese at all.

Over the last several years, North America has continued to see a steady growth in immigration. For example, among the G8 countries (Canada, France, Germany, Italy, Japan, Russia, the United Kingdom, and the United States), Canada has the highest proportion of foreign-born immigrants. The percentage of Canadians reporting a mother tongue other than French or English now hovers at 20 percent (Statistics Canada, 2011). As a result, more and more children are entering Canadian schools speaking a minority language at home and learning both English and French at school. Many enroll in early French immersion programs, so these learners are learning three languages somewhat simultaneously. They are sometimes referred to as third language, trilingual, or allophone students.

What Does the Research Say?

Research indicates that third language or trilingual learners are at no greater risk in language immersion programs. In fact, many surpass their bilingual peers. Trilingual learners have many of the same characteristics as second language learners, but because they are already learning two languages they have "… more language experience at their disposal" (Cenoz, 2003, p. 71). This puts them in an advantageous position over their bilingual and monolingual peers. Studies have found that they have "highly developed learning strategies, metalinguistic awareness and communicative sensitivity" (Cenoz & Hoffmann, 2003, p. 6). In fact, bilingualism favours the acquisition of a third language (see Bild & Swain, 1989; Cenoz & Valencia, 1994; Klein, 1995; Swain, Lapkin, Rowen, & Hart, 1990; Thomas, 1988). There is also some limited research related to allophone students and motivation for learning French (as a third language). These studies indicate generally that families of allophone students and the students themselves tend to perceive the advantages of multilingualism and are highly motivated to learn additional languages (see Dagenais & Berron, 2001; Mady, 2003). Further, it is worth noting that many allophone students may feel more at ease in the language classroom where other students are also having the experience of learning the language.

Figure 1.2 offers a summary of many of the key ideas presented in the previous pages, including recommendations for additional research reading.

Figure 1.2: Myths About Second Language Learning

Myth	What the Research Says	Some of the Scholars Who Say It
Learners need to have a strong foundation in their first language (e.g., they know how to read and write) before they learn another language.	First, there are many individuals who develop two languages from birth, so experientially, that myth is challenged. However, when thinking about when students should start studying a second language after learning their first language, the research has shown that the starting point makes no long-term difference in their oral or writing skills.	Genesee & Jared, 2008; Genesee, Paradis, & Crago, 2004; Turnbull, Lapkin, & Hart, 2001
Learning another language will have negative long-term effects on the first language skills of the learner.	There is often a short-term decline in first language skills of language learners compared to monolingual students, but in the long term, no negative effects have been observed. Generally, students who are proficient in multiple languages have stronger overall skills than monolingual students.	Cummins, 2000, 2001; Mady, 2013a, 2013b; Swain & Lapkin, 1982; Wiss, 1987

continued

Myth	What the Research Says	Some of the Scholars Who Say It
If a student is struggling in his/her first language, the student should not try to learn another language and should not enroll in an immersion program. Learning another language would stress or overburden the student's brain.	In general, there is no evidence that a learning disability or other difficulty within the first language impedes the development of skills in another language or that it is cognitively unfeasible for the student to learn another language. However, there is evidence that students with these challenges who begin language study in late immersion programs will have more difficulty than if they had started earlier (and this is not necessarily due to their age).	Arnett, 2008; Bourgoin & Dicks, 2013; Bruck, 1978; Paradis, Genesee, & Crago, 2011
If a student is already learning one language, he/she should not study another language.	There are two dimensions to this myth. First, there is evidence (as was the case for some of the previous myths) that studying multiple languages increases one's skill with executive functioning, which governs decision making in the brain. Second, there is evidence that students who are adding another language beyond the one they are learning as the language of school outperform monolingual students and students who have access to another language in their home environments in those same language settings.	Bialystok, 2001; Baker, 2011; Mady, 2013a, 2013b
If a student is having difficulty within the new language, it is counterproductive to give support in the first language.	Because learners are able to transfer ideas and information across languages, the issue is not the language of support, but rather that support is offered at all.	Bourgoin & Dicks, 2013; Bournot-Trites, 2008; Durgunoglu, 2002
If a student learns content in one language, he/she will not be able to easily go into other learning environments, in other languages, and apply that knowledge.	Content consists of concepts. Once the concepts are learned, they can be transferred. Though some work may be involved in renaming the knowledge in the new language, this is not a disadvantage to the student.	Culligan, 2010

continued

Myth	What the Research Says	Some of the Scholars Who Say It
For a language learner to do well, he/she must have a parent who speaks the language, or otherwise have regular access to the target language.	Multiple factors influence second language development, including environment. Within that influence, parental knowledge of the target language has not been identified as a critical need; what matters more are the types of interactions that occur within the language environment. (The four factors are identified in Chapter 2.) It is also worth noting that French immersion programs were specifically developed for students whose parents did not speak French.	Ortega, 2009
Fluency or proficiency in the language takes only a year to develop.	Language skills—especially the most sophisticated—will take years to develop. Though learners may be able to carry on a social conversation with relative ease after a few months in some situations, learners are not able to navigate all language situations in such a short time.	Cummins, 2000, 2001; Krashen & Terrell, 1983; Ortega, 2009
New language learners who say little, if anything, in class, are cause for concern.	Silence or non-verbal communication is an expected part of language learning, and this phase can last as long as a year. Because comprehension precedes production, silence is an expected outcome. The challenge is that this natural reality conflicts with classroom expectations for participation and grading.	Cummins, 2000, 2001; Krashen & Terrell, 1983

Beliefs and popular myths about second language learning can make it more difficult for students of particular subgroups to have access to learning an additional language. Therefore, when decisions are made by policy makers and education leaders, it is important to be armed with sound empirical research to ensure that policies do not reflect popular, unfounded beliefs about language learning.

Myths about second language education persist and continue to shape attitudes toward second language learning. Solid research evidence is crucial in influencing good inclusionary practices in second language education.

Closing Thoughts

In our work with teachers and other educational stakeholders, we have found that creating and maintaining an accessible language learning experience has often required us to examine notions of language education, inclusion, and how those constructs intersect. In Chapter 2, we will look at the processes and procedures involved in second language development more closely. Some of the themes that we have explored in this chapter will be revisited or expanded, as we have found them to be critical to explorations of accessible, inclusive language teaching.

We want to be clear: we acknowledge that yes, some students may, at first glance, require some additional consideration on the part of the teacher; nonetheless, when we come to understand these learners, we start noticing a lot of overlap in how their needs can be addressed. One thing to remember as we read about these learner groups is that most children in the world are educated in their second language (Cummins, 2000, 2001); thus, first language education—which has often coloured how we have considered the needs of second language learners in schools—is not as prevalent a model as it is often assumed to be.

As you reflect on the contents of the chapter, consider the following questions:

- How do I define *inclusion*? How is my conception of inclusion similar to or different from the broader school philosophy?
- What experience have I had with various language programs?
- What research would I like to consider further?
- Which ideas challenge my current understanding of language education?
- What myths have I held about language learners and language learning?
- What myths about language education may be held by others involved in supporting the students in my classes?

CHAPTER 2

Second Language Learning: Understanding the Processes and Managing Expectations

To begin this chapter, we want you to think about two pairings that will help us draw an analogy to the core content featured in the pages that follow. The first pairing we want you to think about is that of an apple and an orange. What do they have in common? What is different? They are fruit. They are both round or roundish. They have skins protecting the inner fruit. They have seeds in the centre. One is orange, and the other is a range of colours—red to yellow to pink to green. Oranges tend to be sweet, while apples can range from sweet to tart. Thus, in a lot of ways, they are comparable, but with some appreciable differences. The next pairing is that of an apple and a pickup truck. Outside of the fact that both are used or consumed by humans and that they could be the same colour, there's not much to compare. They are two vastly different entities.

We offer these pairs to help you think about learners in a classroom setting. When students are being educated in their home language (that is, the language they already know well), it is fairly feasible to make comparisons about their work and progress. Their successes can sometimes be compared with norms in mind because insights we have about development and learning are based on data collected from children living and learning in their first language. Thus, learners in this setting are apples and oranges.

When working with learners who are learning another language, comparisons among the students and to any established norms are not really possible; any similarities are typically peripheral. Second language learning is so different from acquiring one's first language that what happens with each student is unique; comparing one student's experience to another student's experience is like comparing an apple to a pickup truck. Consequently, when it comes to thinking about and making decisions pertinent to second language learning and development, using what we know of first language learning and development (and the educational experience that happens in a child's first language) can set us up for unreasonable expectations and, sometimes, ill-informed knowledge bases.

The purpose of this chapter is to establish some baseline understandings about the factors and processes that shape second language development and education—and that make it fundamentally different from learning experiences based in a student's first language. There are multiple influences on the process of second language learning and development, but in the interest of space, we will consider the four most significant and universal in the research: (1) learner age, (2) the language environment, (3) cognition, and (4) first language (Ortega, 2009).

In addition, we will spend some time exploring why second language learners vary so greatly from one another when it comes to the pace at which they develop their new language skills and the depth to which those skills are developed. Learner differences in these two dimensions, in our experiences, tend to arouse the most teacher concern about student progress and success and questions about who "should" access second language learning (answered in Chapter 1) or ways to facilitate that access (answered in Chapters 5 to 9). We begin this chapter with an overview of the general stages of second language development, which will lay the foundation for the discussion of the rate/depth dichotomy.

Why can't we find out if a learner's experience in a second language is "normal"? In English, the word *normal* is tied to the idea of a norm. At a social level, norms are things that are expected, such as a certain behaviour at a certain time. Norms can also be established through mathematical methods, in situations where large numbers of individuals are sharing the same type of experience (e.g., being born and passing through the first few years of life) with comparable conditions or factors. Data can be collected as to when these individuals hit certain milestones (e.g., babbling, saying first words, walking) and calculated to determine the *average* (mean) point of when these events occur and the *range of variation* (standard deviation) between the earliest and latest occurrences of that event. Plotting those values leads to curves that show us the normal trend for that particular event. These curves are what help us know if a child is language delayed in the first language because we are able to compare his or her skills with other children who learned their first language.

Second language learning, as this chapter will reveal, is a lot more variable than first language learning—more factors and conditions can alter someone's experience. Thus, even though there are a lot of individuals who have this shared experience, because there are so many differences among them, it is not possible to adequately control for those variables when doing the kinds of statistical tests that would establish those norms.

continued

Consequently, no curves can be established, and we are not able to capture what should be considered normal. There is thus no normal for second language learning.

The Stages of Second Language Acquisition

There is one notion about first language acquisition that is relevant when considering the process in a second language: the idea that there is a progression of skill development, moving from comprehension of the language to non-verbal and increasingly verbal forms of the language. Outside of that concept, what we understand about language development from the first language—particularly when it comes to deciding what is normal or not about a child's experience—can possibly misinform thinking about what to do with a second language learner.

Stephen Krashen and Tracy Terrell (1983) proposed a five-phase overview of the stages of second language acquisition. Upon close inspection, these five stages somewhat resemble what happens when children are in the process of acquiring their first language, but as is also clear, learners of a second language are already using skills and knowledge in certain stages of the process that convey they have competencies in another language. The stages are presented in Figure 2.1; the information contained therein synthesizes the initial work of Krashen and Terrell (1983) with others (e.g., Coelho, 2004; Fairbairn & Jones-Vo, 2010; Hill & Flynn, 2008).

A downloadable version of Figure 2.1: Stages of Second Language Acquisition is available on the *Access for Success* website.

Figure 2.1: Stages of Second Language Acquisition

Stage of Second Language Acquisition	What Happens at This Stage At this stage, the learner can ...	This stage typically occurs ________ from time of initial L2 exposure
Pre-production	This phase is often referred to as the Silent Period because learners may not speak at all. It is a receptive phase where learners are, for the most part, absorbing the language. Learners may repeat what is being said (parroting) and may have up to 500 words in their receptive vocabulary. In addition to parroting, they can offer non-verbal responses to questions and, sometimes, responses with high-frequency words (Yes/No). They are not generating their own spontaneous language.	0 to 6 months

continued

Early Production	Learners continue to add to their receptive language and are more regularly offering one- and two-word responses to questions. They are able to identify key words and ideas in the language. During this stage, learners have the ability to produce a limited number of words. They use familiar phrases that may or may not have been memorized. They generally use the present verb tense when communicating. Learners in the early production stage have a vocabulary of about 1000 words.	6 to 12 months
Speech Emergence	Learners are more actively balancing their receptive and expressive language. Students can follow the general gist of texts and can identify certain details within those texts. Spontaneous language production is becoming easier, but still may require teacher prompting. Learners in this stage can use short sentences and can produce questions. They have also expanded their receptive and expressive vocabulary to roughly 3000 words. They make errors when communicating, but the errors generally do not interfere with comprehension.	1 to 3 years
Intermediate Fluency	Learners are working with more complex dimensions of language grammatically, in terms of vocabulary, and in meaning. Their spoken language is increasingly smooth, and they can attend to big ideas and details within a text. These learners use more complex sentences when communicating. They are also able to think in the target language and have a working vocabulary (receptive and expressive) of about 6000 words.	3 to 5 years
Advanced Fluency	To a large degree, these learners resemble students who have been using the target language as a first language. Advanced language learners can navigate with ease a variety of social and academic situations. They are comfortable communicating in the target language. They may have errors in some aspects of language, particularly with less common structures and words.	5 to 7 years

It is worth noting that learners do not move in lock-step progression from one stage to the next. Rather, the progression is more gradual, and it is not uncommon for students to be straddling phases for a while or seemingly moving back and forth between two phases (Krashen & Terrell, 1983). Learners do not decide one day to move into the next phase of their learning or to take a step back on a particular day. Given that the reasons for using language at any given point depend on one's situation, certain situations will cause learners to be more or less verbal and linguistically engaged with what is happening.

The time frames offered in the last column of Figure 2.1 are suggestions, not rigid guidelines. The rate or speed at which learners develop skills in another language is one of the individual differences of great interest to researchers in the field of second language acquisition (SLA) (Ortega, 2009). It has been noted by some (e.g., Coelho, 2004; Cummins, 2000, 2001) that learners can need twice as long as these time frames indicate to navigate a particular phase. The reasons for these variations are best explored by considering the role of the four universal influences on second language acquisition.

The Universal Influences on Second Language Learning/Acquisition

Within second language education, there is a fundamental difference between learning and acquisition. Generally, acquisition is viewed as a subconscious development of understanding of how to interpret and use language, while learning is viewed as a more conscious endeavour. Pages upon pages have been devoted to figuring out where acquisition ends and learning begins, and the two are not always easily distinguishable. In this book, we typically use *acquisition* only when referring to the ideas of Stephen Krashen and others who are looking at the "native" elements of language learning, as he is very clear in his theoretical framework about the processes and role of acquisition. We have chosen to use *second language learning* as our general phrasing in all other areas, since learning, at the general level, is an outcome of education.

Broadly speaking, most of the factors that shape an individual's experience in learning another language address one of four areas: age, cognition, language environment, and first language (Ortega, 2009). How these factors work with and against each other varies from individual to individual, which adds to the complexity of determining how to support learners' acquisition of another language.

Age

The first universal we will consider is age. Chances are, you've heard something like "The best language learners are young" or that "You need to start learning a language before adolescence." The age of a learner at the start of the second-language learning experience will shape the learning, but not always in the way that is often expected.

Most of the concern about learner age has been anchored to the idea of a critical period for introducing another language; the premise of this hypothesis is that second language learning needs to begin before adolescence if the targeted outcome is native-like proficiency because of the brain's ability to incorporate the new language. Birdsong and Park (2008) have helped to disprove this hypothesis, and their work and that of other researchers has helped inform understandings of how learner age (but not cognition related to age) can benefit second language learning. Those benefits are explored in Figure 2.2, summarized in part from Wright (2015).

You may want to go back to Chapter 1 and review the section on pages 19 to 20 (learners with limited or no literacy in L1). Here, we review some research findings that consider how the timing of language study has outcomes for reading skills and general language development.

Figure 2.2: Age-Related Advantages to Language Learning

Advantages to Being a Younger Language Learner	Advantages to Being an Adult Language Learner
• Greater access to opportunities to learn other languages, in terms of how much instructional time the learner can access through programs, such as immersion programs • More likely to have less anxiety about learning another language	• Can more readily transfer skills, such as literacy, from first language to second language • More likely to be aware of and skilled with using learning strategies that help support progress

Source: Based on Wright (2015)

It should be noted, however, that language learning occurs with rich exposure to the target language. Learners who begin earlier will likely have more exposure to the target language. For example, as mentioned in Chapter 1, research has found increased language proficiency in students enrolled in early immersion entry points.

Cognition

Cognition is described as the processes by which the brain intakes, interprets, and organizes information. Cognition is concerned with memory, which has been found to be a core factor in language learning. Ellis (2001) advanced the idea that working memory (short-term memory) has a significant role to play in language development. The working memory is where, cognitively, our brain interprets new information and makes connections between this new information and previous knowledge. Understandably, there is a limit to what our brains can hold and navigate within the short-term memory, and similarly, there are differences among individuals' memory capacity, which, in turn, can influence how much language learners in a classroom setting can navigate at any given time.

Some researchers have also considered cognition in relation to one's aptitude or potential for language learning, as measured by various psychometric tests. Historically, these tests have been used as tools to identify students who possibly should not pursue language study or to determine which program was most likely a match for their skills, but such a practice runs counter to most policies in schools today (Lightbown & Spada, 2013). However, what is worth noting is that several studies that explored links between students' aptitude for language learning and the language learning environment found that instructional mismatches between a student's needs and a teacher's practice can limit the degree of student success in developing target language proficiency (e.g., Erlam, 2005; Wesche, 1981).

Language Environment

This universal influence considers the contexts in which the learner accesses (both receptively and productively) the target language and the ways in which the language is used within those contexts (Ortega, 2009). Thus, language environment is both a physical space and a cognitive space.

The physical space occupied by the language environment is typically described in a dichotomous way: natural or instructed. A *natural* environment refers to settings in which the language is used to carry out daily life and expects the learner to use the language to communicate with family members and, quite possibly, the larger community. First language learning occurs within a natural environment, but that is not always true of second language learning. An *instructed* environment is where the learner comes to and by the language through formal instruction, either in a traditional school setting or a schooling situation specifically for that language (e.g., Saturday schools for heritage languages). Either setting can support rich, deep exposure to language, but there is admittedly a question about the degree of authenticity available in an instructed environment. No matter the setting, the ways in which individuals use the language therein (both the students and others around them) varies, which creates the second type of environmental consideration: the cognitive space.

To be clear, the cognitive space is different from the influence of cognition, which was discussed in the previous section. Here, we are referring to what learners are expected to do with the language as the cognitive space. Are they expected to talk about social events? learn about a particular content area? solve a certain type of problem? These interaction demands will shape how a learner comes to understand and use a language. For example, if a learner's only experience with a certain language is with grandparents who speak that language, chances are the learner's language skills are restricted to topics one would discuss within a family—from family history to food to special events—and most likely just at an oral level; the learner probably does not read or write much, if at all, in this language. That learner cannot be expected to offer extended discourse about an academic topic in that language.

Within both dimensions of the language environment, we need to consider the amount of language to which learners are exposed—how much *input* they access as part of their learning. As mentioned in Chapter 1, from a language development standpoint, comprehension precedes production, and one's ability to comprehend and eventually produce the target language depends on the language that is presented to the learner and the ways in which others work to help the learner understand that message (Krashen & Terrell, 1983). The richness of an environment, in both the volume of the language and the volume of the opportunities to meaningfully use the language, will create other considerations for learning.

For example, on average, a fluent speaker of a language will share between 150 and 180 words a minute when speaking at a standard pace; this equates to two or three words a second. If most hours of the school day are spent with some form of spoken language going on, then the average (language) learner is going to be exposed to around 10 000 words in a typical school day. That is a lot of input to manage—and that is not even considering how much print language is also embedded into the school day. What the learner notices or not is shaped by the other universal influences, but also considerations such as previous experiences, existing knowledge of the target language, and personal motivation. It is, therefore, not surprising that language learners will sometimes be overwhelmed and struggle to attend to what is happening in the environment.

For more information about language learners who need support to sustain attention in the target language, see Chapter 7.

First Language

As much as some language educators may want to ignore or exclude a child's first language from the classroom experience, such a practice is not reasonable. Once we have skills with one language, we are predisposed to both subconsciously and consciously draw on our knowledge and understanding of that language to navigate the second language. However, it is worth noting that when looking at the experience of multilingual individuals, it appears that the first language is not necessarily an influence on the acquisition of later languages; instead, later languages may influence subsequent languages (Mady, 2013a, 2013b).

Depending on the schools of thought to which you have been exposed, you've either heard about first language interference or influence (Ortega, 2009). *First language interference* tends to frame what the learner knows and can do within the first language as somewhat of a barrier to overcome, be it in the form of certain types of errors that occur (e.g., errors of gender when the learner is coming from a non-noun-gendered language), certain concepts that do or do not exist from one language to the next (e.g., the number of tenses in English versus the number of verb tenses in Japanese), or even the extent to which the languages are similar in their alphabet, phonology, vocabulary, and structure. Conversely, the idea of *influence* takes a more positive view of the presence of the first language in the life of the learner. Instead of viewing the first language as a barrier to navigate, its dimensions are perceived as assets students can draw on to explore the new language and contrast it with what is already known. Further, the influence paradigm tends to view students' efforts to compare their first language with the target language as natural and something to encourage and acknowledge. We personally prefer the influence mindset because of the constructive view it promotes; in fact, this aligns well with the inclusive model from Chapter 1. We have also found in our work supporting inclusion in language learning contexts that positioning the learner's home language in a positive light can help the student approach the study of another language more openly.

In the Shoes of a Language Learner

In *Languages for All*, Katy (Arnett, 2013c) used a series of simulations to help readers understand the ways in which certain learning needs are manifested in the classroom. The goal was to enable teachers to begin to problem-solve about the supports that would best address those needs. Here, we offer a few of those simulations, retooled for a different purpose: understanding what it is like, cognitively, to try to work within another language. Even if you are a multilingual individual, chances are you are removed from the time period when your brain was trying to figure out another language. And if you're not a multilingual individual, maybe you will be by the time you tackle some of these activities.

In this section we are including three simulations that represent the biggest general challenges facing language learners: (1) decoding the target language, (2) connecting ideas in the target language to what they previously know about a topic, and (3) formulating a response to express their understanding.

These general challenges facing language learners are tied to the four categories of Universal Language Actions that we explore in Access Point 3.

1. Breaking the Code

Every language has its own code system: a series of relationships between symbols, the sounds they make, and how those symbols and sounds work together to create words and concepts that carry larger meaning. Languages can share alphabetic symbols, but the sounds assigned to those symbols change, and sometimes there are additional marks above or below a letter that tell us it makes yet another sound. Languages can also have very different alphabetic or scripting systems, and we have to rethink both the visual and auditory concepts of language we may have established through our first language. In this simulation, we give you a taste of the experience of trying to figure out a message in a symbolically different language. We will be kind and give you a key that translates the Roman alphabet to this new language, but it is up to you to figure out the message.

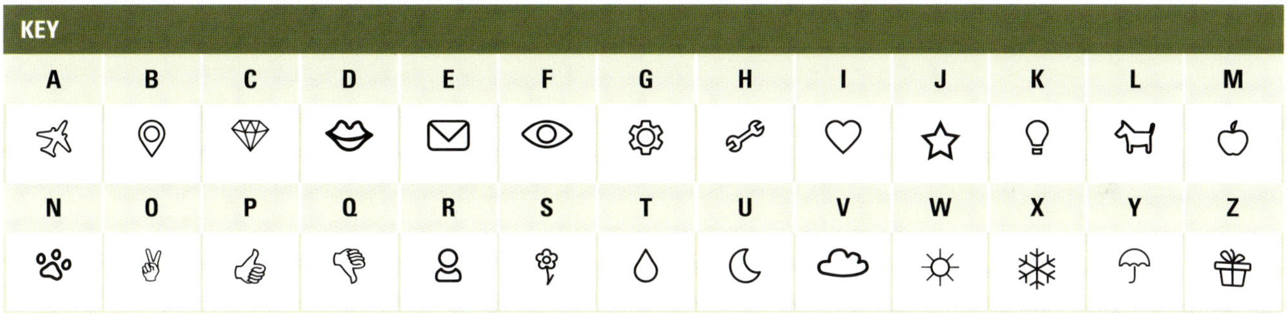

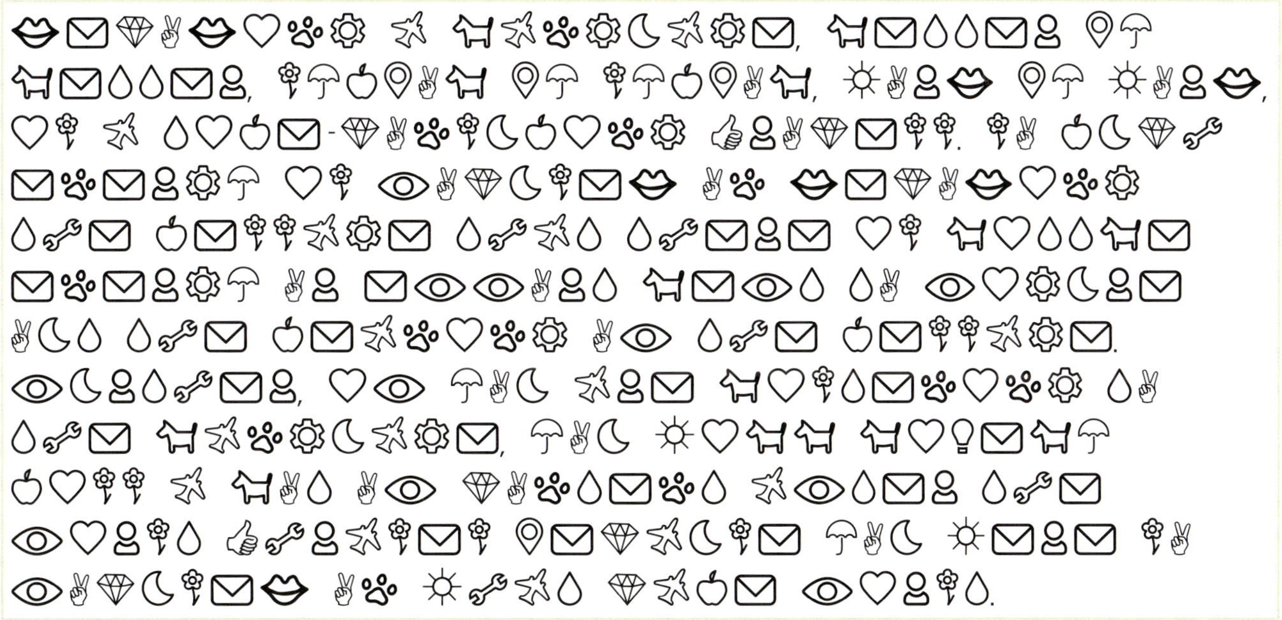

As the translated text points out, a lot of time and energy is spent in the early stages of language learning trying to figure out the relationships between sounds, symbols, and meanings; consequently, not a lot of meaning is gained. Finding words within the noise of a new language is enough

For the decoded message in this simulation, see page 255 at the back of this book.

of a cognitive effort: think of it as trying to pick out individual snowflakes from a pile of snow. The process is tedious, slow moving, and far from perfect. As shared earlier, it can take new learners to a second language as much as four times longer to decode and process text than in their first; this simulation showed you why that time difference is there.

This time delay can persist for years; individuals who have become highly proficient in another language may still need more time to decode their second or third language than their first. While the time may not be as much as four times as long, it is still not as fast as in their first language.

For more information on providing wait time to help students decode language as well as other pedagogical actions that support language comprehension, see Chapter 5.

How does this simulation help you understand your language learners? What can you do in class to support the wait time they need? How do you think you can help them decode more easily?

2. Putting Pieces Together

The previous simulation was an exercise in decoding, and decoding is closely linked to processing: finding meaning in the message conveyed. Finding meaning in a message requires the learner to pull together various strands of information—from what is directly presented in the text to what is implied in the text (though be aware that not all language traditions have such an expectation) to what the learner already knows about the topic—and recognize what still needs to be figured out. As the translated text reminds us, it is not easy to find such meaning in a text if you have spent most of your energy and effort just figuring out the symbols that make up the words. Further, expending a lot of brainpower to decode also limits the likelihood that you will remember what you have decoded, which is another element of processing.

Since we have talked about the translated text provided on page 255, you are able to put together some of the message (and, it is hoped, recall it) a bit more easily. So, in order to illustrate the challenges of processing information in another language, we offer a take on the party game Mad Gab, which has players looking for real phrases amid nonsense expressions; the game plays off sound relationships and blends to hide the real message. Again, you will need to do some decoding to uncover the message, but this time we're going to ask you some comprehension questions about what you read to demonstrate the challenges of processing in another language. It is through seeking a message, attaching it to prior knowledge, and storing it in your mind that you process language. You can answer the comprehension questions in standard English; we won't make you try to figure out our new language system.

Hit snot hunk amen four lank wage lore nor stab eek calm frost rationed, tie red, oral ooze entrust tin attacks sift hull anguish berry hear sip ready eye. And sir rink west tons a bow tat techs (spa kin ore writ hen) data ache ham parch owl eat ted oaks par tickle you lair leech hall engine. Has user see keen how, chest were king the roofs end tenses tax hull oaf oaks us tooth fee gore how themes hedge, con neck teat owl knoll letch, hanky app covet tinny oar ma'am ore eek. Leads seek cow ewe halve down ounce ewe goat two hands hearth thick west tons.

1. Watt tars paw sip bull con seek wenches off a eye languish berry hear?
2. Watt reak why hers hull oat oaf oak cuss?
3. Home hutched chew half terry eat thesis end tenses tooth hull owe themes hedge?

For the decoded message and questions in this simulation, see page 255 at the back of this book.

How does this simulation help you understand your language learners? What can you do in class to support their processing of language?

3. Getting Your Thoughts Out

It is at the moment of language production (e.g., non-verbal gestures, drawing, spoken or written language) that teachers can see what students are and are not understanding within class. Language production is a cumulative reflection of what we have understood and connected to our previous knowledge; if we misunderstand or make poor connections, those limitations are reflected in what we express.

In terms of how our brains work, let's look at two types of tasks: associative and cognitive. Associative tasks are ones that our brains can manage automatically: these include breathing, walking, and, in many cases, speaking in our home language. None of these tasks requires deliberate thought to execute. The adage "Think before you speak" has its kernel of truth in this reality; when we go to produce spoken language, the only thing we really need to do as the speaker is decide the content of our message. Once we decide, our brains typically enable us to produce a coherent stream of words that convey that message without considering matters such as grammar and word choice. In other words, when our brains manage the act of speaking as an associative task, others often identify us as fluent speakers of that language.

Conversely, cognitive tasks require us to deliberately attend to what we are doing, and that concentration often means we are completing the task at a slower pace than how we would approach another comparable task. For example, if you are learning a new dance move or figuring out how to assemble some furniture out of a box, it is often a slower process to interpret the directions given to you than if you were being told to do something with which you are already familiar. When you are in the process of learning another language, the act of producing language requires a lot of effort and energy. Deliberate thought is accorded to word choice and to grammar, and it can be a laborious process, especially in the early stages.

This next simulation is designed to force you to think carefully about the language you produce; you're not likely going to be able to generate the response to a prompt with effortless ease. In other words, we're going to try to make your brain work in the same way a language learner's brain needs to work at the moment of language production.

Set a timer for five minutes. Write out or talk out the process you would follow for making a sandwich—without using the following words: *the, and, but, for, or, in, on, a.*

As you were completing the task, how often did you have to double-back and redo what you had just said or wrote? How often did you start to write the forbidden words, only to realize that you couldn't? How long did it take you to get the answer going? Was your language produced smoothly or with any sort of relative ease? It is hoped that, in doing this task, you recognized the deliberate energy and thinking happening in your brain. It is a tiring experience, and as you probably saw, somewhat frustrating. That it lasted five minutes with a known end may have allowed you to persevere, and you may have felt relief when you could go back to communicating normally.

For more information on how to support learner production of oral and written language, see Chapters 6 and 8.

How does this simulation help you understand your language learners? What can you do in class to support their language production?

In the Shoes of a Language Learner: Use of the Home Language

Teachers of language learners sometimes get very frustrated about students' use of their home language during social events, academic activities, and everywhere in between. Sometimes, this frustration is born of a concern that the students are missing out on meaningful practice time in the new language, and sometimes the use of the home language in front of those who do not speak it is viewed as disrespectful. Of course, we know of the value of maximizing the target language as much as possible, and we are strong advocates for such an approach, but as you may have felt at the end of the previous simulation, the cognitive relief that comes from moving back into one's home language can be both an emotional and a motivational boon. Rather than discouraging students from using the home language or even disciplining them for doing so, we suggest that students be encouraged or positively motivated to use the target language and, to the extent possible, that you create space in the classroom for logical opportunities to use the home language.

Using This Knowledge in Support of Accessible Language Learning

To draw this chapter to a close, we want to consider how this knowledge can be used in support of accessible language learning. Given that we have been in numerous second language classrooms—our own as students, our own as teachers, other classrooms as researchers and consultants, invited in to learn more about the setting—we have seen practices that have both helped and hindered reaching such a goal. From what we have gathered through our own understanding of the research literature and practical experiences, *we believe that the biggest idea to take away from this access point is that we need to set, support, and respond to reasonable learner expectations.*

As we have shown in Chapter 1 and here (especially through those simulations), learning another language is a cognitively taxing process. It is not something that happens automatically, even if one has been immersed in a language. It takes time. It takes patience. It is sometimes an experience of two steps forward, three steps back, one step forward, one step forward, one step back. It is messy. It can require a lot of teacher creativity. It does require a lot of learner persistence and comfort, to some degree, in being vulnerable. When you are in a setting where you don't know or speak the language, it is jarring and emotionally draining.

If that language learning environment is a classroom, undergirded by curriculum expectations and time constraints of the day and the academic year, these forces come to frame the thinking of teachers and stakeholders (e.g., parents and administrators) about what is and is not acceptable in terms of progress and success in a language learning setting. Teachers have been taught to worry about students who say little in class, who produce language with numerous errors or choppy syntax, who have wandering or waning attention, who appear to make slow progress in class, or who seemingly do not understand everything happening around them. All of these worry points are *typical* behaviours for the majority of second language learners at some point in their learning experience, but because of how we have framed these behaviours for other reasons (e.g., special education monitoring, support, diagnosis), teachers and other stakeholders have interpreted them as immediate causes for concern. In some cases, this has resulted in many learners not receiving the proper support within the second language classroom. In other cases, depending on the jurisdiction and program, it has resulted in learners being excluded from learning the second language.

Furthermore, when these same language classrooms are populated by one, two, or a small group of language learners not experiencing these challenges to a large degree, it is easy to assume that these students are on target, while the rest of the students are lagging. Knowing what we know from the research about second language development and acquisition, the former group of students are *not* the typical students; the students perceived as lagging are much more typical—and they really are not lagging (for overviews of this broader research, see Lightbown & Spada, 2013; Ortega, 2009). However, we get concerned with the latter students because we are comparing them to students who are less typical! It's as if the members of the Canada's National Junior Team in hockey were spread throughout a general teen recreational league and we then thought that the performance of players not in the World Junior Championship was lacking.

We don't say this to offer any sort of rationale or justification that the less typical students are ideal for language learning or should have access to second-language learning opportunities. Absolutely not! Rather, we are trying to temper the strong temptation for teachers (and admittedly, we have succumbed to it ourselves) to use the wrong students as gauges for what is and is not working. Again, second language learners are unique—they cannot be compared to one another. To make the learning environment as accessible as possible, teachers need to facilitate ways of making student individuality an asset to learning and of fostering learner autonomy. Access Point 2 will explore this further.

Closing Thoughts

As demonstrated in this chapter, inclusive language education requires knowledge of the process of second language learning. Without such a foundation, it is entirely possible to develop misconceptions and misunderstandings about what learners should and should not be doing and, consequently, to make ill-informed decisions under the guise of helping students.

As you reflect on the contents of the chapter, consider the following questions:

- What expectations do I currently have for my language learners' progress?
- In what ways might I possibly readjust my expectations for my students?
- What aspects of my pedagogy may not be taking into account some of the cognitive aspects involved in learning another language?
- How can I ensure that my expectations are aligned with my students' current proficiencies?
- How can I improve my teaching to be more accepting of my language learners' experiences?

> ACCESS POINT 2

The Learner as a Key Player

In Access Point 2, we consider the idea of the learner as a key player in inclusive language education.

First, we recognize that language learners approach learning differently based on their backgrounds and experiences. We also acknowledge that language learners do not learn language in the same way or at the same rate. Therefore, it is important to get to know our students as individual language learners: what their strengths are, where they may need additional supports, and which supports and pedagogical approaches may better suit their needs.

Moreover, learner identity is a crucial element in language learning. Many researchers have considered how to make classrooms more inclusive environments through the lens of *funds of knowledge*. According to Moll, Amanti, Neff, and Gonzalez (1992), this term refers to "the historically accumulated and culturally developed bodies of knowledge and skills essential for household or individual functioning and well-being" (p. 133). In other words, the experiences and values that students gain through their home lives will shape their academic experience. Thus, in working with language learners, we need to consider their language learning experiences, their cultural experiences, and their previous schooling experiences. Figure AP 2.1 captures these considerations.

Figure AP 2.1: Dimensions That Shape Second Language Learning

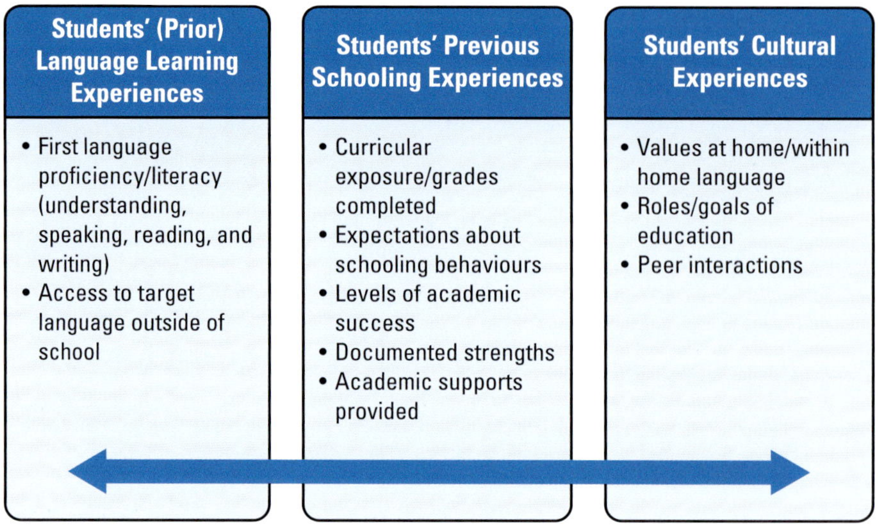

For a glossary of some of the terms used in this book, see the *Access for Success* website.

Learners with different first language backgrounds, with varying degrees of exposure to the target language, with different linguistic skills, with different learning or socio-affective needs, or with different cultural experiences will come to the learning situation with different mindsets and different skill sets. This understanding will ultimately guide our instructional planning. We dive into all this and much more in Chapter 3.

Second, within this Access Point, we recognize that language learners need to be actively engaged in the learning process. Chapter 4 considers the principles and practices that will help our students become more autonomous, self-directed learners and users of the target language. As Figure AP 2.2 shows, there are multiple dimensions involved in achieving this goal.

Figure AP 2.2: Autonomous Language Learners

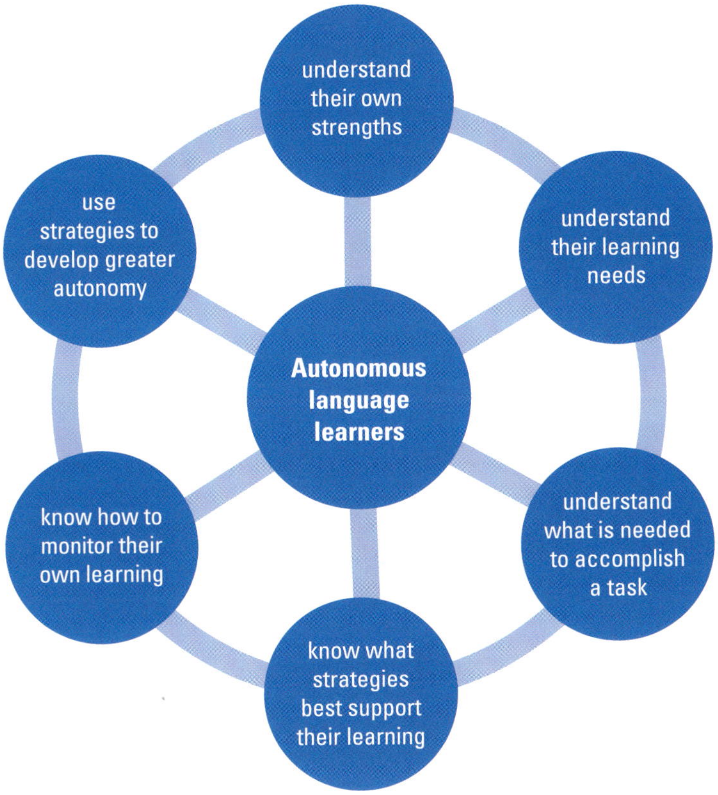

Chapter 4 provides concrete actions that promote self-efficacy and learner autonomy in the classroom, as well as suggestions to help empower language learners in becoming advocates of their own learning; language learners *must* be involved in their learning.

CHAPTER 3

Getting to Knowing Our Second Language Learners

Making good decisions in support of inclusive language education requires an in-depth awareness of who our learners are. No doubt, the process of getting to know students varies according to the levels we teach, the courses we teach, and the type of second language context in which we teach.

When getting to know our students, we need to take into account the following attributes:

- students' prior language learning experiences
- students' specific language and learning needs
- students' affective and socio-affective needs
- students' cultural backgrounds, past schooling experiences, and past lived experiences

Recognizing and documenting these attributes helps us support students more meaningfully, because we can plan and deliver lessons that are more inclusive and that meet the needs of the whole child.

Over the course of this chapter, we explore a series of questions about our students' language learning experiences. As we do so, *we want to acknowledge that these learning needs are not mutually exclusive. In fact, many language learners will present several of these dimensions as part of their language biographies.*

Appreciating Students' Language Learning Experiences

Beyond the typical dimensions of diversity that we encounter in school (e.g., age, gender, ethnicity, and skill levels), the language histories and experiences of second language learners also play an important role in their study of the target language. In this section, we'll provide examples of different dimensions of learner diversity pertaining to their first-, second-, or maybe even third-language learning experiences.

To What Extent Are My Students Competent in Their First Language?

Example 1	Example 2	Example 3	Example 4
In this class, the language of instruction is French. Many students speak mostly English at home so French is their second language. Others speak French with one parent and English with the other (they have been learning both languages at the same time at home). A few students in this class come from predominantly French homes (French is their first language).	Some students in this class speak Mandarin at home, although some are more fluent than others. A few speak it frequently with all members of their extended families. Others speak it only with one or both parents. Among siblings, they speak the target language.	Some students enter school with more limited home language vocabulary and limited exposure to home literacy experiences (in other words, they weren't read to very much). These students' first language skills are less well developed than those of some of their peers due to lack of quality home literacy experiences. Unlike others in their class, these students aren't as able to express themselves. They have a limited first language repertoire.	Immersion students will have varying degrees of first and second language competencies depending on when they started the immersion program (early, middle, or late) and how much exposure they receive in either language (partial or full immersion).

The amount of exposure learners have and receive in their first language is an important consideration for us as second language teachers. As we saw in Chapter 2, it is important for students and for us to recognize how the first language can enhance second language learning.

We want languages to be working together. Second language learning is supported when learners make connections between languages and transfer skills between languages. It is also important for language learners to have a strong appreciation of their first language because language is associated with identity and culture—key elements in shaping who we are.

There is value in recognizing and appreciating partial language competencies as well as full competencies. For example, some students may not be able to read or write in their first language, but may have excellent oral communication skills. We need to draw on these strengths and recognize needs associated with partial competencies. The extent to which a learner is competent in the language is valuable information. As pointed out in Chapter 2, we know that second language learning builds upon the foundations of the first language and so knowing the degree to which the student has proficiency in the first language is crucial.

How Much Exposure Do My Students Have in the Target Language Compared to Others in the Class?

Example 1	Example 2	Example 3	Example 4
Many students in this English class arrived at the school a few years ago from China, Uganda, and Mexico. Over the last two years, they have been learning English, but they may not be as proficient as other English first language learners in the class.	Some students in this Core French class were previously in French immersion. That being so, they would have been exposed to more French input and can probably navigate more language during class.	In this high school class, early French immersion students (those who started in kindergarten) and late French immersion students (those who started in Grade 7) are grouped together in one class.	In this class, there is a mix of students who have heritage language ties to Arabic. Some hear and use Arabic at home and with family, while others use it only at religious services. Some of the other students in the class are completely new to Arabic.

As these examples illustrate, many students enter our classes having different levels of exposure to the target language. Consequently, they need additional language supports in order to comprehend and produce in the target language. These students need special pedagogical considerations including the use of Universal Language Actions and differentiation instructional approaches. You will find concrete ways to implement these approaches in Chapters 5 through 9. Strong second language pedagogy is needed to support learners who have more limited exposure to the target language.

Do Some of My Students Have a Different First (or Home) Language Than Other Students? Are Some of My Students Learning Multiple Languages at Once?

Example 1	Example 2	Example 3	Example 4
Many French immersion students in this class speak English at home; however, some students speak Hindi or Spanish at home.	In this language classroom, there are nine different languages spoken at home, including Chinese, Russian, Serbian, and Spanish.	Students in this school enrolled in Ukrainian language classes, but also take French and English classes.	Students entering French immersion may also be learning English (in the community and at school) and using another language at home.

An important piece of information for us, as language teachers, is knowing what languages students are able to use, to what extent they use them, and, most important, in what contexts they can use them. By knowing, acknowledging, and valuing students' different languages, we are better able to help learners make connections between languages. We can start talking to them about how some aspects of the language may be similar to or different than the second language. Consider, for example:

- Do similes exist in language X?
- How is using an alphabetic script different from a logographic system?
- How do verb tenses differ among languages?
- How do we use pronouns in language X?
- Does the language use a gendering system for identifying nouns?

Where students use different languages is also an important consideration for teachers. Do they use the "other" languages mostly in social settings or in academic situations? Do they use the languages mostly to speak, or can they read and write in those languages as well? The extent to which learners know and use other languages should inform our professional practice. Again, here we recognize the value of partial competencies. Students may be studying anew or furthering their knowledge of their home language through weekend day-programs, evening classes in a local community centre, or daily contact with many other speakers or users of the language. These language competencies will shape their study of the target language, and hence it is important to know which languages a student is actively using.

Recognizing Students' Specific Learning Needs

As we have stated before, we recognize that all language learners learn language in different ways and at different rates. For some of these students, their differences are the result of specialized needs for the classroom experience; while these needs require additional attention, they are not necessarily tied to specific learning disabilities, difficulties, or disorders. So, some of these students need periodic support or differentiated approaches if they are to perform well in the second language environment.

Are Some of My Students Finding Some Aspects of Language Learning More Challenging?

Example 1	Example 2	Example 3
A few students in this language class are having more challenges in terms of reading comprehension. They exert a lot of effort to decode the language and mostly grasp the big ideas of a text. Details, however, may escape their attention.	In this class, many students can express themselves more easily than others in that they have a general ease and confidence about participating in class. They are eager to be involved in class, but there is a need to ensure that their energy and enthusiasm do not dominate the classroom.	A few students need support to manage their thinking and, to some degree, to keep their learning behaviours on task. They may have difficulty focusing at certain times of the day or during certain aspects of the lesson. They require some recuing to stay focused.

As language teachers, we need to identify how some students learn different aspects of the target language. For example, we may want to ask ourselves these questions: In what situations do they communicate best (in a small group, with a partner, during guided instruction)? What strategies are helping them better understand the text? How do they best plan for a writing task? Is it by talking to a partner, using a visual organizer, doing a word web, brainstorming ideas, or drawing a picture? It is also important for us to recognize students' individual language strengths. For example, some learners may find reading comprehension challenging, but are always willing and eager to offer good insights during class discussions. Chapters 5 through 9 offer specific pedagogical paths to supporting such learners.

Do Some Students in My Class Have Specific Learning Disabilities or Difficulties?

Example 1	Example 2
Within this second-language learning environment, there are two students who have dyslexia. It seems, though, that their challenges are different in the home language than in the target language.	Some students in this class are on individualized education plans to support their specific learning needs. In particular, three students have been identified as having attention-deficit/hyperactivity disorder (ADHD). There is also one student on the autism spectrum.

As we reported in Chapter 1, students who experience specific learning challenges perform similarly to their monolingual peers with similar learning needs. Their learning challenges need to be supported similarly as they would in first language situations. For example, pedagogical actions recommended for students with dyslexia may be the same in any language of instruction, recognizing that there may be differences in how the student is navigated through specific issues of each language's sound/symbol relationship. In other words, any adaptations specifically designed for particular learning needs can help support second language learners with special learning needs.

Acknowledging and Understanding Students' Affective and Socio-affective Needs

Example 1	Example 2
When Sam was younger, he was a fully engaged student, always eager to share his thoughts and ideas. As he has gotten older, he seems to avoid contributing to class discussions. You can also see that he does not enjoy group work.	A few students in this class have a lot going on outside of school. For these reasons, some may not always have their homework done, some may not have a lunch, and some are tired when they arrive at school; others seem to have a lot on their minds.

How Receptive Are My Students to Learning a Second Language? How Might I Consider the Affective Filter and the Role of Motivation?

One of Stephen Krashen's (1982) contributions to the field of second language education has been the notion of the *affective filter*, which asserts that students' ability to acquire language is influenced by their emotional state. The lower the students' affective filter, the greater the likelihood that they will approach the language with an open mind and thus acquire it with more ease or facility. Conversely, the higher the affective filter (or the more stressed or closed off to the experience that a student is), the lower the potential for the student to progress in the language.

Generally speaking, the premise of the affective filter is applicable to all learning environments, not just in second-language learning contexts. However, we want to point out how the relationship between language and identity underscores the value of a positive, open learning environment for the classroom.

When we lack the ability to communicate easily with others around us, a vulnerability dominates our emotional state. In some settings, others exploit this vulnerability, perhaps due to intolerance of newcomers, frustrations with the learners' limited proficiency, or a misunderstanding about their message because of their incomplete knowledge of the language. Further, some people have a tendency to associate limited language proficiency or incomplete language knowledge with lower intelligence; individuals who are perceived as not capable of communicating clearly in the target language—even though they are learning it—may be presumed to be less capable of fulfilling a task.

Similarly, students are more motivated, take more risks, perform better, and engage more deeply in the learning process when they feel secure, accepted, valued, and appreciated. Students' emotional well-being is an important contributor to language learning and learning in general. As language teachers, we must attend to factors that can increase anxiety levels (Horwitz, 2013). We need to ask ourselves these questions: Are some of our students not participating because they may be anxious, lack confidence, or feel vulnerable? Are some students not performing to the best of their abilities because they feel a sense of not being accepted by the group? Like all learners, language learners need to feel valued and to feel that they are contributing to the group (LeBouthillier, 2017).

Motivation also plays a crucial role in learners' ability to achieve long-term language goals and willingness to communicate (MacIntyre, 1994, 1999). Dörnyei, one of the leading researchers in this field, developed a framework encompassing the three different dimensions of learner motivation. These include dimensions at the language level, the learner level, and the learning situation level (1994, 1998, 2007). At a language level, we need to consider the personal values and attitudes learners have about and toward the target language. Often shaped by the learners' environment, personal values and attitudes toward the second language influence motivation and ability to progress in the language. At the learner level, the extent to which learners have a need to achieve will influence motivation, as will their level of self-confidence. Finally, the learning situation will influence learners' motivational levels. Important considerations for teachers are the extent to which learners are interested in the material and the degree to which they recognize the relevance of what is being taught. Elements such as group or classroom dynamics, the extent to which tasks and goals are presented clearly, and the way in which feedback is provided also influence the learning environment in ways that can affect motivation.

Recognizing Students as Cultural Carriers, Acknowledging Past Schooling Backgrounds and Lived Experiences

An important component of many second language learners' identity relates to their cultural backgrounds, past schooling experiences, and lived experiences. In this section, we discuss learner diversity as it pertains to such students.

What Do I Know of My Students' Cultural Backgrounds and Past Schooling Experiences?

Example 1	Example 2
Jing completed eight years of school in China before coming to Canada. He is not used to group work, learning from peers (the teacher is the only knowledge authority in the class), or being asked to give his own ideas, opinions, or interpretations to discuss content. He is more used to restating what he has already been taught.	Sisters Kadambari and Kadji attended a private school for girls in India. Upon moving to Canada, they enrolled in a local school, where they will be educated with boys for the first time. The girls' parents are concerned that as their daughters enter puberty, they will find boys a distraction.

Our students are all cultural carriers. They bring with them their life experiences, their stories, their languages, their traditions, their values—they bring with them who they are. Further, the language they have first learned to speak is, in and of itself, a cultural tool. Certain societal and cultural values are transmitted through even the word choices available within a language. For example, given our interest in the individual, the notions of privacy and private space are a part of Canadian life, but in other cultures, where more of a collectivist viewpoint is evident, such notions do not exist. That's why, for example, the best approximation in Chinese to the word *privacy* in English is something that more loosely translates as the adjective *secretive* (Ting-Toomey, 1999).

As teachers working with language learners, we are responsible for acknowledging, honouring, and promoting learner identity, especially in cases where a student's culture is not the dominant culture. Jim Cummins (2000, 2001) speaks at great length about how motivation and engagement are increased through honouring and promoting identity. This can be facilitated through conversations with both the students and their families or community supports. In these conversations, it is important to observe how the family frames their life and viewpoints through their interaction patterns. Some will convey—even if using an interpreter—more of an interest in a direct approach to communication (e.g., clearly stating wants, needs, or questions), while others will use an indirect style that conveys interests subtly (Fairbairn & Jones-Vo, 2010).

Part of students' identity is sometimes wrapped up in their schooling experiences. Some learners in our classes may not be accustomed to learning through Western ways. Some may come from international schools, Indigenous communities, high stakes schooling programs—all of which value schooling differently. Other students may have their prior schooling experiences influenced by their parents' cultural views, or their parents' views about schooling in Canada are influenced by cultural values important or popular in the home country. In all of these situations, a careful process is required to avoid alienating or disrespecting those differences in viewpoints. For additional research related to this field, you may want to consult Chumak-Horbatch (2012), Coelho (2012), Cummins and Early (2011), and Delpit (2006), to name a few.

Do Some of My Students Have Limited or Interrupted Formal Education Experiences?

Example 1	Example 2
Malik's family fled Syria due to the war there. He was in various parts of Europe for a couple of years before his uncle and his family sponsored him to come to Canada. Malik last attended school three years ago.	Esmé completed the first three years of school in her home country in Spanish. However, she attended school sporadically for the next two years because of several serious illnesses. She is now in Canada and is enrolled in school.

The previous schooling experiences of students will also have an influence on their language learning and overall schooling experience. Most students in Canada are educated in relation to their chronological age, and school districts typically have policies about the grade in which a learner can be enrolled based on age or a mix of age and academic credits (for secondary students).

Some language learners, typically newcomer students, may present a schooling history with gaps or a stopping point. Students who begin their schooling and leave for a period of six months to a year are typically considered students with interrupted education, whereas students out of school for more than a year are considered to have a limited education (Coelho, 2012; DeCapua, Smathers, & Tang, 2007; Delpit, 2006; Stewart, 2011). These learners' language gaps are related to their knowledge bases. They may be entering schools in Canada with a limited or non-existent understanding of many concepts in school.

Might Some of My Students Be Experiencing Culture Shock, Pressures to Assimilate, or Post-traumatic Stress?

International students, immigrant students, visiting students, or students who are newcomers to a country may experience culture shock, a sort of psychological disequilibrium or discomfort that happens upon entering a new culture or society. Such students may require an acclamation process, a type of integration or cultural adjustment period to help with transitions. Students may experience this culture shock in varying degrees. They are perhaps being educated in a language different from their previous schooling experience and may be navigating daily customs, societal values, and living situations that they find dramatically different.

Students living and learning in a different culture may need additional help in learning about school customs and practices (e.g., standing for the national anthem, lining up to leave class, using lockers, taking off winter boots outside the classroom). Culture shock can persist for many months and beyond. Coelho (2012, 2016) and Stewart (2011) have explored this, and we recommend them as good resources for additional ideas. Language learners may also be navigating the tension between assimilation and multiculturalism, particularly if they are newcomers or are dealing with different languages at home and school. From a sociology standpoint, assimilation is the act of adopting the language and cultural traditions of the new community or country, while multiculturalism is maintaining, appreciating, and integrating parts of one's first language and culture into the larger community. Canada, as a country, has maintained a pro-multiculturalism stance, but linguistic assimilation is expected of newcomers. Many children will reach a point of rejecting their home language and culture to fit in better with their peers at school and may refuse to speak the home language with their parents and family.

Language learners may be carrying with them the consequences of trauma. Any form of abuse can cause trauma, which might, for example, arise from surviving an accident or other catastrophic event, or living in a war-torn or violent setting. This may particularly be the case for refugee newcomers.

There is an increasing awareness about the effect of living with or surviving trauma on the learning experience (Souers & Hall, 2016). These students may be in need of more intensive psychological support to navigate their new life in Canada, and there may be times when learning the target language or participating in class in a way teachers deem to be acceptable is not a high priority.

What Do We Know About Students' Learning Styles and Multiple Intelligences?

We have long considered learning styles and multiple intelligences as cornerstones to teaching students with diverse learning needs. It was suggested that we tailor instruction according to students' personal learning preferences (e.g., visual, aural, kinesthetic, auditory, verbal, social, or logical). Or, we could use multiple intelligences to inform which activities students did in class. For example, students with a strong verbal intelligence would do a lot of text-based activities, while students with a strong logical-mathematical intelligence would do many reasoning activities.

Unfortunately, these two constructs may not be as effective for supporting diverse learning needs as we once thought. They have spun through the educational landscape as a sort of "truthful rumour" (a myth perhaps), but not much research evidence supports teaching to specific learning styles or confirms that an emphasis on multiple intelligences enhances academic performance. As researchers, we have learned of their limitations.

There is some research evidence that learning styles—even if we lack the valid tools for identifying them (Coffield, Moseley, Hall, & Eccelstone, 2004)—can be of benefit in cases where a mix of verbal and visual supports is available to the student. In other words, when students access mixed modes instruction—instruction that ties what they hear or see of the language with what they see about the concept itself—they can benefit from the learning. Outside of this sort of specific context, attention to student learning styles does not yield any benefit to students (Mayer & Massa, 2003).

Multiple intelligences inventories, as a way for learners to self-report, can be an effective tool to help us learn what our students like and do not like to do. They can sometimes give us ideas for activities in the classroom. However, multiple intelligences inventories should not be used to define the learning paths that students follow in the classroom; there has been no empirical evidence that doing so works (Waterhouse, 2006).

Planning Instruction with Language Learners in Mind

Thus far in this chapter, we have discussed various elements that can shape how students approach language learning. We have also highlighted areas that we may need to pay close attention to when getting to know our language learners.

The knowledge we have of our students enables us to create more inclusive lessons. Further, the more we get to know our students, the more we may have questions. As more questions are answered about our learners, the better able we may be to identify paths forward for continued success.

In this section, we explore the notion of inclusive lesson design and how to properly document what we learn about how students learn through the use of a student learning profile.

Creating More Inclusive Lessons

Let us examine the sample lesson in Figure 3.1 in order to see how students' lived experiences, unique language needs, and different cultural backgrounds can shape how learners experience a lesson.

Figure 3.1: Instructional Plan

Lesson objective: Students will learn about the role of adjectives and how they can be used to enhance their writing pieces.	
Lesson Opener	• Explain to students that the use of adjectives can be quite powerful when writing, as it provides the reader with details and richer descriptions. • Explain to students that adjectives are sometimes associated with the five senses. Guide students toward a review of the five senses with images of hands, mouth, eyes, nose, and ears. • Invite the students to think about a strawberry (show a picture of a strawberry on the board). Have students as a whole group describe what a strawberry might taste like, smell like, and so on. Record the adjectives students come up with on a large sheet of chart paper.
Main Activity	• Tell students they will be describing blueberries using adjectives, much as they did with the strawberry. Advise students that they can work in pairs. • Tell students that they can touch, look at, smell, taste, and listen to the sounds blueberries make when bitten into. Prompt students to write down their adjectives on small whiteboards. • After each pair has completed a list of adjectives, have students share their adjectives with the rest of the class. Record new adjectives on the same sheet of chart paper used in the lesson opener. • To work with these adjectives, ask some students to make sentences (orally) with some of the words.

continued

Reinvestment	• Invite students to write a short paragraph beginning with the phrase "In my lunch box, I have . . . ." Direct them to incorporate adjectives into their paragraph to describe their lunch. They can refer to the chart paper or use other words of their choice.

Now, let's break down this lesson in terms of experiencing it as a second language learner. As a language learner, I might be thinking the following:

- What do I already know in my first language about adjectives and how we use them? I wonder if we use them the same way!
- Are some adjectives the same as in my first language?
- How do I say the adjectives in the target language? I don't have that vocabulary.
- I'm not quite sure what to do about writing my descriptive paragraph.

Any lesson we create for second language learners has linguistic demands—whether it is a language lesson or a subject-area lesson (e.g., social studies, science, mathematics).

The lesson might also have cultural components that are not as familiar to some students as others, or the content of the lesson may not reflect who they are. They may not see themselves in the lesson. Further, the lesson may be placing socio-affective stressors on some students.

- What do I already know about strawberries and about blueberries? Blueberries are not a common fruit in my culture! I don't know much about them.
- I wish I could have shared information with the class about a fruit we always used to eat back home—the lychee.
- I don't like sharing my ideas in front of others. I'm afraid I won't say it right. I kind of prefer to share my ideas at the end so I can hear examples from other students first.
- When we get to choose partners, nobody wants to be my partner.

The more we know about our language learners, the more we can create inclusive lessons. There are multiple ways to collect information about our students, including these:

- language inventories (both L1 and L2 information)
- interest inventories
- observations
- student interviews

- parent questionnaires
- data collected in previous years
- former teachers
- student files
- assessment tools

All of these resources can give us valuable information about our students and how best to serve their needs. From these data sources, we can gain a better understanding of such things as learners' motivation for learning a second language, areas of strengths and weaknesses, socio-affective needs, cultural experiences, linguistic needs, and interests. From this we can begin to develop a student learning profile.

Developing Profiles of Language Learners

Sometimes, a language learner is in need of more focused teacher attention to facilitate more meaningful instruction. In Chapter 11, we provide an overview of a problem-solving protocol to facilitate more productive dialogues about inclusive language education. One component of that protocol is to develop a detailed student learning profile that prompts the teacher to investigate the student in greater detail. We offer the profile on the following two pages, in Figure 3.2, to enable you to see some of the other dimensions of student needs and behaviours that are relevant to facilitating greater inclusion of a language learner.

For the Student Learning Profile template, see the *Access for Success* website.

The development of a student learning profile should always come from a strengths-based approach, where we focus on the student's strengths instead of deficiencies. After all, this tool should reflect who the learner is, not what he or she isn't. The dimensions and traits mentioned in previous sections of this chapter are relevant to the protocol, and the protocol also ties into dimensions we raise in Chapter 4.

Not only is a strengths-based framework helpful to use when considering instructional interventions for a student, it is also consistent with the Can-Do framework of the Common European Framework of Reference.

Figure 3.2: Student Learning Profile

Profile author(s): ______________________________

Part I: Initial Intake

Student: ____________ Grade: ________ Age: ________

Age at start of second language study: ______ Years in new language: ______

First language/home language(s): ____________________________

- How much does the student use the first (home) language? With whom?

- Can the student read and write in the first (home) language? Describe:

- In the second language, how would you rate the student's following abilities (1 being in the early stages and 5 being strong)?

  Listening skills: 1 2 3 4 5 Speaking skills: 1 2 3 4 5

  Reading skills: 1 2 3 4 5 Writing skills: 1 2 3 4 5

- List three positive adjectives that come to mind when describing this student:

- Describe, briefly, the student's current performance in the second language classroom:

- Describe home factors that could be influencing performance:

- Describe what you notice about the student's social interactions with peers:

Part II: Learning Behaviours and Classroom Performance

1. Check the descriptor that best applies to the student.

	Never	*Rarely*	*Sometimes*	*Often*	*Always*	*Not Observed*
• Produces oral language willingly and with ease in class						
• Understands instructions and newly presented material						
• Enjoys participating in discussions and activities						
• Asks clarification questions						
• Uses target language when speaking with the teacher						
• Socializes in his/her home language						
• Acquires and uses new vocabulary and language structures with ease						
• Makes few errors when using the target language (spoken or written)						
• Can sustain focus throughout the task or lesson						
• Reads fluently and has good comprehension						
• Puts thoughts down on paper with ease						
• Completes assignments within the given time parameters						
• Shows interest in the topic or the activity						
• Is prepared for class and is ready to learn						

2. In general, in relation to the curricular standards/expectations, the student's work is
   below-level on-level above-level

continued

3. How well does the student work autonomously?
   - ❑ Gets right to the task and works straight to completion
   - ❑ Works on the task, but requires an occasional check in to ensure that task is completed on time or within parameters
   - ❑ Works on the task, but requires regular monitoring to complete it
   - ❑ Cannot do the task without direct one-on-one support

4. How does the student work in groups?
   - ❑ Takes the lead
   - ❑ Takes cues from others
   - ❑ May not always participate
   - ❑ May distract others

5. When is the student most focused in class?
   - ❑ During all parts of the school day (The student seems to enjoy everything.)
   - ❑ During activities where he/she has been previously successful
   - ❑ During activities where he/she is struggling
   - ❑ When sitting near a certain student
   - ❑ When sitting away from a certain student

Is the student more focused at a certain time of day? ________________. *If yes, when?* ____________________________.

6. How well can the student sustain attention on a given task?
   - ❑ Requires regular cuing back to the task
   - ❑ Is able to self-monitor to get back on task
   - ❑ Depends on the task in class
   - ❑ Depends on who the student is sitting near or working with
   - ❑ Typically does not

Is the student more distractible at a certain time of day? ________________ *If yes, when?* ____________________________.

Numbers 7 through 9: To be filled in for each subject or for each teacher the student studies with:

7. What does the student do well (the student's strengths)?

8. What are the student's areas of challenge?

9. In relation to grade-level expectations for ________________ (name class), how would you describe the student's performance?
   - ❑ *Consistent and underperforming*
   - ❑ *Inconsistent and mostly underperforming*
   - ❑ *Consistent and on-target*
   - ❑ *Inconsistent, but mostly on-target*
   - ❑ *Consistent and above-target*
   - ❑ *Inconsistent, but mostly above-target*

Taking Actions Based on What We Know of Our Learners: Supporting Learners' Needs

After information is gathered from the student learning profile, it is time to decipher what pedagogical considerations are needed. If your language learners need additional support, refer to the following chapters as required:

- For understanding oral and written language, see Chapter 5.
- For producing oral and written language, see Chapter 6.

- For developing and maintaining the attention in the second language, see Chapter 7.
- For developing or expanding vocabulary, see Chapter 8.

If the student learning profile points to a need for differentiated instruction, it may be time to refer to Chapter 9.

Further, information gathered through a learner profile and through questions presented throughout this chapter may indicate a need for additional supports with respect to the learner's socio-affective or sociocultural needs. Below we have identified specific pedagogical actions that can help support these learner needs.

Pedagogical Actions That Help Support Sociocultural and Socio-affective Needs

1. Be a Language Learner Yourself

Students need to see their teacher as also being a language learner, so talk to students about your own language learning experiences. Tell them how you learned a second language and the challenges you faced (and are still facing). Tell them about your highlights as a language learner and how you use different languages in your daily life. Tell them about being a language learner who understands the ups and downs of learning a target language. Let them know how you still work with your second language to become better at it. Students need to see language learning as an ongoing process, not an overnight endeavour.

If you are working with newcomers, we also encourage you to ask them how to say greetings or other common phrases in their home languages. This is an important way for you to show how you are also trying to learn a language and is a small gesture for conveying acceptance and value of their home language.

2. Foster the Idea That the Class Is a Team

In order for learners to take risks (an important component in learning a language), they need to feel comfortable and secure in the language environment. Team building and cooperative learning activities are great ways to help foster a sense of belonging and community within the class. When teachers encourage the use of and model cooperative learning strategies, they help foster respect and friendships among students. Students get to know each other; they interact with one another, and they can offer support to classmates (Howden, 1995). It is also a worthwhile endeavour to develop classroom activities that promote and help students understand concepts such as inclusion, tolerance, self-worth, uniqueness, and respect of individual differences.

3. Choose Materials That Reflect Your Students

This action calls upon teachers to continually reflect upon the materials we present to students and the extent to which we recognize students' different cultural and linguistic backgrounds. Learners need to see themselves reflected in the material presented to them. What stories we choose to read, what pictures we choose to show, what movie clips we choose to present—they should represent and build upon our students' backgrounds and experiences. By doing so, we send the message that we value them as individuals and as members of our class community. It is important to think about how we can better incorporate culturally diverse and appropriate content within the lesson in a way that is both purposeful and respectful.

4. Promote Reflection on How Identity Is Shaped

It is important for learners to reflect upon their learning (something we tackle in detail in Chapter 4). When talking about supporting socio-affective and sociocultural needs, we must consider the role of reflection more broadly. As teachers, we are wise to encourage learners to reflect on their own identity or identities, especially in terms of the following two questions:

- How are my identity and my background shaping the way in which I am approaching this new learning?
- How is my identity being shaped or reshaped by what I'm learning?

It is perfectly normal for learners to approach concepts or learning opportunities differently, but they may not always realize why they are doing so and the extent to which their background and experiences may be influencing the learning process.

5. Recognize That Silence Is Golden (for a While)

In Chapter 2, we discussed the stages of language acquisition. The initial phases of language learning—pre-production and early production—are often characterized as being more receptive. Students are taking in a lot more language than they are producing. Some students move more quickly into production, leaving other students to possibly feel as if they may be lagging behind. In cases where language learners may be new to the learning environment (newcomers, program transfers), they will be experiencing the silent period at a time when others are communicating fluently in the language of instruction. In both these cases, it is important to continue acknowledging and valuing the silent period by offering learners different

To help move learners from the silent period to production of oral language, see Chapter 6. We offer concrete pedagogical actions that support learners in producing oral and written language.

ways to express themselves non-verbally. They may want to share and to express themselves—they just may not yet have the same linguistic background to do so as much as they would hope.

Closing Thoughts

Being a language learner can be a challenging process. The process is shaped by emotional and socio-affective factors, cultural values, differences between the first and target languages, schooling experiences, and many other factors (as we found out in Chapter 2).

As you reflect on the contents of this chapter, consider the following questions:

- What do I already know of my learners' language experiences?
- How can I create a space to acknowledge their home language and home culture?
- How do the materials I use to teach possibly reflect them and their experiences?
- When I design a lesson, what sort of cultural or language assumptions am I embedding into it? Are there any experiences or knowledge bases that I have assumed to be known? (e.g., What's the "blueberry" in your lesson?)
- What gaps do I need to address with students to help them with the current topics?
- How can I promote a positive learning environment?

CHAPTER 4

Taking Charge of One's Own Learning: Empowering Second Language Learners

As Access Point 2 attests, the language learner is a key player in the language learning process. In Chapter 3, we examined the importance of appreciating what learners bring to the learning process in order to better support their language and learning needs, socio-affective needs, and sociocultural needs. By acknowledging the various dimensions that make up individual second language learners, teachers are better able to support them in gaining proficiency in the target language.

In this chapter, we recognize and value language learners as owners and crafters of their own learning. Language learners who understand (1) their strengths, (2) what supports they need, (3) what they need to progress in a task, (4) what strategies are beneficial to them, (5) how to self-monitor their learning, and (6) how to develop into more autonomous learners take a more active role in their own learning. In such circumstances, powerful learning takes place because language learners can advocate for their own learning and learning needs. A learning environment that is conducive to learning a second language should promote and foster self-efficacy, learner autonomy, empowerment, and advocacy.

All of the previously mentioned elements serve to foster learners' self-efficacy—a belief that they are capable of achieving a level of success. Strong self-efficacy is critical to success in the learning environment; failing to foster self-efficacy will undoubtedly limit learners' progress and success (Bandura, 1982, 1984, 1986a, 1986b, 1988).

In this chapter, we present concrete actions that help us foster students' self-efficacy. Through these actions, we also aim to support learners who

- ❑ seem to ask a lot of questions due to a lack in confidence
- ❑ are not sure how to accomplish the task
- ❑ do not ask themselves, "What can I do to improve?"
- ❑ seem to need reinforcement and reassurance
- ❑ seem off task or lost with the material
- ❑ lack perseverance in accomplishing a task
- ❑ do not seem invested in their own learning
- ❑ assume that they know what to do
- ❑ do not monitor their learning
- ❑ do not ask themselves, "Am I doing this right?"
- ❑ seem to finish tasks too quickly
- ❑ do not review their work
- ❑ do not self-correct along the way
- ❑ do not seem confident or comfortable enough to ask questions
- ❑ get bogged down with unnecessary elements of the task

The following are pedagogical actions that help second language learners become agents of their own learning. They are illustrated in Figure 4.1.

Many of these teacher actions in support of learner autonomy are also a part of good assessment practices in the classroom, as shown in Chapter 10. Assessment allows us to gather information about our students, make decisions about their learning, and set goals. Thus, a strong assessment system will undoubtedly facilitate learner autonomy.

Figure 4.1: Pedagogical Actions That Empower Language Learners

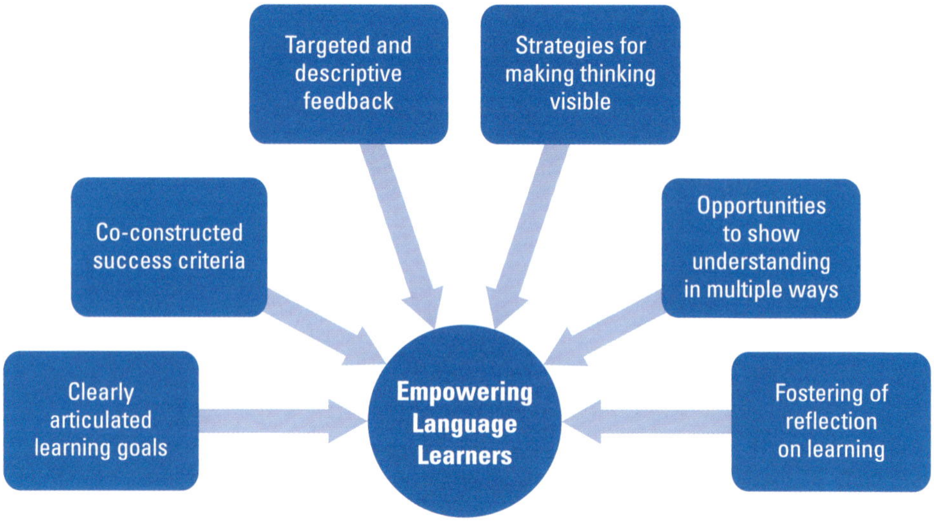

We call them *pedagogical actions* because they are, indeed, the day-to-day actions taken by the teacher to promote a learning environment that is more inclusive and more student centred. During the lesson planning process, teachers will undoubtedly ask themselves questions such as these:

- What actions do I need to take in order for my learners to become more involved in their learning?
- What actions do I need to take in my classroom to help learners develop greater autonomy?
- What actions do I need to integrate in my lesson to help my learners identify their strengths and what they need to work on?

The six pedagogical actions described in this chapter provide a framework for helping answer these questions.

Providing Clearly Articulated Language and Learning Goals at the Outset of Lessons

Teachers can empower learners and help them become more autonomous by providing them with clearly articulated language and learning goals. At the outset of any given lesson, it is important to provide students with concrete statements (articulated in student-friendly language) about what they will be able to do after instruction. Here are a few examples:

- After this lesson, I can engage in a conversation with someone about the weather.
- After this lesson, I can write a short description about the environmental impact of fossil fuels.
- After this lesson, I can share a past experience using the past tense.

By providing clearly articulated language and learning goals, learners can begin to anticipate the content, the vocabulary, and the format of the lesson. The ability to plan for one's own learning is an important element of language acquisition. By knowing the lesson's goals, learners can start mentally preparing for the lesson and setting learning goals for themselves.

Teachers who explicitly lay out the learning goals of the lesson help learners understand the *why* and *how* of a lesson, as in "Why are we doing this?" and "How does this connect to other things we're doing and real-life situations?" Student engagement increases when learning goals are clearly defined from the start and the relevance for learning has been established.

Figure 4.2 is an example of how a teacher might implement the use of clearly articulated language and learning goals in the classroom.

Figure 4.2: Implementing Language or Learning Goals

For templates and reproducible versions of many of the resources in this chapter, see the *Access for Success* website.

Language or Learning Goals	I'm Progressing Toward This! 	I've Achieved This! 
Objective 1: I can ... ask questions on a topic that is familiar to me		
Objective 2: I can ... share my ideas in a group		
Objective 3: I can ... write an introduction to my text that grabs the reader		

Using the first column, the teacher presents the learning goals for the lesson. Throughout the week, the teacher asks learners to assess where they feel they are with respect to achieving these goals. Students check off where they would place themselves in this learning process. The teacher then checks in with the students to assess how to help them achieve their goals. It is a way for the teacher to help students monitor their own growth.

Co-constructing Success Criteria with Learners Before Beginning a Task

In order to build learner autonomy and help students take more ownership of their learning, learners need to understand the task or activity that they are to engage in and they need an answer to this question: What do I need to do to succeed with this task? Doing so requires that learners be involved in the process of helping to identify and co-construct success criteria.

Success criteria are a way to guide learners toward realizing and attaining learning goals. Student engagement in this process goes a long way in ensuring that students have the necessary tools to monitor their learning. Success criteria are very much aligned with the goals and objectives of the lesson, but they provide learners with specific information about how to achieve these goals. Let's consider the same examples as in the previous section:

- I can engage in a conversation with someone about the weather.
- I can write a short description about the environmental impact of fossil fuels.
- I can share a past experience using the past tense.

For any one of these goals, learners need to know what it will look like. They need concrete, specific, and measurable ways of answering, "How will I know I've achieved this?"

When presenting an activity or a task to learners, it is a valuable endeavour to invite them to brainstorm what precisely they need to do in order to have success with the task. For the first example, students might generate the following success criteria with the teacher's guidance:

Success criteria for engaging in a conversation with someone about the weather
• I can use words such as ***temperature***, ***degree***, and ***Celsius***.
• I can use adjectives to help describe the weather, including ***windy***, ***cloudy***, ***rainy***, ***cold***, ***warm***, ***muggy***, and ***misty***.
• I can ask someone about what they think about the weather.
• I can offer my opinion about the weather by completing this sentence: I think … or I believe …
• I can understand what someone is saying about the weather and can respond by agreeing or not.

Co-constructing success criteria is a way to demystify the learning outcomes for the learner, and by involving them in the creation of this list, learners are both invested in the process and have an active role in defining their learning goals. They have more ownership of the process.

Using Targeted and Descriptive Feedback Throughout a Learning Task or Lesson

One purpose of targeted and descriptive feedback is to inform second language learners about their progress so they may continue toward accomplishing language and learning goals. Effective feedback has been linked to increased learning (Black & Wiliam, 1998, 2009; Brookhart, 2008; Chappuis, Stiggins, Chappuis, & Arter, 2012; Davies, 2007; Hyland & Hyland, 2006; Popham, 2016). Therefore, it is important that it be an integral part of any second language lesson or activity, including oral activities, reading tasks, written work, and content-related assignments.

In Chapter 10, we offer specific ways to structure targeted feedback on language so the feedback will be most effective.

When we think of feedback, we tend to think about the formal and informal oral comments we provide learners or the written feedback we jot down for them. But we also give language learners lots of feedback through our facial expressions and gestures (e.g., thumbs-up, a nod, a smile, a frown). Let's consider the necessary elements of effective feedback for second language learners.

Elements of Effective Feedback

Feedback should

- be personalized and identify a learner's strengths
- be timely and done when students are engaged in the task
- offer specific and concrete suggestions and solutions for the task at hand (not vague comments, such as "You're doing well! Keep it up," "Good work!" or "Maybe you should review this one more time.")
- provide clear guidance on how the learner can improve and move forward with the task
- provide positive reinforcement and praise that reflect how well the learner met a particular success criterion
- help the learner recalibrate or readjust, if need be

When providing feedback, teachers are wise to seize the opportunity to make direct links between lesson objectives, success criteria, and student progress, as illustrated in Figure 4.3.

Figure 4.3: The Components of Student Progress

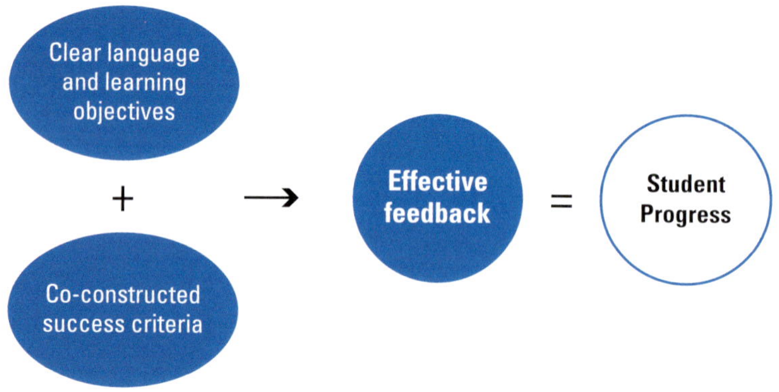

When lesson objectives are clear and success criteria have been co-constructed with learners, it is much easier for teachers to identify students' strengths and where learners may need additional support (Biggs, 1999; Dunn, Morgan, O'Reilly, & Parry, 2004).

So far, we have discussed only the importance of *providing* feedback. In order to motivate learners to become more autonomous and in charge of their own learning, they need to recognize the value of feedback. As demonstrated in Figure 4.4, we want to move students toward understanding the value of feedback to maximize learning, but ultimately, we want to foster an environment where learners seek out opportunities to receive feedback that is valuable to them.

Figure 4.4: Understanding the Value of Feedback

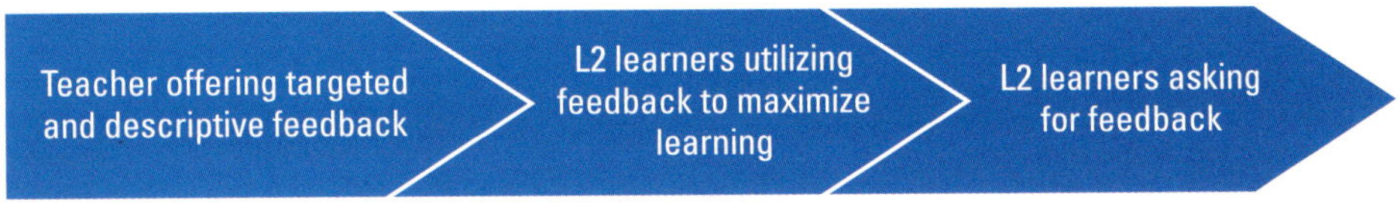

When learners reflect on their needs, understand when they require support, and monitor their progress, they can start advocating for themselves and their learning. They may even start setting their own goals and establishing a plan of action. Thus, feedback that is effective and valued encourages metacognition (Met, 1994).

Hosting Learning Conferences That Build Learner Autonomy

An important way to provide feedback to learners is through student-learning conferences. Conferences between a teacher and a student should focus on getting the student talking about his or her learning. Conferences can take place with respect to any learning task, including oral, reading, and writing tasks and assignments.

Student conferences should be designed to build learner autonomy and help students take ownership over their own learning. The conferences do not need to be long to be effective—a few meaningful minutes to a five-minute conversation is all it takes in many cases. When a student is ready to discuss progress with a given task, a student conference should take place. These conferences can be either formally or informally built into the lesson. For older learners, a more casual approach may work best.

Learning conferences are about giving the learner an opportunity to talk about his or her work. Here are a few ways a teacher may want to start a learning conference:

Helping learners talk about their work in a learning conference
• Talk to me about what you've been working on. Tell me about your work.
• Tell me what you have improved or reworked so far. How did you go about this?
• What are the strengths of your work?
• How did you go about undertaking this task?

continued

• Where would you like to go with this task now? What would you like to work on?
• What are you planning to do next?
• Have you made any changes to your work? How did you go about making these changes?
• What do you need to move forward?
• You set goals for yourself before undertaking this task. How have you met the goals you set out for yourself?
• Talk to me about how you used or integrated the success criteria for this task into your assignment. (See section on success criteria above.)
• How may I help you?

As students discuss and share their thoughts around these questions, the teacher listens, paraphrases, and asks clarification questions. It is also the time to push the learner into offering suggestions that further support his or her learning. Of course, the teacher may offer up suggestions and take formative notes with respect to the learner's progress. Perhaps most important, however, a learning conference is an important time for the teacher to highlight where the learner has taken risks with the language. When language learners are involved in risk-taking, they experiment with the language, play with it, and learn to understand the target language a bit better.

Making Thinking Visible: Language and Learning Strategies

Good language learners use multiple language and learning strategies to support their growth in the target language. But what exactly *are* strategies? We talk about them, but what does the term *strategies* really mean? Much education and psychology literature has been written about strategies, and the general consensus is as follows: strategy is a broad term that encapsulates the different actions, steps, operations, or techniques that learners use throughout the learning process (e.g., Chamot, Barnhardt, El-Dinary, & Robbins, 1999; Chamot & El-Dinary, 1999; Rubin, 1987; Oxford, 1990, 1992/1993).

Fair enough! So, in other words, we use strategies to obtain, retrieve, retain, learn, comprehend, and use information. There are strategies for just about anything related to learning, but for our purposes, we are concerned with the general learning strategies and metacognitive strategies related to planning for and executing the following tasks: listening, communicating, reading, and writing. Here are a few examples of strategies we may employ when planning or executing a learning task:

For additional resources to help plan and execute learning tasks, see the *Access for Success* website.

Examples of Strategies		
• Repeating or rereading words	• Using background knowledge	• Self-evaluating
• Reviewing work	• Taking notes	• Transferring skills/ knowledge from one context to another
• Skimming or scanning	• Asking questions	• Asking for clarification
• Using mental images (visualizing)	• Summarizing information	• Creating mental links between concepts
• Setting goals	• Using context or linguistic clues	• Self-monitoring
• Analyzing	• Guessing	• Paying attention
• Focusing attention	• Using resources	• Using graphic organizers

More often than not, strategies need to be learned and practised if they are to be used effectively. And while second language learners need to develop good learning strategies, they also need to understand how such strategies can help them learn the target language. Our second language students need to develop both good learning strategies and good language strategies. Below, we discuss ways by which we can support students in developing effective strategy usage.

Modelling, Modelling, Modelling

As noted above, strategies are not necessarily innate, and most often learners need to learn how to use them effectively. What makes strategies even trickier is the fact that they are not always visible to learners. Students don't necessarily see strategies when they are used implicitly by others. As a result, they need explicit strategy instruction. They also need many opportunities to learn about and practise integrating strategies into their learning.

It is not enough for second language teachers to discuss the use of language and learning strategies. Students need to see strategies being used explicitly and in meaningful ways throughout daily classroom activities. Research has shown that some second language learners can come up with a list of strategies to use for any given task, but when it comes time to do the task, they may not think to use them or may not use them effectively (Bourgoin & Dicks, 2013). This is why it is so important to demonstrate, model, and share with students how strategies are used in actual learning situations. As part of literacy or content classes, teachers are wise to plan lessons that focus on modelling the use of specific strategies. Figure 4.5 presents two examples.

Figure 4.5: Teachers Modelling Strategy Use

Example 1

"Before I read an information text, I find it helpful to look at the text features. I tend to look at the pictures and read the captions underneath them. I also analyze the diagrams and I read the subtitles. This helps me get a sense of the text. Let me show you what that looks like with this text called *Climate Change—The Facts*!"

Example 2

"Sometimes, when I'm listening to a video clip, I don't always understand. To help me, I use the strategy listening for words I know or the strategy listening for words that sound the same in my other language. Those words are called 'cognates.' In a second, I'm going to put on a clip and I'm going to show you how this strategy is helpful for me. I'll stop the clip every so often to show what goes on in my head and how I use these two strategies."

In both of these cases, the teacher would then proceed in modelling the strategy in a real, meaningful learning situation. Students would then be asked to practise this strategy in similar learning contexts.

Throw Me an Anchor Chart

Anchor charts are visual aids that help learners remember when and how to use particular strategies. They can also be used as a way to identify and help learners remember the concrete steps or procedures needed to complete a task. Anchor charts are meant to be a strong and reliable support that helps link learners to strategies or procedures.

Anchor charts involve a two-part process: creating them and using them. Creating anchor charts with students is a powerful pedagogical action because learners get to "see" the thinking process. Teachers tend to create anchor charts during or right after modelling a strategy or two. In theory, students saw the strategy in use when the teacher modelled it. However, anchor charts go one step further by having the teacher write down how he or she uses the strategy—the step-by-step process. In other words, the thinking process comes to life and strategies become visible through the creation of anchor charts. Figure 4.6 shows a couple of examples of anchor charts.

Figure 4.6: Anchor Charts

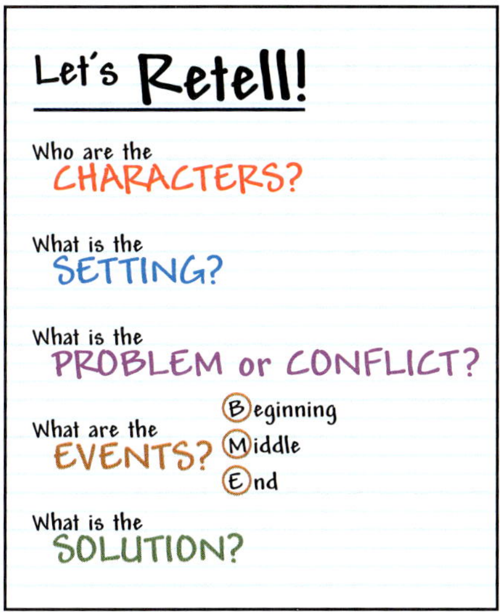

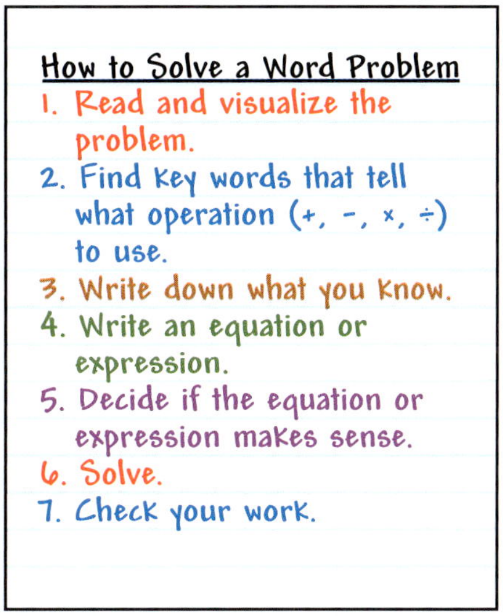

Once an anchor chart is created with students, they should be able to refer to it when necessary to have help in developing the strategy or problem solving. Be sure to revise anchor charts often to add elements as needed.

Some older learners may not feel comfortable consulting anchor charts. Consider providing the same information in other forms (like digital slides) to increase their appeal.

What About Metacognition?

As learners acquire strategies and use them to orchestrate their learning, they also should be moving toward reflecting upon these strategies. This is where metacognition takes place. We want learners to be able to think about how they think and how they learn. Metacognitive strategies are those that help learners gain control over their learning (e.g., their ability to self-monitor, to self-reflect, to plan for and execute a task). The benefits of metacognition for second language acquisition are well documented!

Learners need multiple opportunities to help them develop their metacognitive skills. To foster this in classrooms, we have provided a few concrete examples of ways second language teachers have implemented reflective practices:

Example 1: In this case, the teacher brainstormed with students possible strategies that could be used for a given task. Once strategies were identified, students were asked to keep a running log of their strategy usage.

Strategy Running Log

Type of Activity and Strategies	Date	I used this strategy often	I used this strategy at times	I didn't need this strategy	I don't know how to use this strategy
Reading informational text about dinosaurs	Dec 13th				
• Looking at pictures		X			
• Rereading more difficult passages		X			
• Visualizing the information				X	
• Writing notes in the margins					X

Example 2: In the following example, the teacher provided learners with opportunities to discuss their learning with classmates. When students encountered an issue, they jotted it down on a card and asked a few other students (or the teacher) for some possible strategies that could be useful. Students kept the cards and whenever they encountered a similar issue, they could refer back to the cards for support.

Offer me some suggestions		
I would like to improve		
Strategies That Can Help Me		
1.	2.	3.

Example 3: In this final example, the teacher created metacognitive strips. The teacher would choose a strip that best fit the lesson and then present the question to learners. Students worked independently or in pairs to answer the question. A whole-class discussion often ensued.

Metacognition Strips

In general, metacognitive moments like these can make for meaningful closing activities to a lesson.

We used the following strategy today: ______________________. How could we use this strategy in other learning tasks (e.g., another oral task, another piece of writing, another reading task)?
Today we learned (about or how to) ______________________. To help us learn this, we used the strategy ______________________. How is this strategy helpful?
Based on what we have learned today, how could we now solve the following issue: ______________________? (Possible examples: a text lacking in organization, a particular speech error, a mathematical problem)
Today in class we worked on ______________________.What helped you the most in accomplishing this task/activity?
On a scale of 1 (not at all) to 5 (completely), how well do you think you have understood how to ______________________?
What do you think you still need to learn to move forward?
How did you learn today? What was beneficial in helping you learn?

Encouraging Learners to Suggest or Complete Different Formats for Tasks, Assignments, and Projects

Although we are going to explore differentiation in greater detail in Chapter 9, we want to point out how a differentiated approach to instruction is an important tool for facilitating learner autonomy.

In the differentiated classroom, learners have the option to pursue tasks within larger learning activities that are linked to their needs, interests, and readiness. When students are involved in identifying their needs, establishing their readiness for a particular task, or leveraging their personal interests, they are more motivated to pursue the learning and they are in a position to engage with the learning in a way that is consistent with their current knowledge and skills (Hume, 2009; Tomlinson, 2014; Tomlinson & Imbeau, 2010).

When students know who they are as language learners, they can start advocating for how best they believe they can show what they have learned. Students benefit from being aware that there are multiple forms of representing their understanding of the language or concept being studied. They should, in conjunction with their teacher, be able to reflect on how best they want to demonstrate their learning. Here are some examples:

- For an oral presentation, learners could suggest using videos or audio files.
- For a written narrative piece, learners could suggest using a storyboard or creating a short film.
- For explaining a process, learners could suggest using graphics, drawings, narrations, or any combination of the three.
- For summarizing key ideas, learners could suggest using Sketchnotes, tweets, a blog, an essay, or a graphic organizer.

In all of these examples, learners are still working on the same outcome, but the ways they demonstrate their learning are tailored to their individual needs, interests, and readiness for trying a particular type of task.

Documenting and Reflecting on One's Own Learning

If second language learners are to be recognized as owners of their learning and are to become more autonomous, we need to help them reflect upon their own learning. Self-reflection is a critical element of second language learning and is linked to increased student achievement (Little, 2005).

Self-reflection enables learners to more fully understand their strengths, what supports they need, what strategies are beneficial to them, and how they grow as learners. Although all the actions mentioned so far in this chapter involve some element of reflection, it is important for reflection to take its own prominent place in second language classrooms.

We know that part of the self-reflection process is documenting learning and growth. That is why we speak so often of learning portfolios and language portfolios, admit and exit slips, and journals entries (to name a few) as ways of reflecting on what, how, and why we learn.

- Learning portfolios and language portfolios are ways to connect and gather evidence about one's own learning. A student may want to jot down that he/she went to a French film over the weekend, for example.
- Admit and exit slips are used either at the beginning or the end of class to help consolidate the learning and allow students to reflect on the relevance of the material and its applications. They are also a way to help learners gauge where they are in the learning process.
- Journal entries are ways to document one's learning. The teacher usually assigns a reflection question.

Below are some sample questions that can be used to help support students' self-reflection.

It is important to remember the difference between metacognition and reflection. When we ask students to think metacognitively, we are asking them to think about how they think. When we ask them to reflect, we are asking them to ponder the content they have learned.

Reflection Questions

- When thinking of or examining this ________________ (e.g., word, picture, reading passage, quotation, chart, concept, diagram, visual organizer, text, concept, mathematical formula), what comes to mind?
- Now that you know a lot more about ________________, how could you apply this learning to another situation?
- Today we learned (about or how) ________________. How could having learned this be helpful in the future?
- Now that the lesson is over, name one thing that you are still unsure about.
- Based on what we learned today, can you
  - explain how to ________________?
  - show/demonstrate how to ________________?
  - justify the following statement: ________________?
- Can you explain the following in your own words: this word, this picture, this reading passage, this visual organizer, this text, or this concept? Please do so.
- Draw or illustrate what we learned in class today.
- What part of the lesson or activity did you prefer? Why?
- Evaluate the quality of the following:
  - this paragraph
  - this conversation
  - the way this problem was solved

continued

- What would you say to someone else (e.g., another student in the school) about what you learned today?
- If you had to teach this concept to someone else, what would you say? How would you explain the concept?

Closing Thoughts

In second language contexts, we should place a lot of value on the role of the learner in the language learning process. We want engaged, empowered learners who are able to reflect upon and advocate for their own learning. We want learners who are able to set goals for themselves based on their strengths and progress. We want learners who self-monitor their learning, regardless of their age or their ability level in the target language.

As you reflect on the content of this chapter, consider the following questions:

- What are some of the ways I foster learner autonomy in my classroom?
- How much do I value learners as agents (or advocates) of their own learning?
- How would the actions presented in this chapter help my students grow as second language learners?
- How do these actions also support learners who may
  - lack confidence or need reassurance?
  - be unsure how to complete a task?
  - not know how to improve or self-monitor?
- In terms of my own pedagogy, where do the following fit in?
  - providing clearly articulated language and learning goals at the outset of lessons
  - co-constructing success criteria with learners before beginning a task
  - using targeted feedback throughout a learning task or lesson (including the use of learning conferences)
  - making thinking visible through use of language and learning strategies (including the use of modelling, anchor charts, and metacognition)
  - encouraging learners to suggest different formats for tasks, assignments, and projects to show their understanding
  - promoting student documentation of and reflection on their learning
- How can I integrate these actions more fully in my classroom?

levels, with beginning language learners, with more advanced learners, in different subject areas, and in different language programs. Finally, the list of ULAs was solidified. ULAs are our own creation; they stem from this work and are grounded in strong second language research. They are important actions for any teacher working with language learners to further support students' language development.

What Are Universal Language Actions?

We define *Universal Language Actions* as gestures, procedures, and operations that help create the most favourable and accessible environment in which to learn a language (see Figure AP 3.1, below). ULAs facilitate access to the curriculum and the target language and are specially designed to support language learners. These actions are fluid, flexible, and adaptable based on the following:

- specific language learning contexts
- second-language learning pedagogy
- subjects being taught (language or literacy classes and other subject areas)
- learners' language development and proficiency levels

The actions encourage reflective practice because teachers tailor the ways by which they facilitate access to the language and curriculum based on learners' strengths and challenges. Ultimately, they provide specific additions for making our lessons more inclusive.

Figure AP 3.1: Universal Language Actions at a Glance

Universal Language Actions That Facilitate Learner Understanding of Oral and Written Language

For a convenient checklist of the Universal Language Actions, see the *Access for Success* website.

Action 1.1 Using gestures, facial expressions, images, pictures, drawings, objects, and manipulation materials

Action 1.2 Playing with expression and voice intonation, and pacing rate of speech

Action 1.3 Adjusting the complexity of oral and/or written language

Action 1.4 Assessing the extent of prior knowledge and filling in any major gaps

continued

Action 1.5 Providing wait time when presenting new information, after asking a question, or before inviting learners to start a task

Action 1.6 Repeating or reformulating oral and written language

Action 1.7 Reusing and recycling pedagogical materials

Universal Language Actions That Facilitate Learner Production of Oral and Written Language

Action 2.1 Providing many exemplars of oral and written tasks

Action 2.2 Using graphic organizers to support oral and written production

Action 2.3 Creating and displaying linguistic supports around the classroom

Action 2.4 Offering planning strategies for learners to use before starting a task

Action 2.5 Using pedagogical and language production routines

Action 2.6 Choosing grouping arrangements that favour peer communication

Action 2.7 Asking questions that encourage learners to elaborate

Universal Language Actions That Facilitate Learner Focus and Attention in the Target Language

Action 3.1 Providing specific listening and reading intentions

Action 3.2 Dividing lessons, activities, and tasks into many small steps

Action 3.3 Incorporating discourse markers to oral and written texts

Action 3.4 Providing explicit cues to refocus learners' attention

Action 3.5 Using different modalities to present material

Action 3.6 Explaining the relevance of what is being taught

Action 3.7 Summarizing key points of lessons, activities, and reading passages

continued

Universal Language Actions That Facilitate Learner Development and Expansion of Vocabulary

Action 4.1 Identifying and presenting required language at the outset of a lesson or activity

Action 4.2 Capitalizing on the use of word walls and word maps

Action 4.3 Accessing the senses to facilitate vocabulary acquisition

Action 4.4 Using role-play and games to present or reinforce new vocabulary

Action 4.5 Explaining vocabulary using examples, synonyms, antonyms, cognates, and teacher/learner definitions

Universal Language Actions merge solid second language pedagogy with the framework of Universal Design for Learning (UDL). UDL is a framework for thinking about inclusive lesson design.

The UDL framework was first conceived by Rose and Meyer (2002) to "guide educators in finding innovative ways to make curriculum accessible and appropriate for individuals with different backgrounds, learning styles, abilities, and disabilities in various learning situations and contexts" (cited in Eagleton, 2008, p. 1). It focuses on adapting the curriculum through three guiding principles: providing multiple means of (1) representation, (2) expression and action, and (3) motivation (Center for Applied Special Technology, 2001).

We consider ULAs to be universal because they support language learners of various linguistic competencies at different grades levels, in different subject areas, and in different language contexts. They also align with the three UDL principles noted above. Moreover, through a UDL lens, we view ULAs as an important component to lesson design. They should be integrated purposely as teachers plan their lessons. ULAs act as a sort of safety net within lesson delivery to catch and support language learning, thereby creating more access to the learning environment.

Using Universal Language Actions

As mentioned above, ULAs should be accounted for in the early stages of lesson planning. What's more, our research into the world of ULAs revealed that teachers also tend to use them throughout their lesson delivery as needs occur. They do so spontaneously but purposely. When teachers recognize that learners are challenged to access the language or curriculum outcome, they can deploy ULAs (see Figure AP 3.2). They can do so

- when they are presenting or delivering content
- when learners are working through material or developing new skills
- when learners are demonstrating understanding of newly acquired knowledge and skills

Figure AP 3.2: When to Deploy Universal Language Actions

For each ULA in Chapters 5 through 8, we have identified when the ULA can be used: during the delivery of content, during a learning event, and/or when learners are demonstrating their understanding.

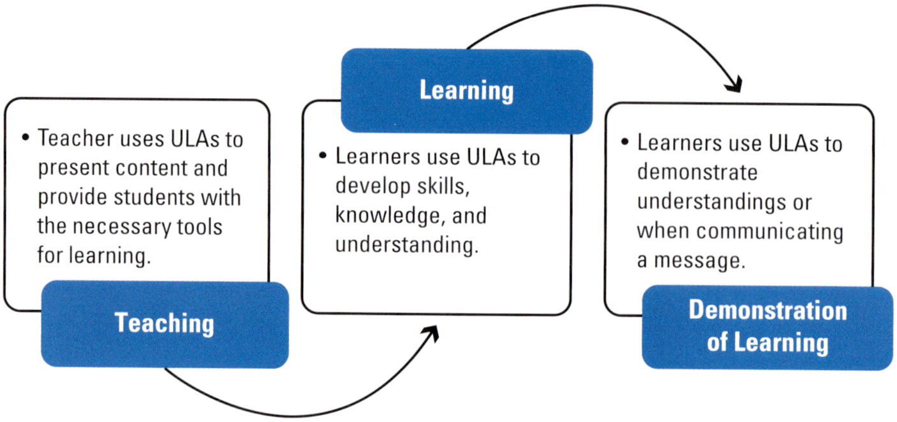

ULAs should be used with intent and purpose. Be it for an individual learner, a group of learners, or the whole class, teachers determine which ULAs to integrate proactively within their teaching practices by carefully considering students' comprehension and production levels, their strengths and challenges, and their motivation levels. In Chapters 5 through 8, where we outline the ULAs in greater detail, you will also notice Action in Action! vignettes, which describe intentional teacher uses of the ULAs.

Differentiation

Originating with the work of Tomlinson (1999, 2001) and her efforts to show how to vary instructional opportunities to support students who are gifted, differentiation is an instructional practice that creates multiple paths of learning to address multiple student needs. Although *differentiation* has been co-opted as a term in some jurisdictions to mean *accommodation* (e.g., teaching acts that respond to a specific learning need), in this text we consider differentiation in the original conception of Tomlinson—as a mechanism for providing distinct learning options to students based on their needs, interests, or readiness. Nonetheless, we do acknowledge that in offering various learning paths to students, teachers are accommodating differences in learning needs.

Tomlinson (1999, 2001) proposed three primary types of differentiation: (1) differentiation by process, (2) differentiation by product, and (3) differentiation by content. While other types of differentiation (e.g., differentiation by resource, differentiation by outcome, differentiation by challenge) have been proposed or advocated for by others (e.g., Heacox, 2002, 2009; Hume 2009), they are largely encompassed in the three original Tomlinson classifications. In *Languages for All*, however, Katy (Arnett, 2013c) proposed that another type of differentiation—differentiation by linguistic complexity—was a separate method that required special consideration for language learners. Figure AP 3.3 presents the conceptualizations of these types of differentiation that will be used to frame the activities featured in Chapter 9 and in some of the discussions of the ULAs. It is worth noting that while the table presents the differentiation methods separately, in most differentiated activities, multiple methods are often at play.

Figure AP 3.3: Types of Differentiation

Differentiation by Process	Differentiation by Product
Students complete different steps—in complexity, sequence, mode, or purpose—in order to arrive at the learning goal.	Students create different pieces of evidence of their understanding or mastery of a topic, varying in particular format or mode.
Differentiation by Content	**Differentiation by Linguistic Complexity**
Students consider different dimensions of a concept or different concepts relevant to the overall learning goal.	Students navigate different types and levels of language, most typically consistent with their current language skills.

When to Use Differentiation

Implementing differentiation has two primary types of application in the classroom. First, differentiation considers the learning activities that are used in the classroom to help the students reinforce, expand, or otherwise develop their understanding or mastery of a topic or skill. When these different activity options are organized in such a way as to facilitate most of a student's exploration of a lesson, **differentiated instruction** is said to be occurring. Figure AP 3.4 offers an overview of how differentiated instruction can be set up in a history class that includes language learners.

Figure AP 3.4: Differentiated Instruction in Action

Learning Goal: To compare and contrast perspectives presented in various media accounts of a historic event; to explore how events can be perceived and presented differently and how that influences what we come to think and understand about an event

Preparation	Line up a willing colleague to help you stage a mock disagreement in class. Write up another mock disagreement nobody witnessed. Prepare a mix of articles (print, video) or other texts (e.g., social media accounts, blogs) that all describe the same event; a blend of first-hand and second-hand accounts is fine. Some accounts should be less linguistically complex than others; the accounts can consider different aspects of the same event.		
Warm-up	As class begins, another teacher enters the room and picks a mock disagreement with the classroom teacher about something that happened in the copy room. The disagreement lasts two or three minutes; students are likely tuning in to different parts of the event. The other teacher leaves, and the classroom teacher asks the students to stop what they are doing, take out a piece of paper, and either draw or write out what they saw to help make an incident report. After a few minutes, students are asked to show or describe what they observed. The teacher asks a few questions to note the differences that have emerged.		
Transition	The teacher writes the word *perspective* on the board and invites students to share other words that explain or complement the term. When needed, the teacher prompts with questions and statements about the opening event to elicit other ideas. The activity concludes with a working definition of *perspective* that will be used in the day's class.		
	Path A	Path B	Path C
Student Grouping	Students will work with two or three first-hand accounts of the event.	Students will work with second-hand accounts of the event.	Students will work with a combination of first- and second-hand accounts.
Task A	Group meets with teacher. Read aloud or provide viewing of least linguistically complex account. Pose general questions: Is account positive or negative? Who tells the story? What do they say?	Half of students in this group are assigned two second-hand accounts to read or view; other half are given two different second-hand accounts. Students review their accounts and complete a guide with questions about the accounts.	Half of students in this group are assigned two second-hand accounts to read or view; other half are given two first-hand accounts. Students review their accounts and complete a guide with questions about the accounts.

continued

Task B	Students individually work with another account, responding to the same questions. Students with limited proficiency either review the first account again or work on a language point relevant to the class (e.g., more work with perspective or writing statements about the first account).	Group meets with teacher. Teacher mediates a discussion of all the accounts the students have read.	Students work with a partner who read the other two accounts; they complete a graphic organizer that allows them to identify areas where the accounts overlap *and* areas where there may be questions about what happened.	
Task C	Continue with task B.	Students work with a partner who read the other two accounts; they complete a graphic organizer that allows them to identify areas where the accounts overlap *and* areas where there may be questions about what happened.	Group meets with teacher. Teacher starts a discussion about noted differences between the accounts; teacher may need to step away to check in with Path A.	
Closure	Teacher asks students to share the personal perspective they have on the historic event based on what they read or viewed. Teacher guides students to notice how the materials accessed about an event influence their personal perspectives.			
Exit Slip	Ask students to explain how they know if they can trust a given account or perspective. Ask students with limited proficiency to provide their own definition of *perspective*.			

As you may have surmised from the table, differentiated instruction requires a solid system of classroom management and a strong well of resources for implementing a lesson. For some teachers, differentiated instruction (DI) at the full-class or lesson level may be feasibly incorporated on a regular basis, while for others it is an occasional instructional method. However, teachers may find it an easier option to implement differentiated activities, which can be the stepping stone before formal differentiated instruction. From the example above, teachers could take the idea of having a mix of first- and second-hand accounts and assigning an account to students, perhaps considering the linguistic complexity of the text as a starting point. Students read or review their account and complete a guide about their text. Then, either at a whole-group level or in small groups, the different accounts are presented. The students then work together to write or create another new account of the event, based on what has been shared. This jigsaw activity offers students paths aligned with their language needs and may present an easier classroom management protocol to navigate in your class.

As will be explored in Access Point 4, deploying the ULAs and differentiation effectively with language learners requires ongoing assessment and attention to those results. Teachers need to assess their students' current skills, levels of mastery, and, in some cases, interests in order to guide students to the learning paths most suited to their current needs and the learning goals.

The Overlap of Universal Language Actions and Differentiation

We think of the ULAs as actions that facilitate and enhance a teacher's delivery of content and students' engagement in the lesson, whereas differentiated activities and instruction offer a way to organize learning events that support specific levels of needs, interests, and readiness. In some situations, ULAs can be implemented within a differentiated activity; in others, they can easily support an overall lesson structure that is differentiated, as teachers can deploy ULAs to certain paths as the needs emerge. Thus, ULAs and differentiation have a strong interconnectedness, but they are not necessarily interdependent for inclusive language education. As Figure AP 3.5 reveals, we do believe that both are needed to facilitate the most inclusive language learning environment possible.

Figure AP 3.5: How Universal Language Actions and Differentiation Support Inclusive Language Education

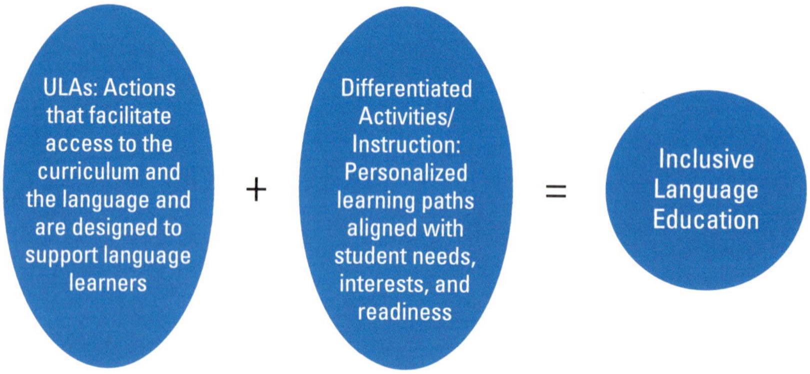

Response to Intervention: The Role of Universal Language Actions and Differentiation for Inclusive Language Teaching

In thinking about ULAs and differentiation within language education, we found another paradigm to be helpful: that of Response to Intervention (Fuchs & Fuchs, 2006). While we are not necessarily positioning ULAs and differentiation as tools to use within Response to Intervention (RTI), we do acknowledge how both ULAs and differentiation offer the kinds of supports and opportunities that are consistent with what has been described as solid Tier 1 and Tier 2 instruction.

RTI has its origins as a method for identifying students who may be in need of special education services (Fuchs & Fuchs, 2006). RTI considers what happens at three tiers of the instructional experience and recommends certain actions at each tier to determine whether a student's response warrants further attention and perhaps eventual evaluation for a special education need. The RTI protocol is positioned as an alternative to special-education identification processes that call for psychometric assessments earlier in the process.

We see the value in conceptualizing the supports offered by the ULAs and differentiation through the lens of Tier 1 and Tier 2. Time and time again, second language teachers tell us that they want and need professional dialogue and resources that will support them in providing quality Tier 1 and Tier 2 supports for their language learners.

- Tier 1 supports are generally described as high-impact, high-yielding teaching practices implemented to support the whole class (Fuchs & Fuchs, 2006). We strongly believe that ULAs and differentiation offer such high-impact, high-yielding practices to use to support language learners.
- At Tier 2, a teacher continues to use high-impact practices and supports, but these supports are provided to individual learners or groups of learners in a specific and deliberate way as instruction occurs. Again, we argue that ULAs and differentiation can be used at this level to support inclusive second language learning.

The chapters that follow this overview offer practical suggestions for making your language learning environment as inclusive as possible, and we hope that you are inspired to try them with your students.

CHAPTER 5

Language Learners Who Need Additional Support in Understanding Oral or Written Language

The Importance of *Understanding* for Language Development

As mentioned earlier in this book, "comprehension precedes production." Language learners need to develop strong oral and reading comprehension skills if they are to become strong, independent communicators. As comprehension skills increase, so do learners' abilities to communicate, both orally and in writing.

Comprehension is an outcome of repeated exposure to the same words and messages followed by actions that allow learners to decode the meaning of the ideas being conveyed. To facilitate comprehension of messages, language learners should be exposed daily to a large amount of authentic oral and written input in the target language. This input should include traditional sources of information and multimedia-based materials (e.g., videos, audio files, and web-based shared material, such as blogs and podcasts). Whether language learners spend all or a part of the day surrounded by the target language, this variety of input is critical to establishing a solid foundation. Language development within an individual is a direct result of much exposure to different input by different speakers of the target language (e.g., Krashen, 1977, 1981; Lightbown & Spada, 2013).

Although we often associate the need to develop comprehension and listening strategies with beginning language learners (Vandergrift, 1999), more fluent speakers also need to continue building comprehension. At times, more advanced learners may take language comprehension for granted and may not always interpret the message as quickly as they hear or read it. As advanced learners are exposed to more complex oral and written language, their need for strong comprehension skills increases.

It is quite typical for language learners to occasionally understand some words but not the whole message, or they may miss important details that have an impact on overall comprehension. You may also notice that they quickly forget what they heard or read. Language learners may not always grasp nuances found within messages or be able to create mental representations. Again, this is quite typical.

In a classroom context, teachers may notice some characteristics that could signal learners' difficulty in making sense of information being presented to them. Granted, on some days, all learners will engage in at least one of these behaviours. However, learners who are having more difficulty with comprehension will exhibit many of the following behaviours daily:

- ❑ offer irrelevant answers or information
- ❑ avoid taking risks
- ❑ be overly quiet
- ❑ guess answers
- ❑ try to finish tasks quickly
- ❑ avoid eye contact
- ❑ have delayed response times when asked questions
- ❑ seek attention
- ❑ seem lost with the material
- ❑ avoid putting their hands up
- ❑ pretend to understand
- ❑ avoid certain tasks
- ❑ answer with a yes or no
- ❑ follow exemplars and examples too closely
- ❑ put their heads down
- ❑ have a hard time getting started
- ❑ get emotional or anxious
- ❑ seem to be daydreaming

Language learners contend with potentially large amounts of daily language input. Since they are working in the second language, they need more time to process the language and work through challenges with recall or by attending to detail. Therefore, it becomes essential for classroom teachers to facilitate learners' understanding of the target language.

Universal Language Actions That Support Learners in Understanding Oral and Written Language

We have identified seven ULAs designed to support language learners in understanding and grasping the target language (see Figure 5.1). At minimum, a combination of these actions should be regularly incorporated into our daily pedagogy to help facilitate comprehension for all language learners. If you have a learner (or several learners) who is often challenged to understand oral and written messages, we recommend the following actions.

Figure 5.1

Universal Language Actions That Facilitate Learner Understanding of Oral and Written Language

Action 1.1	Using gestures, facial expressions, images, pictures, drawings, objects, and manipulation materials
Action 1.2	Playing with expression and voice intonation, and pacing rate of speech
Action 1.3	Adjusting the complexity of oral and/or written language
Action 1.4	Assessing the extent of prior knowledge and filling in any major gaps
Action 1.5	Providing wait time when presenting new information, after asking a question, or before inviting learners to start a task
Action 1.6	Repeating or reformulating oral and written language
Action 1.7	Reusing and recycling pedagogical materials

Because ULAs are not mutually exclusive, some actions found in other chapters are also beneficial in supporting students to understand the target language. Action 2.1 *Providing many exemplars of oral and written tasks*, Action 3.1 *Providing specific listening and reading intentions*, and Action 4.3 *Accessing the senses to facilitate vocabulary acquisition* are but a few examples of other actions that can be used to support comprehension. In this chapter, we highlight Actions 1.1 to 1.7.

ACTION 1.1 Using gestures, facial expressions, images, pictures, drawings, objects, and manipulation materials

As mentioned above, language learners are exposed to a large amount of oral and written language. This language may, at times, be incomprehensible to learners without some level of visual support (for examples, see Figure 5.2). By integrating meaningful gestures, facial expressions, images, pictures, objects, or manipulation material with oral messages and written texts, teachers provide a concrete reference point for learners to find meaning in what is being presented.

This ULA can be used

- ✓ When teacher is presenting content and/or language
- ✓ When learners are engaged in a learning task
- ✓ When learners are demonstrating learning and understanding

Figure 5.2: Examples of Visual Supports

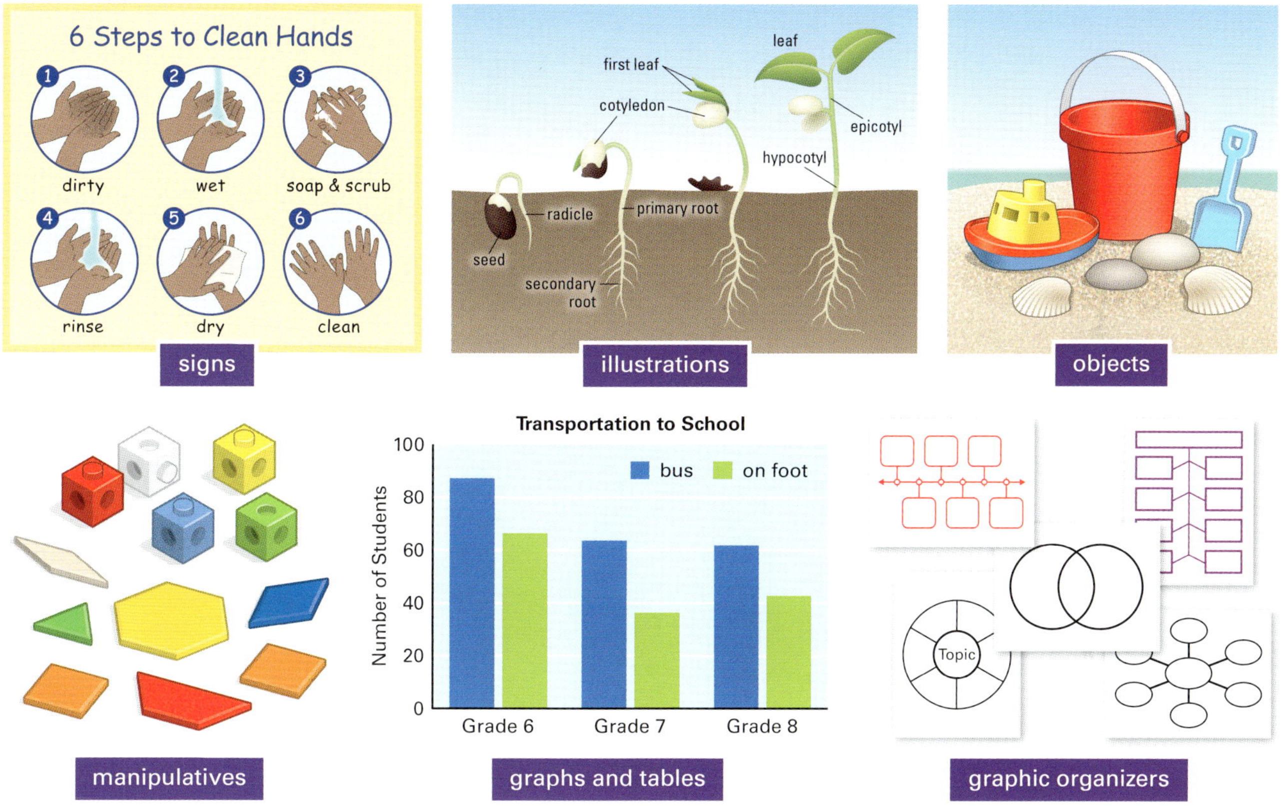

Visual supports draw learners toward the key elements of oral or written messages (e.g., vocabulary, communicative function, concept). They are a very effective way to activate prior knowledge.

It is estimated that 55 percent of all communication is done through gestures and expression, hence the need for them in second language contexts. As for images, pictures, objects, and manipulation materials, they help contextualize the learning for learners and enable them to quickly make connections to what is being heard or read.

For more examples of visual supports, see the *Access for Success* website.

Along with supporting instruction and delivery of content, visuals aids offer great support for learners engaged in a learning task or trying to demonstrate understanding. In particular, inclusive teachers working with beginning language learners and those teaching more complex material understand the importance of being strategic in the ways by which they assess learners' oral or written comprehension skills.

The use of visual supports reinforces input and strengthens learners' oral and written output. As learners become increasingly comfortable with new or more complex material, verbal and written output increases and the use of visual scaffolds diminishes.

REFLECTION ON PRACTICE

Tactile Input

- For this lesson, are there any objects that I could bring in that learners can touch, smell, and manipulate? Could I bring in items such as clothing, foods, textiles, building materials, toys, and household items—that is, realia—to enhance the delivery of my lesson?

Visual Input

- What pictures, images, or illustrations could I share with my learners to depict the concept being studied?
- When learners are discussing or working in small groups, what visual aids could I provide to support the interactions and the learning?
- Are there enough visual supports in the text to help my learners' understanding? If not, what images could I add to the text or put up on the board to help support their understanding?

Gestures and Expressions

- When reading aloud a text to learners, where can I include more meaningful gestures and facial expressions?

Alternative Ways to Show Understanding

- Am I providing alternative ways for my learners to show me their understanding?
  - Can learners use gestures or point to things to convey understanding?
  - Can learners draw their understanding of a reading passage?
  - Can they sketch out what they learned in class today?
  - When learners communicate in a more formal way with the rest of the class, do they have access to images, drawings, or objects to help them get their message across?
  - Can learners glance at pictures or images for cues and reminders?

BROADENING ACCESS

- To build learner autonomy, could I share with my learners the value of this action so that they, in turn, use it in oral communication to support other learners' comprehension?
- With respect to targeted support (e.g., Response to Intervention), are there any specific language learners in my class who could benefit from this action?

Action 1.1 in Action!

For this particular lesson, I wanted to work with my students on adding adjectives to the text they were working on. Many of my students have limited vocabulary in the target language. I decided to provide the class with a word bank of adjectives. We would create a chart together full of adjectives. I know that many of my students would not *understand* the meaning of certain adjectives. To support my learners, I brought in different types of fruit. When discussing adjectives such as *rough*, *smooth*, *prickly*, or *fuzzy*, students were able to touch the different fruits. Then we tasted them. They really understood *sour* when they bit into the lemon! No additional explanation needed.

—K. Horne

I notice that many of the reading passages I give to my students have only one main picture or illustration somewhere on the page. My language learners tend to rely heavily on this picture to support their comprehension of the text. However, that picture often portrays only one idea from the page/text. I now create a visual support that I project on the board or hand out to students. For each paragraph of the students' text, I find a picture that depicts the main idea. Students can refer to each picture as they move from one paragraph to another.

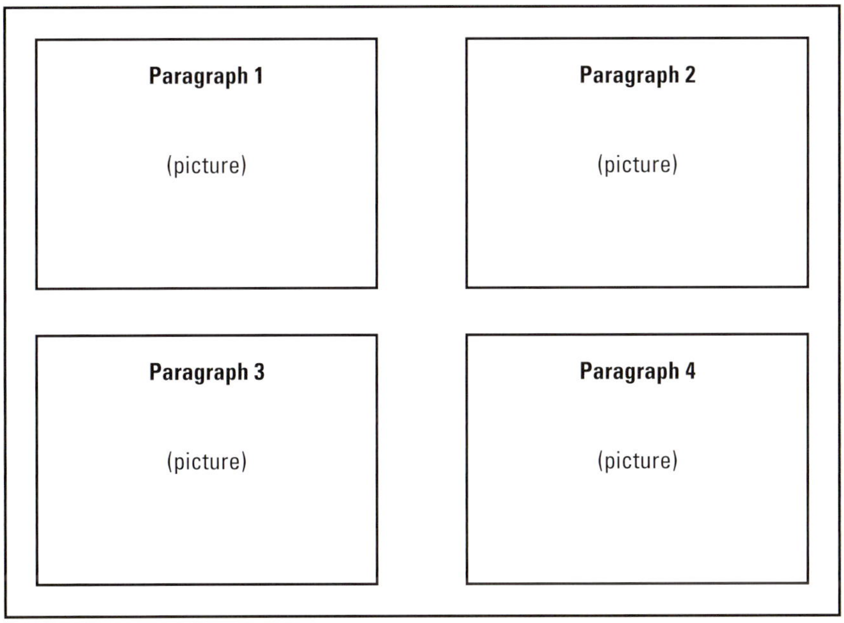

Students can refer to this visual aid to further support their *understanding* of the text.

—K. Hennessey

This ULA can be used

✓ When teacher is presenting content and/or language

When learners are engaged in a learning task

When learners are demonstrating learning and understanding

ACTION 1.2 Playing with expression and voice intonation, and pacing rate of speech

Expression, intonation, and rate and rhythm of speech are essential to the way we understand and communicate messages. These elements affect how messages are heard, said, and read, and how they make the input more comprehensible (Krashen, 1981; Lightbown & Spada, 2013; VanPatten & Williams, 2007). All languages have a unique musicality and rhythmicality (prosody), so language learners need lots of exposure in the target language to become familiar with its nuances and rhythmic features.

To make oral or written messages more comprehensible, at times teachers will choose to exaggerate the use of expression and intonation. The overt use of expression and intonation makes the rhythmicality of the target language more explicit for language learners. Moreover, these elements draw learners' attention to the specific linguistic features of oral and written texts that a teacher wishes to emphasize. Learners are better able to hear things such as (1) the emotions related to certain words or a concept and (2) the spot in a sentence or word where the voice could be inflected.

This ULA also encourages teachers to slow down the pace when learners experience a breakdown in comprehension. By slowing down, teachers offer additional time for learners to process information in the target language, allowing them to catch up.

BROADENING ACCESS

- To build learner autonomy, could I share with my learners the value of this action so that they, in turn, use it when talking or reading to support other learners' comprehension?
  - How can students be using intonation, expression, and pacing while reading or talking?
- With respect to targeted support (e.g., Response to Intervention), are there any specific language learners in my class who could benefit from this action?

REFLECTION ON PRACTICE

Expression and Intonation

- When presenting a concept, could I be emphasizing key words or phrases by lowering, changing, or amplifying my voice?
- During class discussions, do I use expression to convey my feelings? (Examples: Exactly! / Umm. I'm *not* quite sure ... / What seeeems to be happening?)
- When reading aloud instructions or information to students, which key words or phrases should I emphasize through voice intonation? (Example: "For examples 1 and 2, work with a **partner** to find **two** solutions.")
- When reading narrative pieces, how am I bringing life to the words? How am I portraying the characters and the story's narrator?
- When choosing materials for students to listen to (video, audiobooks, songs), am I considering if and how expression and intonation are used?

Pace

- When delivering this lesson, where should I slow the pace by talking more slowly?
- Could I bring in software/devices that have adjustable text-reading speeds?

Action 1.2 in Action!

I just love doing readers' theatre with students! It's a good way to teach the importance of using expression and intonation when reading and it also increases students' reading fluency (a double whammy!). During readers' theatre lessons, students perform by reading scripts or stories. The goal is for their voices to do the "acting"—hence the need for pacing, expression, and intonation. I remind students that these elements need to be used meaningfully to help the audience *understand* the story.

I've also done a modified readers' theatre with information texts. I asked my students to read aloud a scientific text to their group members. Students needed to read the text using different voices. Some group members read passages using the scientist's voice (affirmative expression), others used a concerned little old lady voice (trembling voice as she is scared of the outcome of this scientific discovery), while others used the voice of confused students.

—M. Sanchez

I noticed that most of my students do fairly well when I'm presenting new concepts. However, *comprehension* tends to break down a bit when I'm giving instructions to a task or explaining a group activity, as I'm often explaining the different steps they'll need to do. I now slow down quite a bit when doing this. I tend to hang on every word just a little longer and I emphasize key words (e.g., "In your **group**, you will be looking for the **big** ideas" or again, "You'll have **five minutes** to **sort** these words." I find that works much better to help students understand what's going on.

—N. Michaud

ACTION 1.3 Adjusting the complexity of oral and/or written language

Stephen Krashen (1981) advanced the idea that language learners should be exposed to language that is comprehensible, in other words, language that is just beyond their current language skill, but within the realm of understanding because of support provided with that language. Ideally, learners should be able to understand the general meaning of oral and written messages, but not necessarily all the words and language features of a text presented to them.

Within that realm of support is the dimension of *complexity*—or how direct and simple is the language presented to the student. Playing with the complexity of the language shared with the students will support their understanding of the language.

This ULA can be used

- ✓ **When teacher is presenting content and/or language**
- ✓ **When learners are engaged in a learning task**
- **When learners are demonstrating learning and understanding**

Linguistic complexity is also a method through which we can differentiate learning paths in a language classroom. We explore that in Chapter 9.

Linguistic complexity can and should be adjusted as students' language proficiency increases. In this case, input should increase in complexity. Conversely, for beginning language learners or for learners learning new or more complex material, the language may need to be adjusted for simplicity. Ways of making oral and written language simpler include using

- short sentences with simple structures
- words and phrases that are repeated throughout; simple, known words, adverbs, and adjectives
- concrete examples linked to students' experiences
- limited use of abstractions and inferences
- simple verb tenses
- many cognates (words of the same linguistic family)

This action works well in combination with other ULAs from this chapter in making input more comprehensible for learners.

REFLECTION ON PRACTICE

- Is it time to take stock of my learners' current linguistic levels? Are all my learners at similar levels? Who may be stronger linguistically?
- When explaining a concept, am I using language that is comprehensible to them?
  - Am I choosing to use short and simple sentences?
  - Am I using familiar words and cognates?
  - How often am I repeating key words and phrases?
- When I choose reading materials for students to read, is the material comprehensible to them?
  - Does the text use sentence structures appropriate for students' reading level?
  - Does the text have a lot of repetition of words, phrases, and ideas?
  - Does the text contain many high-frequency words?
- When talking with my language learners, am I challenging them enough? Am I providing language that is just slightly above that of my students?

BROADENING ACCESS

- With respect to targeted support (e.g., Response to Intervention), are there any specific language learners in my class who could benefit from this action?

Action 1.3 in Action!

To see this ULA in action, you will need to go to Chapter 9. Of all the ULAs we present, this action has the most overlap with the dimension of differentiation explored in this book. That is because one of the methods of differentiation we explore in Chapter 9 is differentiation by linguistic complexity.

For the purpose of clarity at this juncture, we want to say that when a teacher adjusts the complexity of the language at a more general level to support all students, the teacher is said to be using the ULA. If the teacher is using differentiation by linguistic complexity, all students are being offered distinctly different learning paths that are shaped by their proficiency needs.

ACTION 1.4 Assessing the extent of prior knowledge and filling in any major gaps

This ULA can be used

- ✓ **When teacher is presenting content and/ or language**
- **When learners are engaged in a learning task**
- **When learners are demonstrating learning and understanding**

When students consciously and explicitly link new knowledge to concepts or frames of reference they already possess, then meaningful learning can take place (Ausubel, 1963). Indeed, there is a strong relationship between learners' background knowledge and achievement. It has been shown that learners who know more about a topic are better at retaining new information and find learning much easier (Bruner, 1996). Moreover, learners who have sufficient knowledge and prior life experiences with respect to what is being taught find learning more meaningful. Learners bring to class different experiences, values, and knowledge based on their own lived experiences. Wessels (2012) reminds us to value such diversity and richness when assessing learners' prior knowledge.

How Prior Knowledge Is Constructed

The process of acquiring prior knowledge is twofold. First, students need to develop the ability to process and store information to long-term memory. Second, learners need to be exposed to a number of authentic experiences related to what is being learned and, what is more important, learn from these experiences and make connections to move ideas into long-term memory.

For second language learners in particular, background knowledge is often learned in the first language, which makes up part of their prior knowledge. From a language teaching standpoint, it is a different process to teach students the word *butterfly* in a target language if they already know what a butterfly is. However, if students are learning the concept and the word at the same time, through the target language, a different pedagogical tactic is needed. Here are the steps to assessing prior knowledge and filling in gaps:

1. Teachers engaged in inclusionary practices consider the lived experiences and home languages that learners bring with them to the classroom.
2. They identify key background knowledge and language needed to successfully learn a topic.
3. They account for possible gaps in learners' backgrounds and understand that learning can be more challenging with limited prior knowledge or limited target language.
4. They then offer rich and significant experiences to help learners build a sufficient knowledge and linguistic base for the concept being studied.

When to Assess Prior Knowledge

Assessing learners' background knowledge should first take place at the beginning of a lesson or unit or any time new oral or written material is presented. Background knowledge serves as a springboard to the construction of new learning, brings to the surface what learners already know about the subject, and allows teachers to validate language learners' lives, cultures, and experiences. It also enables teachers to assess the following: (1) the amount of knowledge learners have about the topic and (2) the extent of the target language that learners already possess. With this information, teachers can begin to fill in possible knowledge and language gaps.

Learners' prior knowledge should also be activated and acknowledged throughout the unit of study because learners need multiple occasions to reflect upon and discuss the relationship between new concepts and language and their lived experiences. Making connections to prior learning or experiences enhances learner engagement; it also further supports learners who need additional support with oral or written comprehension.

REFLECTION ON PRACTICE

This action works well in combination with Action 1.1 *Using gestures, facial expressions, images, pictures, drawings, objects, and manipulation materials*. Often, drawings, pictures, and objects help activate learners' prior knowledge.

- At the beginning of my lesson or unit, how do I assess students' prior knowledge?
  - Do I ask questions? Do I do a pre-assessment? Do I give examples? Do I provide visual supports to identify what they know and don't know?
- How could students show me the extent of their prior knowledge at the beginning of a new unit of study?
  - Could they draw what they know about the topic?

continued

- Could they talk it through with a partner?
  - Could we do a whole-class brainstorming activity?
  - Could they find concrete examples in the classroom (e.g., shapes, words that rhyme with *cat*, working mechanisms, things that float)?
- Could I use concept maps, word walls, or labelled pictures to support discussions centred on activating prior knowledge?
- When choosing reading materials, do I consider the extent of prior knowledge students need to have on a topic to understand the text?
- How could I be using students' prior knowledge more meaningfully as a springboard to new learning? Am I making clear connections between prior knowledge and new concepts being presented?
- During this unit of study, are there any cultural elements that may be unfamiliar to some of my language learners?
- Are there visual supports or objects that I could bring in to help trigger students' prior knowledge?
- Do students understand the concept in their first language? If so, what connections could I be making to students' first language? (Example: "In Spanish we have adjectives—words that describe objects. We also have adjectives in English.")

BROADENING ACCESS

- To build learner autonomy, could I share with my learners the value of this action so that they, in turn, can decide to use or build prior knowledge?
- With respect to targeted support (e.g., Response to Intervention), are there any specific language learners in my class who could benefit from this action?

Action 1.4 in Action!

One of our class units is on sustainability. We work on this concept from an urban and a rural perspective. I teach in a more rural area and some of my students have never gone to a big city. In terms of activating prior knowledge of rural sustainability efforts, students could generate quite a few ideas that I could then build upon throughout the unit.

However, I noticed that some of my students didn't have the same amount of prior knowledge about urban life. That's when I realized that I needed to assess where they were at with respect to their prior knowledge of urban life. There are things I could have easily taken for granted that they knew (e.g., the concept of a high-rise, taking a train to work, the lack of green spaces in city centres). I knew then that I had to fill in these knowledge gaps before even going into "sustainability." To fill in these gaps, we Skyped with an urban class, we watched live stream videos from city-placed cameras, and we had a few people from the school staff, who had lived in a big city, come to talk to the class. These were all authentic, meaningful experiences that really helped to fill in the gaps.

I gather that the opposite is also true for city folk who have never been to farm country. I'm sure there are gaps to fill there, too! We just don't know what the gaps are and how big they are until we assess students' prior knowledge.

—T. Gauvin

This ULA can be used

✓ When teacher is presenting content and/or language

When learners are engaged in a learning task

When learners are demonstrating learning and understanding

ACTION 1.5 Providing wait time when presenting new information, after asking a question, or before inviting learners to start a task

Providing wait time is an important action to embed within instructional practice as part of an inclusive pedagogy. We know that language learners need additional time to interpret and process information in the target language (Marzano, 2007). So, wait time should be provided intentionally when presenting new information, after asking a question, or when preparing learners to begin a new task.

As mentioned in Chapter 2, second language learners need more time to process words and messages in the target language, more so than in their first language. First language learners need about nine seconds of wait time (Woolfolk, 2012). Second language learners, however, need up to four times as long to process language and meaning—up to 36 seconds.

When language learners are being asked a question, wait time is needed if they are to properly understand the question, come up with possible answers, and then formulate answers in the target language. For some, wait time is particularly crucial if they are to participate in class conversation and do so confidently.

The same premise applies when learners are asked to respond to written questions or when we provide directions about an upcoming task. In these cases, it is important for teachers to provide wait time so learners can (1) decipher what is being asked of them, (2) formulate or collect their thoughts, and (3) respond in the target language. Wait time allow learners to be better equipped to answer the question or undertake the task.

When new information is being presented, either orally or in writing, effective teachers pause frequently. Doing this allows learners to process the information and monitor their comprehension. Providing wait time between statements or reading passages enables learners to better grasp the material. It also helps those who need support in keeping up with the pace of the lesson.

REFLECTION ON PRACTICE

- After asking students a question, how long do I wait before calling on them for answers?
- Could I be making an explicit statement about wait time to my students? Should I say, for example, "Before answering this question, I'm going to give you a minute to come up with an answer"?
- Could I provide additional time for my learners when they are working on a written question?

continued

- Are my students conscious of the fact that they may need extra time to read the question in the target language, make sense of it, and formulate their answers in the target language?
- Do my students know that it's normal to take a little longer to answer questions in the target language than in their first language?
- When I'm explaining a new concept, do I stop between chunks of information to allow my students to digest the information?
- When giving multiple-step instructions to students, do I pause between steps so students can decipher the information?
- Do I encourage my students to pause after every page, paragraph, or sentence to take in the information before moving on with the reading?
- What else could I do to more consciously provide wait times in my class?
- Could I encourage my students to share their answers with a partner before sharing them with the class?
- Could I offer my students the opportunity to draw or sketch out their thoughts, take a few notes, or write a few key words during wait time to help them make sense of the material?

BROADENING ACCESS

- How can I help learners become comfortable with wait time and learn how to use the pauses to help them manage their thinking?
- What strategies can I teach students to use during wait time to help them process the information?
- With respect to targeted support (e.g., Response to Intervention), are there any specific language learners in my class who could benefit from this action?

Action 1.5 in Action!

As a result of what I teach, we do a lot of discussions in my class. I was noticing that it was often the same couple of students who took part in the conversations. Initially, I thought perhaps this was due to a lack of engagement or motivation, but again, the less active students seemed to be paying attention and they did seem to be listening. I wondered how I could better bring them into the conversations.

In my class, as in many other classes, I have students with a range of linguistic abilities. The ones dominating the conversations were, for the most part, my stronger language communicators and my very confident students. So, I started providing additional wait time after I asked a question. I also explained to students why I was doing it—to give them time to *understand* the question, reflect upon it, and formulate their ideas in the target language. I must admit that giving the wait time was tough for me at first—I wasn't used to the silence. We tend to want to fill up the silence during conversations, don't we? However, that's exactly what my students needed. That wait time gave students time to prepare. Honestly, students' confidence levels grew, too!

—P. Manson

I tend to link the idea of wait time with the ability to check students' *understanding* throughout my lesson. It's a good way for me to see how

continued

well the students are grasping the material I'm presenting. When I deliver my lesson, I make a conscious effort to pause every so often (I even put an icon on my PowerPoint slides to signal I need to pause).

I call this my "mirror activity": I ask students to think about what I just presented and how they could explain it to someone else. I give them about a minute or two to think it through. Then I say, "Turn to your mirror partner!" One of the students explains what he or she has learned while the other partner fills in additional information, if need be. With this mirroring activity, students work through the material twice (once with me and once with their partner). Students have a chance to consider the extent to which they *understand* the lesson and I get to see students' levels of understanding as I walk around and listen to the different explanations.

—D. Toner

This ULA can be used

✓ **When teacher is presenting content and/or language**

When learners are engaged in a learning task

When learners are demonstrating learning and understanding

ACTION 1.6 Repeating or reformulating oral and written language

Repeating or Reformulating Oral Instructions and Directives

When teachers give instructions or directions, language learners need to simultaneously decipher the meaning of the message (in the second language) and place the information in short-term memory. Doing this can be daunting, especially in cases where there is a lot of input to interpret and retain. In order to facilitate comprehension, inclusive teachers repeat or reformulate the questions they ask learners, the key phrases learners need to learn, the directions they give, and the explanations they provide to their learners.

Repeating or Reformulating Learners' Questions, Answers, and Comments

This action is particularly effective for language learners participating in large-group or whole-class discussions. When teachers repeat or paraphrase learners' questions, answers, and comments, they ensure the following:

1. They ensure that other learners in the class can hear what their classmates are saying. Oftentimes, when learners participate in group discussions, they do not speak loudly enough for all to hear. By repeating or paraphrasing learners' questions, statements, comments, announcements, and accounts, teachers ensure that all learners can

hear what is taking place. Students who find it particularly challenging to focus in and decipher information coming from different speakers will benefit greatly from this ULA.

2. Teachers are able to clarify the learner's comment or question and ensure that the message produced was what was intended. When teachers repeat learners' utterances, they may choose to add more intonation and expression, slow down the pace, or even simplify the language. By doing so, they help learners who need additional support in understanding input coming from various sources. Moreover, the act of repeating a question or a comment more than once has the same benefits as those associated with Action 1.7 *Reusing and recycling pedagogical materials*.

3. Teachers add or reinforce linguistic precision to learners' utterances (error correction). When repeating or reformulating, they are also wise to take the opportunity to offer or ask for the proper language structure, especially in cases where precision is an issue. The repeated utterance will, therefore, offer learners the proper language model (Lyster, 1987, 1998, 2001).

For research related to correcting errors and providing feedback, see Chapter 10.

Involving Learners in Repeating and Reformulating

In some instances, teachers may choose to turn the responsibility of repeating or re-explaining over to the learners. Teachers can ask learners to repeat or re-explain the steps to follow for completing a particular task, for example, or they may choose to ask a student to repeat what another student said. Teachers can then formatively assess learners' comprehension. Moreover, they gain an excellent opportunity for evaluating the effectiveness of their instruction. By involving students, teachers can get a real sense of learners' level of understanding.

Reading Aloud and Reformulating Written Questions, Instructions, and Directions

Language learners also need additional supports in comprehending written instructions or questions. By reading aloud this material, teachers provide oral support to written texts. Doing this is particularly important in cases where learners' oral comprehension is stronger than their reading comprehension. In such cases, these learners may not be able to fully comprehend written questions or texts, but may be capable of accomplishing the required task or answering the question once they hear the language. We do not want to stifle learners' ability to accomplish a task or produce language simply because they do not comprehend written directions.

REFLECTION ON PRACTICE

- When I ask a question of the class, how many times do I repeat it before asking students to offer answers? Should I be repeating my questions more?
- When I ask my students a question, could I be asking it in different ways?
- When I'm giving the directions for a task, should I be repeating these directions a further time?
- When my students ask a question or provide an answer or comment, can the other students in the class hear? Should I repeat students' utterances more often?
- When students ask a question or provide an answer or comment, could I use reformulations more often? Examples: "If I'm hearing you correctly, you are saying that …," "So, in other words, you are saying that …," "Is this what you mean … ?"
- When students are engaged in oral communication tasks, how am I helping them use proper linguistic structures (if errors occur)? Could I be pushing the students more to offer me the utterance error-free?
- What could I do in class to engage my students in repeating and reformulating tasks? Could my students repeat the steps of the activity to a partner? Could they repeat a classmate's answer?
- When presenting my students with written questions or written instructions, could I read this material out to them more often? Could I also reformulate the questions to allow learners to hear them in different ways?
- What could be preventing some learners from completing written questions or tasks? Could it be that they do not understand the questions or tasks? How could teacher (or student) repetition or reformulation help in these cases?

BROADENING ACCESS

- How can I help students learn to ask for repetitions or reformulations to help support their understanding?
- With respect to targeted support (e.g., Response to Intervention), are there any specific language learners in my class who could benefit from this action?

Action 1.6 in Action!

I work with language learners and I tend to use group work as part of my teaching philosophy. Before putting students in their groups, I always go over and model the task with them and explain the different steps for properly completing it. Most of my students can then get in their groups, get organized, and start tackling the task—for the most part. However, it seems like there are always a few students who take longer to get organized and under way.

To try to support my learners a bit better, I now include my students more actively when I'm providing the instructions. Sometimes, I ask different students to repeat the instructions: "Who can tell me what you're

continued

going to do first? Who can tell me what you're going to do after?" Other times, I'll ask students to turn to a partner and they go over the steps together. I can then answer any questions they may have. I think the whole class benefits—they understand better and they get to communicate a bit more in the target language!

—J. Wilson

I remember last year, I was doing some team teaching with another teacher, and we were both noticing the same things. First, a few of our students would ask a question that had already been asked, and second, some students would offer irrelevant comments. So, we kept a closer eye on this for a few weeks. Being in a team-teaching situation really gave us an opportunity to see what was going on when the other one was teaching.

That's when we realized that some students couldn't hear other students' comments (primarily because my students' voices didn't carry across the whole room—some have low or soft voices).

This really had an impact on class conversations (and admittedly, affected some students' ability to understand what was going on). A few of our students would quickly lose track of the conversation because they were missing out on some parts of the group exchange.

Sometimes, a student would be offering a comment to something that had been discussed a few minutes prior but hadn't realized the conversation had taken a different turn. The same was true for questions. They hadn't heard the question being asked the first time around. All this to say that I now repeat a lot of what the students are saying: "Julie just said that ..." "That's an excellent question, Sam! Let me repeat that for those of you who may have the same question." "Ben agreed with me—Thank you, Ben!"

—B. Nguyen

I really take the time to go over any written directions or questions with my students. I let them get a feel for the written text first, then I read it aloud. I'm also reformulating questions or information for them as well. There is a time to assess students' reading abilities, but when I'm working on something else, I really wouldn't want a student to not be able to do the task simply because he or she doesn't understand what I asked of him or her.

I find that, by doing this, I greatly eliminate the amount of re-explaining I'm doing at individual students' desks.

—C. Cloutier

This ULA can be used

- ✓ When teacher is presenting content and/ or language
- ✓ When learners are engaged in a learning task
- When learners are demonstrating learning and understanding

ACTION 1.7 Reusing and recycling pedagogical materials

Teachers working with language learners know that newly presented material needs to be reviewed several times, especially in cases where learners need additional support in understanding oral or written messages. This ULA encourages teachers to reuse and recycle pedagogical materials throughout a lesson or unit. It also ensures that learners get repeated exposure to authentic materials.

Reusing and Recycling Pedagogical Materials

Teachers should not be afraid of reusing or recycling pedagogical material. For example, a particular activity, a favourite children's book, an interesting reading passage, a video clip, or a game can be reused several times within a unit of study. Engaging with familiar material boosts vocabulary and comprehension. Exploiting a text several different times allows teachers to fully take advantage of its teaching/learning potential (Fisher & Frey, 2014; Tierney & Pearson, 1983). Similarly, reusing vocabulary and language structures several times aids learners in storing them in long-term memory.

Teachers who wish to reuse material that students have already been exposed to are wise to consider changing its goal or purpose. In other words, learners need to be provided with different intentions for reused tasks, activities, or pedagogical materials. For example, when wanting to reuse a certain reading passage, a teacher may, one day, ask learners to read the text for general comprehension. The second time, the teacher may ask learners to underline the arguments made for and against an issue, while the third time, learners may read the text to determine the author's point of view. By reusing and recycling newly presented material, teachers provide much needed language reinforcement to language learners.

Re-encountering the Language Orally and in Print

Learners need multiple opportunities to engage with oral and textual elements such as key vocabulary, specific language functions, key concepts of the lesson, and important explanations. As part of their inclusive pedagogy, teachers need to present these elements both orally and in writing. In other words, what is presented orally should be seen in print as well. Learners benefit from rehearing and reusing newly presented material through multiple listening, reading, writing, oral interaction, and oral production activities.

For example, students not only need to say key vocabulary or language structures, but to reuse this vocabulary in their writing and reading—re-encountering this vocabulary through reading, viewing, writing, hearing, and talking. This helps strengthen learners' comprehension and production skills.

REFLECTION ON PRACTICE

- How could I recycle or reuse a passage I am giving my students to read throughout the week (unit, or lesson)? In what other ways could the students be using this text?
- Having done a particular activity, what elements of that activity could I use again?
- How many other ways could the students use the word wall, the concept map, the word web, the song of the week, their library book, and so on?
- Could I find alternative and interesting ways to reuse some of the material I use for this unit?
- Could I be making more direct links between oral communication, reading, and writing when using this pedagogical tool (e.g., this children's book, this lab experiment, this group task, this poster, this video, this audio story)?
- Are my students exposed to concepts and new language, both orally and through print?
- Could my students be reusing language and the concept under study through all these different formats: pair work, team assignments, and whole-class activities?

BROADENING ACCESS

- To build learner autonomy, could I share with my learners the value of this action so that they, in turn, use it to support their understanding of oral and written language?
- With respect to targeted support (e.g., Response to Intervention), are there any specific language learners in my class who could benefit from this action?

Action 1.7 in Action!

In my class, we work on developing reading skills. To build fluency and comprehension skills, we tend to tackle a text several different times throughout the week.

1. I read the text to students and we work together on building general comprehension.
2. Once students are comfortable with the text, we read it again, this time to work on a particular sound—the sound of the week.
3. We may then read the text again to tease out the words that are part of our thematic word wall.
4. We revisit the text: it now serves as a springboard to an oral or written task. For example, I may say, "Talk to your partner about whether you would have acted in a similar way to the main character."
5. Finally, students could read the text to a reading buddy or class partner.

The point is that I reuse the text a lot. Interestingly, the students love it. They are confident with the text, and they're learning so much faster because they are familiar with the content.

—A. Desveaux

continued

Whenever I'm presenting a thematic activity—like students creating their own design plan for a new zoo in town—I make sure students read, talk about, and write about this theme. I want them to be exposed several times to the new vocabulary, the prevailing issues, and the linguistic features.

I make sure we talk about zoos both in terms of personal experiences and about their general knowledge of zoos. We also read fiction and non-fiction books about the zoo, we write a letter to the principal asking permission to go on a class trip to a zoo, we do a virtual tour of a zoo, we do a Skype interview with a zoo employee, and we watch a film about animals in captivity. It's really great that my students get to learn the language through different mediums.

My next step is to start working with a colleague of mine—who also teaches the same students—to see how we could make cross-curricular links between our subject areas. Maybe students could reuse newly acquired vocabulary in their different classes.

—M. Carmel

Universal Language Actions Acting as Comprehension Checks

The Universal Language Actions described in this chapter facilitate learners' understanding of oral and written language while also helping those who are experiencing a breakdown in comprehension. Because a student's comprehension of an idea or concept (the input) is gauged by monitoring nonverbal and verbal production (output), there is a very close, symbiotic relationship between checking for student comprehension and engaging in actions to support the comprehension.

Quick and frequent comprehension checks are an important feature for teachers working with language learners because, in comparison to original oral or written production, capturing learners' precise level of understanding can be a bit more challenging, in part for the following reasons. First, some language learners may not be able to fully articulate the extent to which they understand what is being presented because of limited language abilities in the target language. Second, students experiencing comprehension difficulties may refrain from taking part in a given activity or may act as though they fully understand when they do not (e.g., by nodding or remaining silent when asked "Does everyone understand?"). These students may be embarrassed to show a lack of understanding in front of others; such responses, however, likely diminish teachers' ability to monitor comprehension. Finally, some learners may not even be aware that they do not fully understand what they are hearing or reading.

As outlined in Figure 5.3, the following ULAs from this chapter enable teachers to do frequent checks of learners' comprehension throughout a given lesson.

Figure 5.3: Checking Comprehension Through Universal Language Actions

Universal Language Actions	How They Check for Comprehension
• Action 1.1 Using gestures, facial expressions, images, pictures, objects, and manipulation materials	Because some learners may not be able to fully articulate the extent to which they understand, teachers can assess comprehension by having learners draw or point to objects or images.
• Action 1.4 Assessing the extent of prior knowledge and filling in any major gaps	By assessing learners' prior knowledge or language, teachers gauge where they were when they began versus how much they retained throughout the lesson or activity.
• Action 1.6 Repeating or reformulating oral and written language	Teachers who ask learners to repeat or reformulate instructions or information from texts monitor learners' comprehension. Teachers who repeat or paraphrase learners' questions or comments invite learners to monitor their own understanding: "If I hear you correctly, you're saying ________. Is this what you mean?"
• Action 1.7 Reusing and recycling pedagogical materials	Teachers who reuse pedagogical materials can assess the extent to which learners are working through the materials toward mastery.

Through the use of these actions, teachers are better able to identify learners who may need additional supports with comprehension.

Closing Thoughts

Besides the chapter activity ideas and suggestions for varying the ULAs, we want you to take away two key points about facilitating student understanding in the language classroom:

1. Comprehension precedes production. Students cannot produce language on their own if they do not understand the language around them. The ULAs are critical to helping the students build that understanding.

2. To be able to gauge what students understand about a topic, you have to look at their production. So, there is a lot of back and forth between observing what students say, do, and convey through body language and adjusting the information you give to them to ensure that they understand the ideas around them. Observing a lack of understanding could mean that the student has not been given the right tools (e.g., language prompts, activity formats) to convey that understanding; hence, it is critical to be really mindful of what learning activities and resources require of students.

As you reflect on the contents of this chapter, we invite you to think about the following issues related to student comprehension:

- What kind of language do I assume that students already understand within the lesson?
- How do I currently support student language comprehension?
- What supports could I add to foster understanding?
- How can I support student energy and attention so that they support student understanding?
- How do my students reveal they are not understanding what is happening in class?
- How can I empower students to be more open about admitting a lack of understanding?
- How can I better use what students produce or create to gauge the depth of their understanding?

CHAPTER 6

Language Learners Who Need Additional Support in Producing Oral or Written Language

Students produce oral and written language to express feelings, opinions, and ideas; to transmit information; to retell events; and to ask questions. They also produce language to explain or elaborate upon their thoughts, feelings, and opinions. As you may recall from Chapter 2, early and less proficient language learners expend a lot of cognitive effort to produce language; the lack of immediate automaticity in second language production can be frustrating to students and requires additional consideration from the teacher.

Students who need additional support to produce oral or written language may exhibit some of the following characteristics:

- ❑ limit themselves to non-verbal output (gestures, facial expressions, pointing)
- ❑ rely too heavily on their first language to communicate
- ❑ overuse basic and simple vocabulary, sentence structures, or language functions
- ❑ ask repeatedly: "How do you say ______?"
- ❑ avoid participating
- ❑ write little, if anything at all
- ❑ provide only one-word answers
- ❑ avoid eye contact
- ❑ get easily discouraged or frustrated
- ❑ seem off task
- ❑ cannot elaborate
- ❑ provide few details
- ❑ need constant reassurance
- ❑ seem unmotivated
- ❑ have difficulty with syntax and sentences (incomplete or jerky sentences)
- ❑ do not take risks
- ❑ allow others to accomplish the task for them

Factors That Can Affect the Oral or Written Task

When it comes to language production, we need to first consider four factors that have a bearing on the classroom experience before we look at how to support the students' language learning. These four factors may account for why certain learners require more support with certain oral and written tasks—not all written and oral tasks are the same. Some tasks may be more challenging than others depending on how interactive they are and how much planning is involved. The four factors discussed below are (1) types of oral communication tasks, (2) planning for production, (3) types of language required, and (4) silence and the student affect.

Types of Oral Communication Tasks

All oral communication tasks can be defined by their level of interactiveness. Some are very interactive while others are not—they are more non-interactive and non-reciprocal. During interactive communication, students share their ideas, feelings, and opinions with others. Here, we think of class discussions, peer sharing, debates, and small-group conversations. In these situations, students need to share information and negotiate the meaning of these exchanges in order for the interactions to move along. Non-interactive communication tasks are about presenting or transferring information to others without much interaction. Here, we think about group or class presentations, monologues, and speeches. Some of our students may favour one kind of communication task over the other (interactive versus non-interactive), and some of them may require additional supports with respect to producing language in oral communication tasks of either type.

Planning for Production

There are important differences with respect to how much planning is involved with any given oral or written task. For oral production, in the case of a class presentation, a speech, or an interview, students can spend time planning for the task: what ideas they want to share and how they will go about sharing those ideas. The same holds true for certain written tasks, including those where students follow the writing process: planning, drafting, editing and revising, and publishing. Here we think of pieces of writing such as a story, a non-fiction essay, or a procedural piece.

Some oral activities and writing situations, however, require more spontaneity. Discussions and conversations done orally or through writing (e.g., text messaging) require students to process information coming in from other speakers or writers and analyze this information in order to produce contextually appropriate second language output almost immediately. Other writing tasks that are given by the teacher may also have less planning time involved: these include drafting reflections, learning journal notes, diary entries, and exit slips. Spontaneous language production is different from planned language production.

Types of Language Required

There is a clear distinction between social and academic situations for oral and written production. Vocabulary, linguistic demands, vernacular, and types of languages will differ in these situations.

Jim Cummins (1983) outlines two basic types of language in the classroom: basic interpersonal communication skills (BICS) and cognitive academic language proficiency (CALP). BICS language is more social and less cognitively demanding, and many students can communicate easily about social and daily living needs within one to three years of starting language study. It is often very concrete, in that students can typically point to an object and use that to help build meaning. CALP language is academic. It is more abstract and is often framed as "words to talk about other words." Students will take anywhere from five to seven years, in most cases, to develop the language depth necessary to navigate CALP language. Further, students with a strong grasp of BICS—which often is used in oral language—could be misjudged by teachers when submitting written work (which often uses CALP language); it is not uncommon for their written language to not flow as well as it should. For example, we tend to speak in run-on sentences, but in written language, we want to avoid this.

The range for both types of language is influenced by many of the same factors outlined in Chapter 2, including how much access students have to the target language and when to use it, the similarities between the student's home language and the target language, and, to some degree, learner personality.

Silence and Student Affect

Recall from Chapter 2 the stages of language acquisition. As was pointed out, in the earliest stage, student silence is a typical characteristic—production is not a given, nor should it be expected. The student is in the process of managing a lot of new input in the target language, and the brain and emotions are overwhelmed with all of the new information. Thus, silence is a natural response to the situation—and somewhat of an emotional response.

Certainly, from the start, students can reproduce or mimic language that is presented to them orally or in writing, but it is another thing to ask students to produce language on their own. *Silent period* is used to describe this time (Krashen & Terrell, 1983). It is also worth noting that the time frame can be anywhere from several months to a year, depending on several factors in the student's life, including language similarities between the home and target languages, how much the student is still using the home language outside of school, student personality, access to the target language outside of school, and past traumas that may have had an influence on the student's need to attend school in another language.

Universal Language Actions That Support Oral and Written Language Production

Some language learners need additional support if they are to produce oral or written language at the desired level. The following seven ULAs, listed in Figure 6.1, facilitate learners' ability to produce oral and written language.

Figure 6.1

Universal Language Actions That Facilitate Learner Production of Oral and Written Language

Action 2.1 Providing many exemplars of oral and written tasks

Action 2.2 Using graphic organizers to support oral and written production

Action 2.3 Creating and displaying linguistic supports around the classroom

Action 2.4 Offering planning strategies for learners to use before starting a task

Action 2.5 Using pedagogical and language production routines

Action 2.6 Choosing grouping arrangements that favour peer communication

Action 2.7 Asking questions that encourage learners to elaborate

ACTION 2.1 Providing many exemplars of oral and written tasks

Exemplars are models or examples of what the task or assignment should look like once completed. Language learners need to see, read, and hear what is expected of them. Exemplars provide concrete models of the task. In order to maximize the use of exemplars in the classroom, teachers must carefully select them to represent exactly what is expected of students. Exemplars should also be presented several times during the course of a unit or a longer lesson. Here are a few examples of different types of exemplars in use:

- students watching an interview before doing a similar task
- the teacher and a student in front of the class modelling language structures associated with greeting someone before students are asked to practise those language structures
- students listening to songs before being asked to produce one
- students watching a short play before producing their own
- the teacher asking students to read exemplars of a procedural piece before they do a similar writing task
- the teacher writing an introduction on the board in front of students before asking them to write an introduction

Once an exemplar is provided to students, it is essential that this exemplar be analyzed; using exemplars should be recognized as a type of noticing activity. Students sometimes examine, see, listen to, and read exemplars without noticing what is exemplary about them. Students needing additional supports are particularly prone to this. So, the teacher is responsible for helping students notice the features that make the exemplar so stellar. Teachers can highlight important features of an exemplar by saying things such as

- "You'll notice that I looked at the person as I was greeting him and my facial expressions were pleasant. You probably also notice that I said, 'Hello! How are you?' Saying those two things together is a good thing."
- "You'll notice that the introduction in this text answers the questions who, what, when, and where. When you write your introductions, you'll want to do the same. Let's underline where the author answers these four questions."
- "You'll notice in the songs we'll listen to that there is a lot of repetition and many words that rhyme. Those are things we'll be working on when we write our own songs."

This ULA can be used

- ✓ When teacher is presenting content and/ or language
- ✓ When learners are engaged in a learning task
- When learners are demonstrating learning and understanding

Providing students with language models and reference points during a task de-emphasizes the role of memory and allows students more of a chance to focus on using the language. This is really helpful for early language learners.

Inclusive language teachers not only provide exemplars, but also clearly highlight the important features to notice from these exemplars. They write these down for students. This list becomes a reference for learners doing the production task and helps learners who need additional supports to produce oral or written messages become more aware of the expectations. Learners have a better sense of what is needed to accomplish the task.

Oral and written exemplars help contextualize the production task for language learners. The learners may not always understand the oral explanations associated with a task, but the exemplars provide an excellent reference point for them. By seeing, hearing, reading, and, most important, analyzing exemplars, language learners can observe and start internalizing the linguistic features they need to produce (Kristmanson, Dicks, LeBouthillier, & Bourgoin, 2008).

BROADENING ACCESS

- To build learner autonomy, could I share with my learners the value of this action so that they, in turn, use exemplars to support their own oral and written production?
- With respect to targeted support (e.g., Response to Intervention), are there any specific language learners in my class who could benefit from this action?

REFLECTION ON PRACTICE

- What do I see as being the value of an oral exemplar? a written exemplar?
- Do I provide exemplars for written tasks? Which writing tasks do I provide writing models for? formal writing and informal writing tasks?
- Do I provide a model for oral tasks? Do I provide an exemplar of what a pair discussion should look like or what a show-and-tell presentation should sound like?
- What forms do my exemplars take? Might there be audio files, video clips, and teacher-produced ones among them?
- What kind of analysis is done of the exemplars I provide? Can my students pull out the strengths, or look-fors, of the exemplars I provide?
- Do I see myself as an exemplar provider?

Action 2.1 in Action!

At the start of every year, I ask my students to write a language autobiography that tells me about the language(s) in their lives and how they use them. For some students, it is a difficult endeavour to write about themselves; they have come from schooling traditions outside of Canada where writing about personal experiences is not acceptable. Further, because I have students working at different levels of intermediate proficiency in English, many get nervous about trying to write something extended.

We do a lot of pre-writing work to develop the needed vocabulary, and there are several graphic organizers to help structure their thinking. However, I have found that the most helpful resource is examples

continued

of past autobiographies. With student permission, I kept copies of past submissions—all with varying degrees of detail and skill with writing. I post about eight of them on the wall and ask students to go look at them right after I explain the assignment. Then, when students return to their desks, I have them make a note on their planning guide for the day which past exemplar most resembles what they think they can do, writing-wise. When I collect the papers for review, I make a note of the essay they think is their target, and from there, reference that essay as we continue to plan. The students get copies of the biography for their own reference, and as part of the preplanning, sometimes have to make notes on their copy to support the planning. Though the students can certainly review the exemplars that remain on the wall to see how the assignment can be approached differently, I have found that the focused exemplar is a really good help to the students. It increases their confidence to know that no matter where they are with their writing, they can do the assignment well.

—S. Gagnon

Over the years, I have come to see the value in providing my students with good exemplars of how to do various oral activities. For big presentation assignments, I now have a bank of past student recordings to play for them as I outline the assignment expectations and have for them to reference as they do their own planning. I also have made it a point to role-play interactive speaking activities before I have students do the activity. This is particularly beneficial when the students are using a new interaction structure. For example, when I wanted to start using Inside-Outside circles with my class, I asked six students to join me at the front of the room so we could show the rest of the class how they would be moving and talking with each other. Student production is a lot easier to foster when the students understand the mechanics of the activities they are doing.

—D. Morris

ACTION 2.2 Using graphic organizers to support oral and written production

Graphic organizers are visual displays of ideas that help learners see how different parts of a message work together. They guide learners' thinking by helping them see and organize ideas and information. Students can use graphic organizers to help them explain cause and effect, compare and contrast (e.g., Venn diagram, T-charts), convey information, provide a sequence (e.g., timelines, cycles, chain of events), or even show problems and solutions.

The importance of using graphic organizers with language learners cannot be overstated: these organizers help support reading, listening, speaking, and writing. Students can fill in graphic organizers as a way to track listening skills or reading abilities (working on listening and reading comprehension skills). In these cases, students would pull out key information and jot it down in

This ULA can be used

- ✓ **When teacher is presenting content and/or language**
- ✓ **When learners are engaged in a learning task**
- ✓ **When learners are demonstrating learning and understanding**

graphic organizers. Graphic organizers are also effective in supporting oral and written production. At times, students may be unsure about the ideas they need to produce and in what order they should be presenting them—this can be the case for an oral task or a written task. In terms of oral production (e.g., sharing an experience, discussing a topic), students are able to use the layout of the organizer to guide them through the task. The same is true for written production. Graphic organizers are a great way to help learners plan for what they want to write. Organizers tend to be used most frequently when working on formal pieces of writing, but should also be used to support students in meeting less formal writing tasks, such as demand writing tasks, reflections or learning journal entries, and summaries.

BROADENING ACCESS

- To build learner autonomy, could I share with my learners the value of this action so that they, in turn, can start using graphic organizers in different oral and written contexts?
- With respect to targeted support (e.g., Response to Intervention), are there any specific language learners in my class who could benefit from this action?

REFLECTION ON PRACTICE

General Use and Modelling

- What types of visual organizers do I use in my classroom?
- To what extent do I model the use of graphic organizers to organize my ideas?

Oral Communication

- To what extent do I use graphic organizers to support oral communication?
- What language structures or vocabulary could I add to visual organizers to further support students in producing oral language?

Written Production

- To what extent do I use graphic organizers to support written production?
- For what types of written tasks do I provide an organizer—formal writing tasks (description, procedural piece) and informal writing tasks (learning journal, daily writing log, lesson summary)?

Action 2.2 in Action!

The kids in my class love to share. They love to share what they did over the weekend; when I introduce a new book, they'll all want to share how the topic of the book reminds them of a similar experience they've had. I was noticing, though, that some students found it a bit more challenging to present their experiences. Some students would provide the class with every little detail, while others would limit themselves to one thing. To help them organize enough of their ideas in chronological order, I provided them with a graphic organizer. It is displayed in front of the classroom.

continued

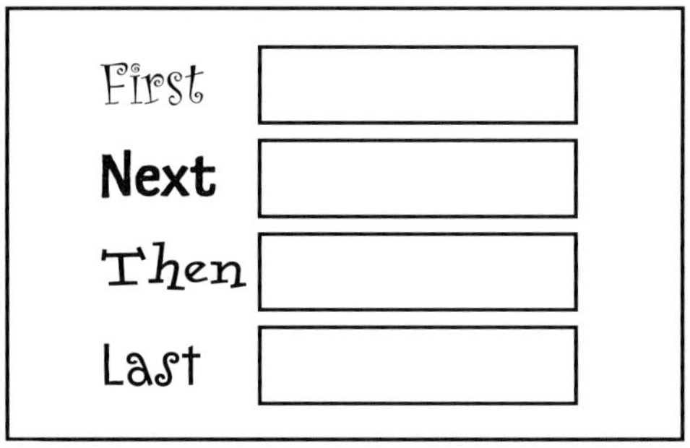

I've noticed now that when my students want to share a personal experience or a story, they look at the organizer to make sure they're covering all the different parts. This has really helped my students organize their thoughts. All of a sudden, they knew how much language they were expected to produce. Some of the students who tended to just say a line or two, such as "I've gone skating, too," will now elaborate on their stories when I ask them to describe their experience using the graphic organizer for support.

I've also noticed that after we read a story, I'll ask the kids to summarize the story, and some turn toward the graphic organizer to help them with the words: *first, next, then, last.*

—C. Samson

In my class, we discuss a lot of social issues. We generate many ideas during whole-group discussion. However, sometimes students don't immediately learn to use the new language produced during whole-group discussions. They need more opportunities to practise using this new language.

I use graphic organizers to support my language learners. During whole-class conversations, I'll take notes in a large graphic organizer I display on my board. As students provide ideas, I jot them down. I write down key ideas and words students may need in order to discuss the topic we're studying. I use Venn diagrams, cause and effect organizers, and problem–solution organizers.

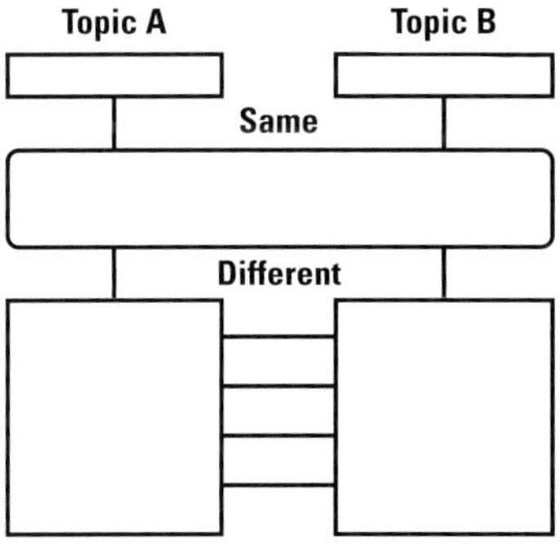

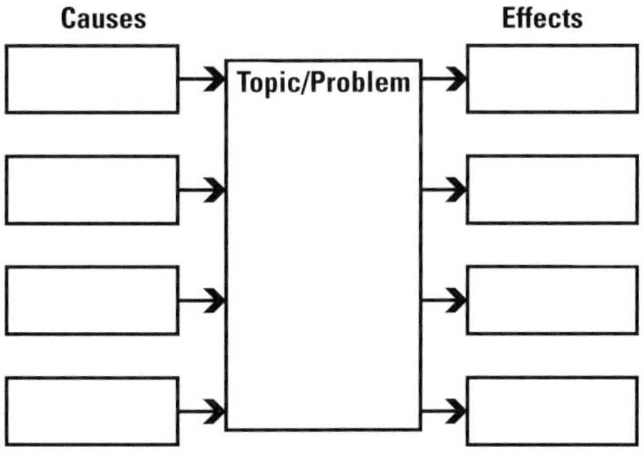

To reinforce the current issue we're studying, I'll place students in small groups to further discuss the topic. Many students will glance up at the

continued

graphic organizer to remember a word or to help them formulate an idea. Graphic organizers work really well in my class!

—S. Arsenault

For many subjects, I ask my students to keep a learning log. At the end of a lesson, I ask students to summarize what they've learned. Some students are quicker at putting their thoughts down on paper and tend to write more than others. Others seem to need support because they wouldn't write much in the allotted time. There are always a few students who wouldn't know where to start to write, so I created this graphic organizer.

Today's lesson was about ...		
What I learned	**What I learned**	**What I learned**
Question or something I'm wondering about ...		

Since students started using this graphic organizer, they know how to organize their thoughts and they know what they need to write. All my students now produce proper summaries.

— N. Harvey

This ULA can be used

- ✓ **When teacher is presenting content and/or language**
- ✓ **When learners are engaged in a learning task**
- ✓ **When learners are demonstrating learning and understanding**

ACTION 2.3 Creating and displaying linguistic supports around the classroom

When we think of linguistic resources, often the first things that come to mind are dictionaries, thesauruses, and grammatical reference books. To navigate these tools effectively, second language learners need quite a bit of linguistic knowledge in the target language. They need to know enough in the target language to be able to know what to look for, understand the explanations, and choose appropriate actions. Here is an example:

Alex wants to work on choosing better words for a piece of writing. The first thing he needs to do is decide which words he would like to change (e.g., synonyms). Not all words require a synonym, though, so the student needs to have enough knowledge of the concept of synonyms to decide which words are more appropriate to change. In this case, Alex decides that the word *student* comes up often in his text. When looking at the word *student* in the thesaurus, Alex sees the following suggestions:

continued

graduate, *junior*, *pupil*, *learner*, *scholar*, *grad*, and *apprentice*. Of course, some words in this list are used to define students in specific contexts. Alex needs to choose an appropriate synonym, but in order to do so he needs quite a bit of linguistic knowledge in the target language.

As this example illustrates, it may be necessary, at times, to create more cognitively appropriate or linguistically appropriate resources that students can use more independently. These resources can include personal dictionaries, million-dollar word charts, thematic word walls and maps (see Action 4.2 *Capitalizing on the use of word walls and word maps*), brainstorming idea-webs, no-excuse word charts, grammar notes on chart paper, lists of survival phrases, and graphic organizers (see Action 2.2 *Using graphic organizers to support oral and written production*).

For adaptable and reproducible linguistic supports, see the *Access for Success* website.

Such linguistic resources should be co-created in class with students in order to foster student ownership (Rivard, Dilk, & Barnabé, 2007). Once created, these supports should be proudly displayed in the room—for easy access. It is important for teachers to model how to use these resources when speaking and writing, all while encouraging students to use them to support language production. Through modelling and making good use of these resources, students begin to understand (1) the purpose of the resources, (2) why they are beneficial, (3) how to use them effectively, and (4) when they can be used, that is, the learning situations in which they would be most helpful.

These types of classroom resources are not only an excellent way for students to learn new language, but they also help learners apply this new language when producing oral and written language. Linguistic supports ensure that the language is visible and at students' disposal. They thereby allow students to use them to further produce oral and written language.

REFLECTION ON PRACTICE

- When I think of linguistic resources that help students communicate more effectively orally or in writing, what types of resources come to mind?
- What linguistic resources are currently available to my students (online or print)? Are these resources linguistically and cognitively appropriate for my students?
- How can I get my students to take even more advantage of the linguistic resources we have around the classroom?
- How do I get my students to help me co-create linguistic resources which we'll later display in the classroom?
- How accessible and visible are the linguistic resources we co-create?

BROADENING ACCESS

- To build learner autonomy, could I share with my learners the value of this action so that they, in turn, use co-created linguistic resources more purposely?
- With respect to targeted support (e.g., Response to Intervention), are there any specific language learners in my class who could benefit from this action?

Action 2.3 in Action!

When I'd look at my students' writing, it was evident that certain words were getting overused: *big, small, good, happy, going, want.* So I decided to create a linguistic support in my class that would provide my students with synonyms for these highly overused words. I explained to my students that a word such as *big* was a nice word, but that we could replace this word with words such as *huge, large, gigantic,* and *massive.* On the visual, I placed the word *big* at the top of a recycling bin. Under the bin, we added the synonyms. Students then helped me brainstorm synonyms for our other overused words. Some looked in thesauruses to find words and we talked about which ones made more sense for us to use.

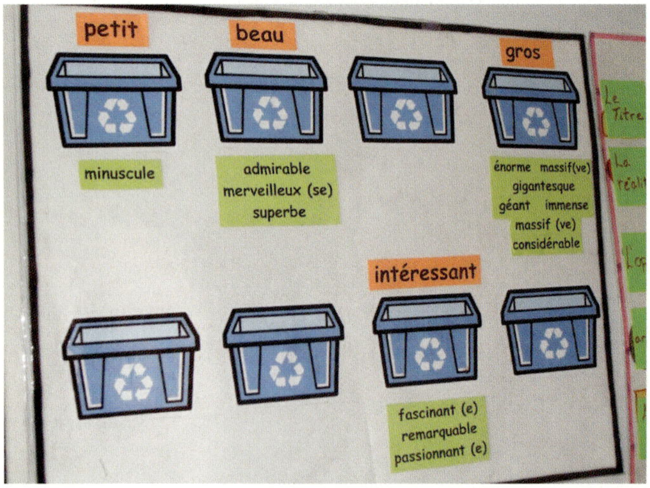

I must say that students really use this resource when writing, but what surprised me was that they also use it when speaking. They glance at the poster as they're speaking to find a better word. Every so often, we'll rework the poster to add different words and I've actually asked my students to suggest words they think they overuse.

—M. Dunbar

Because we do a lot of group discussions in class, I want to maximize that time to discuss the topics we're studying, but at the same time, I want students to work on their language abilities. I created this linguistic resource in my class called "Let's talk." It's a corner of my board. I explain to my students that when we have discussions, there are words that can move the discussion along. Here are some of them: *I agree because, Also, To add to this, An example of this is, On the other hand, In my opinion, Similarly.* We discuss the meanings of these words and how to properly use them. We then add these words to the board. As students get used to using these words during class discussion, we'll add more. It's been a great way for students to express themselves more effectively.

—D. Bullock

ACTION 2.4 Offering planning strategies for learners to use before starting a task

An important factor to consider when students are asked to produce oral or written language is planning. Because the students we teach are working in their second language, they often require additional time to process information and formulate their ideas into words.

As we discussed in Chapter 5, wait time (Action 1.5 *Providing wait time when presenting new information, after asking a question, or before inviting learners to start a task*) is an important thing to offer to help students process and comprehend new language. Planning, however, is also an important action to support learners in producing language (e.g., Chamot, Barnhardt, El-Dinary, & Robbins, 1999; Oxford, 1990). It allows sufficient time for second language learners to not only think about their ideas, but also how to organize them in order to produce an oral or written message.

Some learners may experience difficulties producing language because they require additional planning time and strategies. Language learners who use planning strategies tend to produce more language. When using this action to support written or oral production, teachers can offer students planning strategies such as these:

- drawing and labelling before students write or talk about an event
- talking to a peer about a concept before students are asked to explain it, either orally or in writing
- having students sketch out how something works before inviting them to describe its functioning
- brainstorming ideas in a small group or individually
- using graphic organizers (see Action 2.2) to help students organize their ideas before talking or writing
- peer conferencing to generate and talk through ideas before doing an oral or written task

REFLECTION ON PRACTICE

- How much planning time do I provide my students with before an oral task?
- How much planning time do I provide my students with before a written task?
- When I offer planning time to my students before a written or oral task, how many of them take advantage of it?
- What types of planning strategies do I offer my students? Can my students draw, sketch, talk to a peer, do a brainstorm web, or fill in a graphic organizer to help them produce language?

This ULA can be used

- ✓ When teacher is presenting content and/or language
- ✓ When learners are engaged in a learning task
- ✓ When learners are demonstrating learning and understanding

BROADENING ACCESS

- To build learner autonomy, could I share with my learners the value of this action so that they, in turn, ask for planning time or independently use planning strategies when needed?
- With respect to targeted support (e.g., Response to Intervention), are there any specific language learners in my class who could benefit from this action?

Action 2.4 in Action!

I've used drawing and labelling with younger learners as well as older learners. It works just as well with either group. I've used this action frequently as a way to support students' writing, but I've also used it several times to help support students producing an oral presentation.

If I'm going to ask students to write about a particular topic, I'm first going to ask them to draw a picture. The picture helps students generate ideas about the topic and, by labelling their drawing, students are making choices about what is important about the image that should be discussed in their text. For older learners, I've brought in images about a particular topic (e.g., medieval times) and asked them to choose one. They then proceed to label different elements of the image. Again, this helps students focus their ideas before writing about the image.

For oral presentations, before, my students would read their notes—it was a reading task instead of an oral production task. Now, they don't need their notes because they use the pictures and labels to support their presentations. There is just enough information from the pictures and labels for students to be able to articulate their ideas.

—K. Winters

In an effort to build in more "think time" to my lessons—which is another ULA—I have found it is helpful to officially carve out moments in lessons when I give students a specific moment to try out a planning activity. It's a stop-and-think moment—and I use them a lot when I'm doing a lot of teacher talk. After about two or three slides, I stop and ask the students to spend a minute or two sketching out a summary of what I just said, using their own words. Sometimes, I ask them to do this like a tweet or as a picture, but whatever they do, they need to be prepared to share it with the class to help reinforce the information I just shared.

—A. Ryan

This ULA can be used

- ✓ **When teacher is presenting content and/ or language**
- ✓ **When learners are engaged in a learning task**
- ✓ **When learners are demonstrating learning and understanding**

ACTION 2.5 Using pedagogical and language production routines

Regardless of age, grade, or subject matter, routines are very useful in helping students produce language because learners know what to expect and they are familiar with the language expectations. Consequently, less risk taking is involved.

Pedagogical and production routines are synonymous with the elements of a lesson that we do on a regular basis. They are the predictable and established procedures we carry out in many of our lessons. Some examples of pedagogical and production routines are as follows:

- morning calendar/lesson agenda
- daily message
- math warm-up
- daily journal entry
- question of the day
- daily review
- homework review
- daily lesson objective
- debrief discussion
- specific work or learning station
- daily talk about the weather
- Monday morning weekend discussion

By implementing pedagogical and language production, students become accustomed to and comfortable with the expectations. For some language learners, it may be the only time they will communicate in the target language because the content is familiar and the language structures and vocabulary are predictable.

Once pedagogical routines are firmly in place and students have received sufficient exposure to specific language structures, it may be time to push students' language development further. For example, once students are comfortable with the basics of talking about dates yesterday, today, and tomorrow, we might ask them such questions as "What will be the date in seven days?" "How many more days till the 24th?" "What is the difference between a partly sunny day and a partly cloudy day?" "What is another way you can say this?"

When teachers ensure that routines increase in language complexity, students will still receive the benefits of predictability, but also work at developing additional language abilities. This ULA is particularly beneficial for students who may not be risk takers. The content can easily be anticipated so students can more easily prepare for the task (Arries, 1999; Hurst, 1996; Met, 1994; Snow, 1989).

REFLECTION ON PRACTICE

- What pedagogical or language production routines do I embed in lessons?
- How can I add some routines in my lessons to further support some learners who may not produce language otherwise?
- Is the language that students are expected to produce during routines at the appropriate level? Do I add a bit of complexity to the routines as time goes on?
- Am I helping students plan for their own learning (in this case, listening or reading)? Could I further foster metacognitive strategies?

BROADENING ACCESS

- To build learner autonomy, could I share with my learners the value of this action so that they, in turn, see routines as a safe place to produce language?
- With respect to targeted support (e.g., Response to Intervention), are there any specific language learners in my class who could benefit from this action?

Action 2.5 in Action!

Monday mornings can be a challenge to get students back into school language since they spent the weekend with their home language. Every Monday, I expect students to do a short exchange with neighbours about what they did over the weekend. However, I will vary how I ask students to prepare for the exchanges. Sometimes, I ask them to make a list of 10 words linked to what they did. Sometimes I give them a blank "game board" where they need to draw pictures or write words that give the sequence of what they did over the weekend, or even draw a scene from their favourite activity from the weekend. This planning time helps shake off the weekend cobwebs.

—A. Johnson

This ULA can be used

- ✓ **When teacher is presenting content and/or language**
- ✓ **When learners are engaged in a learning task**
- ✓ **When learners are demonstrating learning and understanding**

ACTION 2.6 Choosing grouping arrangements that favour peer communication

Some students will produce more oral and written language in particular settings. In recognition of this, this ULA recommends we increase the ways by which we ask students to communicate. Grouping arrangements can affect the amount of language students may produce. For example, some students may produce more language during whole-class discussions, while others will produce more when talking in small groups of four. The same can be said for writing. Some learners may write more when working in pairs rather than working independently. Carefully considering grouping arrangements can thus lead to increased language production.

There is some research that can inform how we group students in the language classroom to maximize their learning; Neomy Storch (1998, 2001, 2002) has given us some important insights. First, we need to think about two dimensions of their personalities and skills in the classroom: (1) their overall proficiency (as low, middle, or high, relative to the class) and (2) their general personality in working with others (openness to being collaborative, likelihood of being dominant or passive, and comfort with moving from expert to novice status depending on the situation).

Storch's research has found that student pairings are more effective in certain combinations. Student pairings where one or both students are more dominant or assertive do not result in a lot of interaction and, thus, production. However, if there is more of an openness to idea sharing and work division (e.g., the students are collaboratively oriented or comfortable trading off work as an expert or novice, depending on the situation), the interaction will be more effective. Pairings of students where the proficiency differences are very strong (e.g., a student with strong proficiency and a student with low proficiency) are likely to be ineffective; the same is true when two strong students work together. More effective pairings consist of either two students with lower proficiency working together or one student with mid-level proficiency working with either a stronger or lower proficiency student—in other words, the proficiency differences are not that great.

Language Needed to Participate in Group Tasks

An important element that goes hand in hand with this ULA is group collaboration language. When students are placed in pairs or in small groups, they need the language associated with the task (see Action 4.1 *Identifying and presenting required language at the outset of a lesson or activity*), but they also need the language necessary to negotiate content collaboratively.

Language learners don't necessarily have the collaborative language skills needed to encourage one another, to ask for clarification, to negotiate different points of view, to interject new ideas, or to voice their needs. It is thus essential to teach the necessary language structures to support group discussions. Here are some examples:

- Who wants to start?
- In my opinion ...
- I think that ...
- Does everyone agree?
- I can help!
- What do you think about ...?
- What else?
- I really like that you ...
- What's left to do?
- Please ...
- What's the next step?
- I'd like to suggest ...
- Can I add an idea?
- I don't agree.
- Just a second! I'm thinking.
- We have five minutes left!
- Who else has an idea?
- Can you give an example?
- Thank you.
- Who else would like to share?
- I'm not sure how to say/write ...
- I would prefer ...
- However, ...
- I wonder if ...
- I have another idea.
- I'm not sure.
- May I ...
- I'm not sure I understand.
- Excellent idea!
- It's true!
- I think we're going off task!
- It's your turn.
- Can someone help me?
- Great work!

BROADENING ACCESS

- To build learner autonomy, could I share with my learners the value of this action so that they, in turn, can see the value of working in pairs to produce the target language?
- With respect to targeted support (e.g., Response to Intervention), are there any specific language learners in my class who could benefit from this action?

REFLECTION ON PRACTICE

- What types of grouping arrangements do I tend to favour when I ask students to participate in a discussion? whole class, pairs, small groups? Why?
- What types of grouping arrangements do I tend to favour when I ask students to record their ideas about a topic? pairs, small groups? Why?
- To what extent do I consider students' abilities when forming groups?
- How much collaborative language do my students have? What language structures do they need to further work in groups?

Action 2.6 in Action!

I've come to realize that my whole-class discussions were looking more like question-and-answer periods rather than true discussions (an exchange of ideas). It seemed like I was involved in every exchange. I'd ask a question, receive an answer, only to ask another question to another student. During a 20-minute discussion, only some students were actually talking as part of this exchange.

Oftentimes now, I switch my whole-class discussion to a think-pair-share. I'll ask a question, then ask students to think about possible answers for a few moments before turning to a partner to share their thoughts and ideas with each other. Only once both students have shared will I bring the question back to the whole group. By doing it this way, all students are communicating during discussions. Students are a lot more involved.

—L. Moore

Being that I teach secondary students who can be both very shy about sharing opinions and then very open to such sharing—sometimes within a minute—I have found managing whole-group discussions to be a challenge.

For my class, I have found better luck with rotating small-group discussion set-ups. I have told my students that as adults, particularly at work, they will often have to have short discussions with small groups of people about what they are doing. Sometimes, those discussions are more social, and sometimes they are more serious. So, I set up our discussion groups that way. I have a couple of social small-group configurations, where I've been mindful of including a range of language skills, and a couple of serious small-group configurations, where I've tried to make the most efficient pairings, thinking about their proficiency levels and personalities. Then, depending on the activity, I tell them which group they'll be with. This also lets them know about the expectations I have for their language for the activity.

—L. Muilenburg

ACTION 2.7 Asking questions that encourage learners to elaborate

Some language learners are capable of producing more language than they are currently producing. For example, they may be content to answer questions with very few words. This ULA is tailored for such learners as it pushes them to use more language to elaborate on their ideas and answers. A prompt such as "Tell me more" or questions such as the following encourage further elaboration:

- What do you mean by that?
- Can you explain this a bit more?
- How do you know that?
- What pushed you to think that?
- Why do you think that is?
- How so?
- Why is this the answer?
- Why is this the case?

Such questions require learners to produce more oral or written language because they need to further express their ideas, opinions, understanding, or feelings. By asking these types of questions, teachers move away from closed questions (which have only one or two possible answers) to open-ended questions. Asking open-ended questions is a very effective way to get students producing oral or written language because such questions allow for original answers or multiple responses. Open-ended questions and questions that require learners to elaborate are an effective way to encourage risk taking. Moreover, this action encourages learners to find alternative ways to communicate their message, especially in cases where students may have more limited vocabulary (Snow, 1989).

REFLECTION ON PRACTICE

- What percentage of the questions I ask my students would I consider to be open-ended?
- To what extent do I ask my students to elaborate when answering oral questions? What types of questions do I ask?
- To what extent do I ask my students to elaborate when writing?
- Am I helping students plan for their own learning (in this case, listening or reading)? Could I be further fostering metacognitive strategies?

This ULA can be used

✓ **When teacher is presenting content and/or language**

✓ **When learners are engaged in a learning task**

✓ **When learners are demonstrating learning and understanding**

Some students may need prompts or sentence frames to construct answers to open-ended questions.

BROADENING ACCESS

- To build learner autonomy, could I share with my learners the value of this action so that they, in turn, can start coming up with their own open-ended questions to help them elaborate on their thinking?
- With respect to targeted support (e.g., Response to Intervention), are there any specific language learners in my class who could benefit from this action?

Action 2.7 in Action!

Last year, I asked a work colleague to come and observe me teach so she could provide me with some feedback on my lesson and my instruction. One of the things she noticed was that students were giving a lot of yes or no answers or they would provide very short answers: "The answer is 34!" "The king is at the top of the social hierarchy." "The characters are Jane the fish and Joseph the boy." Once I received this feedback, I created sentence strips, and on each one I wrote a question or prompt that encouraged students to elaborate on their answers.

What do you mean by that?

Why is this the case?

How do you know?

Tell me more!

Can you explain that?

I've posted these strips on my board, and when we have class discussion I try to use as many of them as possible. At first, the students were a bit uneasy because they weren't used to having to produce additional language, but after a few weeks, they became really good at going beyond simple short answers and explanations.

—T. Filbert

One day, we were having a conversation about how to build a snowman. One of the students said, "We should put a *foulard* on him." (She was looking for the word *scarf*, but didn't know it in the target language.) Instead of providing her with the word *scarf*, I asked her to explain what the word meant. She said, "It's something you put around your neck, you know ... a scarf! Yes, a scarf."

I was floored. She knew the word, but didn't recall it when she first put her hand up. When I pushed for an elaboration, though, she talked it through and the word just came.

—S. Mackey-McCarthy

It's amazing how many of my students are very "thin" in their written descriptions when I have heard them use a lot more detail when talking about the same topic. I have found that sometimes, the students aren't writing in these details because they end up spending more energy writing than they do when they talk. So, to pull out more language in their writing, I have a two-prong approach. First, I have them partner with someone with whom they collaborate well. They tell the partner about their paper and what they want to say. The partner takes some notes about what they share. Then, they switch roles. The students have to go back to their paper and find areas where they can add in this information. After they do this, I read over their drafts, looking for areas where ideas are underdeveloped. In the margins, I write things like, "Tell me more," or "How is this connected to X?" or "Why is this important?" It certainly makes for a longer process of drafting and revising, but I've found that investing the energy in several quality essays, rather than trying to have them constantly write different things, has been helping them develop the thinking skills needed for good academic writing.

—K. Koch

Good Language Production Pedagogy

Along with the seven ULAs proposed in this chapter, we also want to acknowledge the following general principles of good language production pedagogy.

- Students need clear oral and written production task goals.

- There needs to be a well-defined and articulated audience.
- The oral and written tasks need to be authentic—the more the tasks resemble how they need to use the language in real life, the more students become invested in them.
- Oral communication is an important precursor to written tasks (Weissberg, 2006). Students write like they speak. Doing so is developmental; on average, students write the way they speak until about age 13 or 14.

Moreover, good language production pedagogy involves teachers in providing students with many opportunities or formats to do an oral or written task. By having several occasions to practise, students deepen their understanding of concepts and increase their abilities to use the language. It is important for teachers to provide many occasions for students to practise in order to build confidence and encourage risk taking. With repeated practice, students develop fluency and are helped in developing additional language skills (Long & Porter, 1985).

Having many opportunities for practising does not mean doing the same task, oral or written, over and over; it is not drill. Practising is about reviewing, revising, and reusing the language orally and in writing. Students need many opportunities to practise reusing the vocabulary, language structures, and language features of the unit being studied. Here are a few examples of how they can get repeated practice using language through various oral and written formats:

Fiction Unit	**Unit on Persuasion**	**Unit on New Technologies**
Students could write a comic strip and a story map before writing fairy tales. They could then create a movie poster for their stories. They could also write a song or rap (from the perspective of one of the characters).	Students could produce a sales pitch and a video to convince their audience. They could also produce a brochure and a jingle for their advertisement.	Students could produce a webpage and a magazine article. They could also do a show-and- tell or a PowerPoint presentation. They could then prepare an infomercial.
Restaurant Unit	**Science Unit**	**Current Events Unit**
Students could write or discuss the features of a menu. They could produce a restaurant critique. They could debate the merits of particular restaurant chains and participate in a restaurant simulation (role-play).	Students could take their new knowledge of concepts and produce a game show, a scientific report, or a questionnaire. They could also teach a review lesson.	Students could produce a news report, a timeline, a mock interview or trial, write an email, or text a friend.

Closing Thoughts

Besides the chapter activity ideas and suggestions for varying the ULAs, we want you to take away these key points about helping students produce oral and written language:

1. Language production takes time to develop automatically. Along the way, students need explicit support to help move language production from a cognitive task to a more automatic one.
2. How you structure language production opportunities in the class will have a bearing on what the students produce. Certain types of activities and certain expectations for language production and interaction will generate different types of language from different students. Don't assume that a student's limited production within an activity is necessarily due to a lack of understanding about the content; the student may be unsure of how to produce the language in the format needed.
3. Producing social language is different than producing academic language. Do not compare how easily or readily students use language outside of class with how readily they use it in class.
4. How students are grouped together will influence the kind of language they produce. Random pairings or groupings can be inefficient for student learning.

As you reflect on the contents of this chapter, we invite you to think about the following issues related to student language production:

- What kinds of language do I expect students to produce in class?
- How do I currently support student language production?
- What sorts of graphic organizers, prompts, or cues could I make available to students on a regular basis to foster language production?
- How can I use exemplars (either past student work samples or ones that I create) to better support student language production?
- How do I need to balance quantity of production with quality of production in my classroom?
- How can I group students most effectively for my class?

CHAPTER 7

Language Learners Who Need Additional Support in Sustaining Their Attention and Focus in the Target Language

The Links Between Language Learning and Attention

We know that language learning is accelerated when learners are exposed to lots of authentic input within language-rich learning environments (Lightbown & Spada, 2013; Ortega, 2009). Such environments help learners develop stronger receptive and production skills in the target language. We also know that learning a second language requires learners to process large amounts of language and information (input). Figure 7.1 highlights a few key elements at play during the learning process.

Figure 7.1: How People Process Information

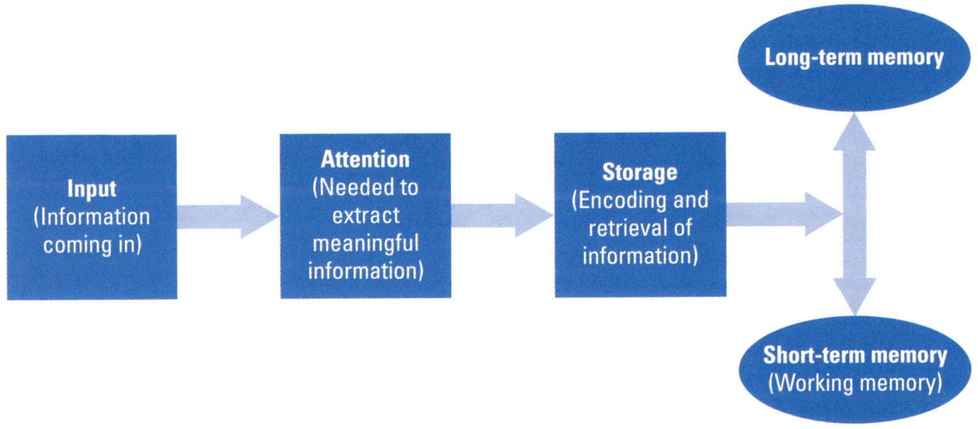

Our students need to focus and pay attention in order to extract what information is most important: they continuously make judgment calls about what information to store in memory and what information to exclude. That is why paying attention to and focusing on the information is so essential to the learning process.

Sometimes, language or cognitive demands are greater than what students can process. The input (information) is just too much. When can this occur? It can happen when the information or the language a student encounters is too great or too complex. It can also occur when learners negotiate more complicated tasks or when they face too many tasks at once. More advanced learners can experience overload because they have a greater number of linguistic choices at their disposal. For example, as vocabulary and grammatical understandings increase, learners have to determine which words or which grammatical rules to follow for any given situation.

When a language or cognitive overload happens, it can seriously hinder a student's ability to sustain focus and attention. The sheer amount of information being presented in the second language may make it impossible for some learners to properly comprehend what is being presented, which, in turn, affects their ability to sustain their focus in the classroom.

Some learners are unable to sustain their focus when experiencing an overload and so cannot meet the demands of the learning experience. You may notice that these learners consistently exhibit a combination of any of the following behaviours:

- ❑ shut down
- ❑ seem off task
- ❑ fidget with objects (e.g., in desk, shoelaces)
- ❑ do not seem to know what they should be doing
- ❑ avoid tasks
- ❑ want out of their seat (wander around the room, want to leave the room)
- ❑ seem overwhelmed
- ❑ require constant monitoring to stay on task
- ❑ are easily sidetracked
- ❑ are daydreaming or have a blank stare
- ❑ get frustrated or discouraged easily
- ❑ get bogged down by the task
- ❑ require lots of breaks
- ❑ need more time to complete a task
- ❑ have difficulty following the pace of the lesson
- ❑ offer irrelevant answers or information

Universal Language Actions That Support Learner Attention in the Target Language

To facilitate access to language learning, we need to limit the amount of overload learners experience by ensuring that the cognitive, linguistic, and task demands we impose on them are manageable. The seven ULAs recommended in this chapter and listed in Figure 7.2 help make the learning more manageable for language learners who need help focusing their attention for sustained periods of time.

Figure 7.2

Universal Language Actions That Facilitate Learner Focus and Attention in the Target Language

Action 3.1	Providing specific listening and reading intentions
Action 3.2	Dividing lessons, activities, and tasks into many small steps
Action 3.3	Incorporating discourse markers to oral and written texts
Action 3.4	Providing explicit cues to refocus learners' attention
Action 3.5	Using different modalities to present material
Action 3.6	Explaining the relevance of what is being taught
Action 3.7	Summarizing key points of lessons, activities, and reading passages

ACTION 3.1 Providing specific listening and reading intentions

Any time students are presented with new language or new information, orally or in print, it is important that teachers establish a listening or reading goal. Some learners need additional support in determining what pieces of information are most important and what should be filtered out (unimportant details). In such cases, students think all information is essential. They try to understand and decipher every word and every idea. This effort can create a language or cognitive overload. Students need to learn how to use listening strategies to meet the demands of listening tasks.

Listening and reading intentions help learners focus on worthwhile aspects of the message. They help learners understand the purpose of the task

This ULA can be used

- ✓ **When teacher is presenting content and/or language**
- ✓ **When learners are engaged in a learning task**
- **When learners are demonstrating learning and understanding**

because they answer the following questions: (1) What are we listening or reading for? and (2) Why are we listening to or reading this? This increases the relevance of the task for learners and enables students to more easily store information in memory.

By setting a clear listening or reading intention, we are giving students permission to focus on a smaller amount of information. We are helping learners to identify what is truly essential so they can shift and focus their attention to the specific listening or reading intention. Let's consider the following examples. What are we asking learners to focus their attention on?

Examples of listening intentions:

- Class discussion: "Some of you might agree or disagree with ... I'd like to hear your thoughts on this. As others share their opinions, *listen carefully to the arguments your classmates are making.* We're going to make a list of these arguments after our discussion."
- Listening to a news report: "We're about to listen to a news report about a tragedy that happened at a zoo. Zoo officials give three ways the tragedy could have been avoided. *Please listen carefully for these three points."*
- Listening to a song: "We will be listening to a song. As you listen, *focus on the words you know."*

Examples of reading intentions:

- Reading a story: "This story is about a student in the same grade as you. As you read it, *think about how your school experience is similar to or different than* that of the student in the story."
- Reading a procedural text: "This text lists the six steps to becoming a better athlete. As you read, *think about which step is most important."*
- Reading a piece of non-fiction: "This information text is about tigers. As you read it, focus on two things: *identifying one fact you knew already and one new piece of information.*
- Reading a paragraph: "As you read this paragraph, *consider what words are used to describe the house."*

By providing listening and reading intentions, learners are better able to retrieve relevant vocabulary and knowledge to support the decoding and comprehension of the message. This action is designed to narrow the learner's focus. Learners should be fully concentrating on interpreting the message rather than just simply hearing or reading the words.

REFLECTION ON PRACTICE

- When I'm about to present new information, do I ask my students to focus on a specific element of my message?
- Do I use the following sentence when I'm about to present a new concept to students: "Please listen carefully for …"?
- When reading a text aloud to my students, do I provide them with a specific listening intention? For example, could my students be listening for words we could add to our thematic word chart?
- If I'm going to ask my students to listen to an audio or video clip, do I narrow the focus to something specific they should listen for?
- When I ask my students to read a longer text, do I provide them with specific things to keep an eye out for in different parts of the text?
- When I give my students a text to read, do I provide them with opportunities to reread the text for different purposes: reading for general comprehension, reading to discover new words, reading to find key ideas for a summary?
- Am I helping students plan for their own learning (in this case, listening or reading)? Could I be further fostering metacognitive strategies?

BROADENING ACCESS

- To build learner autonomy, could I share with my learners the value of this action so that they, in turn, can start coming up with their own listening or reading intentions as a way to monitor their own learning?
- With respect to targeted support (e.g., Response to Intervention), are there any specific language learners in my class who could benefit from this action?

Action 3.1 in Action!

Every Monday morning, I facilitate a class discussion about the weekend. I've noticed that students want to share their experiences, but more important, it gives me an opportunity to learn more about my students. I ask them to share activities they did, people they spent time with, sports they played, interesting foods they ate, or places they visited. Before we start the discussion, I always give students a particular listening intention: something I want them to pay special attention to. Here are a few examples that I've used:

- As others share their weekend experiences, please listen carefully for someone's weekend activity that is similar to (or different from) an activity you did. After the discussion, we'll go over some experiences that were similar.
- As people share something about their weekend, please listen carefully for places they've been. After the discussion, I'll be asking you questions about who went where.
- As we listen to others, please keep in mind one thing you've learned from someone else today.

When I give a specific listening intention, student participation increases during the "post-discussion." I get the sense that they keep on sharing what they pulled from their good listening skills.

—S. Arsenault

Sometimes, I feel that certain students get overwhelmed by some of the reading material. They don't seem to know how to tackle the text: they start reading, but get discouraged, they lose interest, or they try to get through it as quickly as possible. To help them, I now provide a clear reading focus. I'll say something like: "When you read this passage, look for one new thing you've learned" or "When reading this paragraph, look for answers to who, what, when, and where" or "When reading this passage, look for words that we could add to our thematic word chart." These types of prompts really help focus student attention throughout the reading task. I do the same now when I read aloud to students. I'll give them one of these prompts to guide and monitor their listening.

—S. Jenkins

This ULA can be used

✓ **When teacher is presenting content and/ or language**

When learners are engaged in a learning task

When learners are demonstrating learning and understanding

ACTION 3.2 Dividing lessons, activities, and tasks into many small steps

As we've been discussing, learning another language requires a huge amount of concentration. Second language learners are continually deciphering messages, constructing meaning, clarifying their own understanding, translating, making connections to their first language, or working on some aspect of language production (e.g., planning, formulating, producing oral or written texts), all the while trying not to look too lost in class.

To ensure that all these processes do not overwhelm learners, it is important to consider the overall structure of a lesson, an activity, or a task. To the extent possible or reasonable, lessons (or activities or tasks) should be structured as a series of steps to complete. This helps ensure that learners do not become overloaded, either with the amount of language they have to manage or with the cognitive demands of the task. Each step of the lesson or the activity is explicitly and clearly explained prior to learners executing the step.

Such chunking does look different at different levels of instruction due, in part, to the developmental needs of the learner. In general, learners working within a second language—especially in the early stages of learning—process language at one-quarter of the rate of learners working in their first language (Collier, 1987, 1995). That being so, teachers need to carefully craft the autonomous windows of a lesson. These times should be short and focused in order to account for how developmental needs intersect with language skills. Here is an example of chunking an activity, lesson, or task:

1. Planning: The teacher evaluates the linguistic and cognitive demands of a particular activity or task and decides where natural breaks should occur.
2. Teaching:
   a. The teacher presents the goal(s) of the activity or task to the learners, as well as the steps to accomplish the activity or task. "We will be doing (activity) to (goal). This activity has three steps. First, we will ... Second, you will ..., and finally, you will ...."
   b. The teacher re-explains the first step of the activity and then guides learners through the first step and monitors their progress.
   c. The teacher signals the end of this step and checks in with learners to ensure that they are where they should be.
   d. The teacher repeats steps b and c, or each step of the activity or task.

By dividing a lesson, an activity, or a particular language task into smaller steps, the teacher provides the necessary scaffolding for learners to better process language. This support leads to increased oral and written production in the target language.

Moreover, inclusive teachers use chunking as a way of assessing learners' level of comprehension. They get a sense of how much language and content learners can manage for each step and make adjustments to the amount of support they provide.

Transitions

This ULA also covers the need for proper transitions. For some language learners, transitions can be particularly challenging because they have to redirect and refocus their attention quite quickly. On average, learners experience approximately 30 transitions during the day and, often, these include a fair amount of linguistic input. It is often during transitions that teachers will ask students to wrap up the previous activity and offer ways for them to do so. They may start explaining the upcoming task or, at the very least, provide learners with instructions on how to get ready for the next part of the lesson. Transitions are also a time when teachers reinforce expected behaviours.

In such cases, it is often difficult for some learners to distinguish more important information from verbal clutter. Some learners may not even realize that a transition is taking place, and if they do, they likely miss important information being shared during this time. As a result, they take longer to settle into the next activity.

To support language learners in managing transition times, the learning environment needs to be fairly predictable. Learners should be able to anticipate upcoming changes in direction and have enough time to refocus their attention. To enable this, teachers provide explicit cues that alert learners to a transition and an imminent change of focus. Here are some examples of explicit cues:

- reviewing the daily schedule
- mentioning that a change is about to happen
- reminding learners of the amount of time left to complete a task
- informing learners that they should start putting their materials away
- presenting visuals or auditory signals (stop signs, timers, photos depicting next step or activity)
- providing a checklist of tasks that learners need to complete as a larger activity and suggested time frames for those tasks

Explicit transition cues help learners avoid confusion and anxiety by helping them shift and redirect their attention in a timely fashion. They also minimize transition times because they allow learners to shift their attention smoothly.

REFLECTION ON PRACTICE

Considering a Lesson

- How easy is it for me to see where natural breaks in my lesson should occur?
- Before starting my lesson, do I explain to the students the lesson's main components?

Dividing a Task into Steps

- When I ask my students to do a task or activity (e.g., a group activity, a writing task, a reading task, a listening activity), do I break the task or activity into two to four steps?
  - If so, after each step, do I informally check to ensure that the step has been properly completed before moving on to the next step?
- For the different parts of the task or activity, do I review the language my students require in order to complete that step?
- When asking my students to do a writing, oral, listening, or reading task, do I provide them with the steps they need? Do I explicitly review the steps of the activity with my students? Do I record these steps on the board for them? For example:

Writing	Oral	Listening	Reading
• Think about what you want to write. • Write your ideas down. • Revise and edit your work. • Share your work thus far with a partner and get feedback.	• Think about what you want to say. • Share your ideas with a partner. • Share your ideas with the larger group.	• Listen to the song. • Listen to it one more time and try to pick out words you know. • Listen to it one more time and try to sing some of the lyrics.	• Look at the pictures and diagrams. • Read the titles and subtitles. • Read the first page and pull out the main idea. • Read the second page and pull out the main idea.

Chunking

- Before reading a text, do I talk to my students about the importance of reading in chunks and good places to stop reading to monitor comprehension? Do we look at how the text could be chunked?

Transitioning

- Am I providing too much information (input) at the same time as students are transitioning from one thing to the next?

BROADENING ACCESS

- To build learner autonomy, could I share with my learners the value of this action so that they, in turn, can start dividing their work into chunks?
- With respect to targeted support (e.g., Response to Intervention), are there any specific language learners in my class who could benefit from this action?

Action 3.2 in Action!

We do a unit in my class on nutrition and healthy eating. Throughout this unit, we learn about healthy food options and such. One of the activities I get my students to do is a role-play activity where they are at a restaurant and they want to order a healthy option. Before doing this activity, we go over the logical steps to ordering food at a restaurant.

- Step 1: an exchange between the waiter and the customers—general greeting and pleasantries
- Step 2: a discussion between the customers at the table about food choices on the menu
- Step 3: an exchange of information between the customers and the waiter—customers asking questions about specific things on the menu and waiter taking orders
- Step 4: receiving food order and discussion about the quality of food

I tend to write steps on the board or have pictures for each step of the activity so students can see the actual steps. I've noticed that this really helps them focus and stay on task. They know what they need to do for each step and don't get so overwhelmed by the overall activity.

—J. Bourgoin

I was noticing that when students were transitioning from one part of the lesson to another, things were a bit chaotic—students would move around, put stuff away, take stuff out, chatter, et cetera. It was never as smooth as I would have liked, and some students just took longer to settle back in.

I asked one of my colleagues to come observe some of my transition times, as I thought she could provide me with some suggestion. She made the comment that I attempted to provide "directions/clarifications" during transition times. I'd ask students to quiet down or I'd remind them they needed to take their pencils out, et cetera. She was right. I was trying to talk over the noise.

Now, I provide students with a few minutes of winding-down time—time to finish up what they were doing. Then I refocus students' attention toward me. I'll say something like, "In a few minutes, we'll be doing such and such. But first, you'll need to put your book back on the shelves quietly. Then, you'll find your seats. Finally, you'll take out a pencil. Please use the next few seconds wisely as you get yourselves ready to do the next activity: books away, back at your seat, take out your pencil."

To be honest, I no longer talk as students do transitions. The noise level has gone way down, and all my students seem to know what they need to do. They are ready for the next task a lot more quickly than before.

—H. Lyons

This ULA can be used

- ✓ When teacher is presenting content and/or language
- ✓ When learners are engaged in a learning task
- ✓ When learners are demonstrating learning and understanding

ACTION 3.3 Incorporating discourse markers to oral and written texts

Discourse markers are words or short phrases that connect and organize ideas within oral and written texts. Teachers use discourse markers as a ULA to draw learners' attention to the different parts of a message, especially when a lot of input is involved (e.g., lengthy explanation or presentation, longer reading passage).

Since discourse markers act as a way of separating the information into segments, learners can process the information in smaller chunks. They also guide the listener or the reader in the direction the message in taking. They allow learners to predict upcoming content. Teachers can use discourse markers for the following purposes:

Purpose	Examples of Discourse Markers
To order or number ideas	first, second, finally, in conclusion, to begin with, after, next, to sum up
To add something	also, moreover, on top of that, what's more, as I was saying, in addition to
To clarify	I mean, for example, in other words, it's like, essentially
To link ideas together	similarly, likewise, and, such as
To show contradictory information	however, on the other hand, anyway, in contrast, that being said
To show cause and effect	so, as a result, therefore

Discourse markers may not be noticed immediately by beginning language learners. It is thus important for language teachers to use key discourse markers intentionally when speaking. They should also explicitly draw attention to them during reading aloud or when preparing learners to autonomously work through a written text.

As learners become more proficient in the language and are transitioning from understanding single ideas to multiple ideas, explicit use of discourse markers can provide students with hooks that enable them to better understand the language and, thus, maintain their attention.

This ULA is also particularly useful to help learners demonstrate understanding. When teachers provide language learners with specific discourse markers to use during oral presentations or when writing things down, as in a learning journal, learners can organize and focus their thoughts and ideas. In this sense, discourse markers point to what learners should say or write next.

REFLECTION ON PRACTICE

- When I choose a text for students to read, do I draw their attention to the discourse markers within the text? Do I get them to see how discourse markers guide their focus?
- Based on students' language proficiency, which discourse markers could I add to explicitly help students focus more on the message?
- How much intonation and expression do I use to emphasize the discourse markers?
- When I write on the board (e.g., examples, comments, explanations, morning messages, questions), do I add discourse markers to help draw students' attention to certain aspects of the lesson?

BROADENING ACCESS

- To build learner autonomy, could I share with my learners the value of this action so that they, in turn, use discourse markers when talking to support other learners' comprehension?
- With respect to targeted support (e.g., Response to Intervention), are there any specific language learners in my class who could benefit from this action?

Action 3.3 in Action!

I know I always used discourse markers when I talked to my students, but I never really emphasized them or gave much thought to their importance until recently (after receiving a professional learning session about Universal Language Actions).

It's true! Students cannot hang on our every word, unfortunately. Sometimes, their attention might wander. By using specific words, such as *for example, to finish off,* and *however,* I can actually see some students re-shifting their attention. I find that the more emphasis I place on these words (tone, expression), the more effective they are. What's really neat is that some students are now using them as part of their regular vocabulary.

—K. Kertson

We do a lot of journalling in class, like reflection journals and learning logs. After the lesson, I'll get the students to write what they've learned, for example. To help my students focus their ideas, I always provide them with the day's discourse markers. Here are a few examples:

First, Second, Third, Last,	Today, I learned . . . In other words, Unfortunately,

I've also started to use these examples as charts in my classroom to help students talk about concepts. Sometimes, I feel that my students need something to anchor their thinking. They may have too many ideas, not enough ideas, or their ideas may be all over the place. By having these examples as charts on the wall, students can use them to guide the way they frame their comments.

—T. Simon

This ULA can be used

- ✓ When teacher is presenting content and/or language
- When learners are engaged in a learning task
- When learners are demonstrating learning and understanding

ACTION 3.4 Providing explicit cues to refocus learners' attention

Let's face it. Our students hear us talking a lot. We provide lots of instruction, we give directions, we clarify those directions, we talk about what goes on in the class, we review expectations, and so on and so forth. The fact is that our students are exposed to a large amount of input daily.

Consequently, second language learners are not always capable of determining which pieces of information are more pertinent than others (at a given time). As a result, they may overly focus on all aspects of the message, including irrelevant information. With so much energy going to understanding and interpreting less useful information, learners' sustained focus can be compromised.

To support learners in interpreting which pieces of information are most important, teachers can provide explicit clues to refocus learners' attention. This ULA draws learners' attention to the essential components of messages. The following are some examples of explicit cues:

- *Listen carefully!* I'm now going to explain the four steps of the task.
- What I'm about to say is *very important*!
- I'm now going to explain [the concept] another way!
- Here is the *one thing* to consider ...
- I'm now going to repeat ...

By providing such explicit cues, teachers help learners decipher what information is deemed most important.

REFLECTION ON PRACTICE

- Do I reflect on the amount of input my students hear for any given lesson?
- How much teacher talk is there in my class in comparison to student talk?
- What does the following statement mean to me: "It's not about talking more, but about talking more directly deliberately"?
- What explicit cues do I currently give to students I need to bring back to attention? Can I move away from calling out the student's name to using cues such as "Listen carefully now!" or "What I'm about say is really important" or "Let me repeat this" or "Here is what you need to know"?

BROADENING ACCESS

- With respect to targeted support (e.g., Response to Intervention), are there any specific language learners in my class who could benefit from this action?

Action 3.4 in Action!

I have access to a visual projector. For many of my lessons, I use it to project PowerPoints, Smart lessons, and Word documents. Since I work with second language learners, I've noticed that sometimes they need help to maintain or re-shift their attention, especially when I'm presenting quite a bit of content to them. I wanted to find a way to help my students refocus to help them follow along with the lesson.

I ended up creating slides in my lessons that have explicit attention-getting cues embedded in them. I integrate these attention-getting slides in my lessons when I use the visual projector. Here are some examples I've used for different lessons:

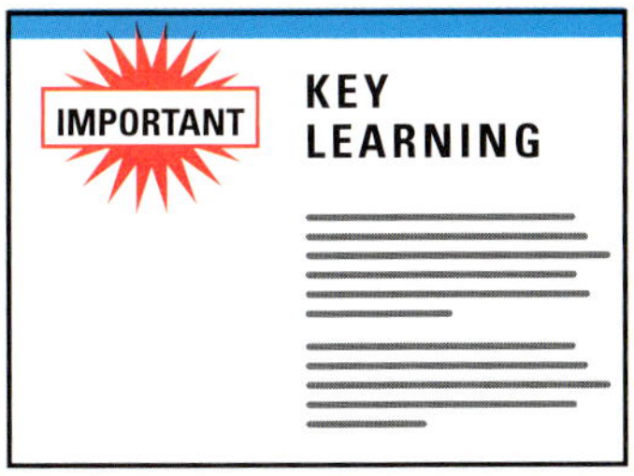

When we get to one of these slides, I remember to bring students back into the lesson. The slides really help the students re-shift their attention to the message.

—D. Crawford

ACTION 3.5 Using different modalities to present material

Research has shown that teachers who use different modalities to present material create an enhanced, interactive, inclusive, and more engaging learning environment for learners. Multimodal teaching has also been linked to increased student achievement (Fadel, 2008), and as we know, this is part of the overall principle of Universal Design for Learning. Using

This ULA can be used

- ✓ When teacher is presenting content and/ or language
- ✓ When learners are engaged in a learning task
- ✓ When learners are demonstrating learning and understanding

multiple ways of representing new content allows for deeper processing of information and helps learners stay focused. For learners who need support maintaining their attention, the use of different modalities is essential.

Through multimodal teaching, learners experience the learning in different ways and access information through various formats. Inclusive teachers use as many mediums as possible to convey information, including various multi-sensory approaches and instructional techniques.

Multi-sensory Approaches	Instructional Techniques
• visual (e.g., videos, images, animation) • auditory (e.g., music, audio files, read-alouds) • tactile and kinesthetic (e.g., games, manipulation material, hands-on tasks)	• teacher demonstration • student demonstration • cooperative learning • problem solving • experiments

Additionally, language learners need to access new learning through different language modalities—through reading, writing, speaking, and listening tasks. It is crucial for them to see words, hear them, say them, and write them. The same is true when teaching concepts. Learners need to see concepts in action while also hearing, talking, and writing about them.

At this point, we want to reiterate the information shared in Chapter 3 about the relevance and benefit of teaching according to learning styles or multiple intelligences. Those dimensions are not effective to the degree often believed; for more details, see page 56.

Overlaying two or more language modalities at once is always a good idea for language learners. For example, teachers could combine listening and writing by providing written backup to content presented orally (e.g., briefing notes, videos with subtitles). They could also choose to combine reading with listening through a read-aloud activity. By exposing learners to two language modalities at once, learners find it easier to store new learning in long-term memory.

The use of different modalities is an effective way to access language and information, but it is also helpful when learners are demonstrating their learning. Multimodal learning environments can more easily facilitate differentiation, in that students can showcase their learning through different processes and products.

REFLECTION ON PRACTICE

- How do I usually go about presenting new language or new concepts to my students?
- How much do I value teacher-led instruction versus other forms of instruction, such as student demonstrations, students experimenting with the material, cooperative learning, and problem solving?

continued

- Do I tend to favour using more visual approaches (e.g., videos, images, animation), auditory approaches (e.g., music, audio files, read-alouds), or tactile and kinesthetic approaches (e.g., games, manipulation material, hands-on tasks)?
- What lesson format do I tend to gravitate toward to deliver my lessons?
- When presenting new language or new concepts, do I get my students to experience this language or concept through different mediums? Do they get to read it (read about it), listen to it, write it (write about it), and talk using it (talk about it)?

BROADENING ACCESS

- To build learner autonomy, could I share with my learners the value of this action so that they, in turn, can start asking to learn using different modalities?
  - Can my students advocate for the ways they prefer to learn material?
- With respect to targeted support (e.g., Response to Intervention), are there any specific language learners in my class who could benefit from this action?

Action 3.5 in Action!

We do a unit on the human body. In this unit, we cover the heart and the circulatory system, the way by which oxygen circulates through our body, and so on. I wanted this unit to be as multimodal as possible. We read and talked about the circulatory system. We watched a video online, but I also wanted students to "experience" the circulatory system.

I went to my local hardware store and bought a white 3 by 3 metre tarp. I drew and painted a large heart on it (the four chambers, main arteries, valves, etc.). To teach students about oxygen delivery, I got students to be red blood cells. They physically had to move (walk) through the heart in the appropriate chambers, exit the heart to body extremities, go back to the heart, move toward the lungs, and so on. They did this in pairs to promote discussions about the circulatory system.

We also reconfigured the school so it became a human body: principal's office = brain, gym = heart, cafeteria = lungs, classrooms = body extremities. We would physically move through the school, going from the gym (heart) to a classroom, where we would deliver baggies full of oxygen, and walk back to the gym.

I also wanted students to write about this concept, so I gave them the following prompt: "The human body is a manufactory company with many different types of workers (those working for the circulatory system, those working for the digestive system). You work for the circulatory system and you are seeking a raise for yourself and your circulatory system colleagues. Write a letter to the boss outlining why you feel your system deserves a raise."

This unit was extremely popular. The students loved it and I really enjoyed teaching it! Students really got to learn about the circulatory system in so many different ways.

—L. Albert

This ULA can be used

- ✓ When teacher is presenting content and/or language
- ✓ When learners are engaged in a learning task
- When learners are demonstrating learning and understanding

ACTION 3.6 Explaining the relevance of what is being taught

To maintain focus, language learners need to be engaged and motivated, particularly when faced with longer or more demanding tasks. This ULA provides an essential support mechanism to help learners sustain focus throughout a task or lesson.

We know that one of the most important ways of motivating language learners is to establish relevance. If teachers do not explain the relevance of what is being taught, learners may disengage, quickly forget, or lose the motivation to try. Learners who clearly understand why the learning is important and useful invest more time and energy in it (Dörnyei, 2005, 2009; Dörnyei & Csizér, 1998). Further, as they experience success with the learning, they are more likely to continue with it.

Activities and learning experiences that are designed to be relevant and meaningful help learners engage emotionally with the material, enabling them to more easily make connections to what they already know. To establish relevance and promote inclusion, teachers should

- plan activities and learning experiences that are meaningful and personally relevant for learners
- make the goals and the purpose of the lesson explicit
- explain the purpose of what we are asking learners to do, pre-emptively eliminating the question "Why are we doing this?"
- provide opportunities for learners to discuss why the material is worth learning
- link the learning to real-life experiences (see Action 1.4)
- explain how the learning operates in the real world
- explain and demonstrate how the learning is transferable and reusable, either to other learning contexts or to learners' daily lives
- make explicit cross-curricular connections
- pique learner curiosity by dropping hints about the new unit or putting up new posters or displays
- invite learners' input by asking them what questions they want answered throughout the next unit and what types of activities they may want to undertake

Making the goals and purpose of the lesson explicit directly ties to the issues raised in Chapter 4 about promoting learner autonomy. Supporting student attention is a way to further develop this independence.

It is important for learners to establish personal and real-world relevance between what is being taught and the world in which they live. By doing so, they can more easily start constructing their own understanding of the material.

REFLECTION ON PRACTICE

- Do I notice specific types of activities or tasks in which my students are less engaged and motivated? What are these types of activities or tasks? How could I add more relevance to the activities or tasks?
- When covering new language or content, do I explain to my students how this relates to the overall unit, an upcoming task, or a future assignment or project?
- When I'm about to teach a lesson, do I explain to my students the value or the benefits of this lesson? How do I explain to them that this is an important element they need to know?
- When covering an outcome, do I explain to my students the goals and purpose of this outcome for future learning?
- Can my students finish the following sentence starters: "I am doing this because it will help me ..." or "I am learning this because ..."?
- How easily can my students link new learning to real-world situations? How can I help them do this more easily?

BROADENING ACCESS

- To build learner autonomy, could I share with my learners the value of this action so that they, in turn, can find the relevance of new learning more independently?
- With respect to targeted support (e.g., Response to Intervention), are there any specific language learners in my class who could benefit from this action?

Action 3.6 in Action!

Sometimes, I must admit that it is a bit easier to establish the relevance of some concepts more than others. For example, when teaching Grade 5, I needed to teach my students about simple machines in science. I really had to think this through. How would I make simple machines more engaging? How could I make this relevant to them? Then it came to me. Without simple machines, we wouldn't have a playground. Play structures are filled with simple machines. And that's how I started the unit. I showed a picture of a school without a playground and one with a playground. We discussed how playgrounds are a big part of our lives as kids, et cetera.

This led nicely to talking about how people who design playgrounds need to know many things in order to design and plan structures, including knowledge of simple machines. Most important though, I told the students they would be creating playgrounds for their upcoming project so they needed to learn about simple machines to accomplish their project. I always find it works best when I link learning to an upcoming task. Students tend to naturally pay a little closer attention when I say, "You'll need this because it will help you with ..."!

—R. Piercy

This ULA can be used

- ✓ **When teacher is presenting content and/ or language**
- **When learners are engaged in a learning task**
- ✓ **When learners are demonstrating learning and understanding**

ACTION 3.7 Summarizing key points of lessons, activities, and reading passages

Inclusive teachers understand the importance of reviewing material more than once. This is especially the case for learners who do not fully grasp important content the first time around. Teachers who summarize key points at the end of a lesson, an activity, or a reading passage offer learners an extra opportunity to hear essential elements in a concise fashion. Doing summaries requires re-explaining key learning points logically, using main ideas. When teachers summarize, they help learners identify and determine essential ideas.

Summaries also provide learners with extra exposure to the target vocabulary and language functions. They are yet another way for teachers to reuse and recycle newly presented material. Summaries help learners consolidate their learning because they act as a reinforcement mechanism. They can appear in many different formats, including highlighted key words, a written synthesis of the information, and even drawings of key concepts.

Similarly, teachers may ask learners to take ownership of doing oral or written summaries. Instead of teachers doing a lesson or task summary, they can invite students to do this summary as a whole-class or as a small-group activity. By doing so, teachers offer another opportunity for learners to communicate their learning in a meaningful way. Having learners summarize is also an effective way for teachers to monitor learners' comprehension of the material.

BROADENING ACCESS

- To build learner autonomy, could I share with my learners the value of this action so they, in turn, take time independently to think about what they've learned?
- With respect to targeted support (e.g., Response to Intervention), are there any specific language learners in my class who could benefit from this action?

REFLECTION ON PRACTICE

- When do I tend to summarize what has been taught? at the end of the day? at the end of a lesson? after finishing an activity? after accomplishing a particular task—an oral, reading, or writing task, for example?
- Can my students finish the following sentence starter: "Today I learned ..."?
- In my class, who tends to summarize the key concepts of a lesson? Do I do it or the students? How can I have both do it a bit more?
- When we summarize key learning in my class, do we do so as a whole group, in pairs, or in small groups?
- Do I vary the ways we summarize key learning? Do I tend to choose oral discussions over written summaries, drawings, word webs, or other means of summarizing key learning?
- What do I learn about my students when I get them to summarize what they've learned from a lesson, task, or activity?

Action 3.7 in Action!

I've integrated the action "Summarizing key points of lessons, activities, and reading passages" in a couple of different ways in my class. One of the ways I've used it is by creating a reusable poster where we keep track of our learning. Throughout the lesson, we'll take stock of what we've learned and we'll start a list. We keep adding to it throughout the lesson (or the day). At the end of the lesson (or day), students can use this list to monitor where they are with their learning and can use the key points to help them summarize to a partner what they've learned.

Wall Poster

I've also used a student self-tracking sheet. I give students a sheet and sticky notes. They keep track of new things they've learned throughout the lesson, day, or week and write them on sticky notes. At the end of the day, for example, they review their sticky notes and can formulate a great summary of what they've learned.

Student Self-Tracking Sheet

—B. Kane

Closing Thoughts

Besides the chapter activity ideas and suggestions for varying the ULAs, we want you to take away these key points about helping students sustain their attention and focus in the target language:

1. Language learners cannot and will not attend to every detail of language and of a lesson; it is important to help them focus their attention at the critical learning points.
2. Attention is not an automatic process and is something that can be lost or hard to manage when you do not have a strong proficiency in the target language. Simply telling students to "pay attention" (a kind of abstract command, if you think about it) is not enough to help them know how to focus or when to focus.
3. Understanding and attention are closely linked in the classroom. For students to attend easily to tasks, they need to understand both what is expected of them and what they are learning from a content standpoint. For students to understand what they need to do and are learning, they need to be able to focus at key points.
4. Supporting student attention may sometimes feel as if you are making ideas too obvious to learners. In other words, you may think it will deter them from paying attention because they know that you will provide summaries, recues, and other ways to engage with the content if they don't understand. However, this sort of view fails to recognize how much supporting student attention in the classroom is really about helping them to manage all of the information they are being given. And they are being given a lot of information.

As you reflect on the contents of the chapter, consider the following questions:

- When do I notice learners having a hard time managing attention? Is it a certain time of day? in a certain content area?
- How closely could learner attention be tied to learner anxiety or nerves about the learning experience in these situations? What can I do in my class to keep students' nerves in check?
- What cues/markers do I already use in an effort to focus learner attention?
- Are there ways I can use colour, font choices, or sound to help focus learner attention at key points?
- What standard summary or reflection questions could I use in my class to promote learner attention at the end of lessons?

CHAPTER 8

Language Learners Who Need Additional Support in Developing and Expanding Their Vocabulary

Throughout the last few chapters, we explored ways by which to promote and facilitate comprehension and language production in the second language. Since vocabulary knowledge is central to understanding and producing messages, it goes without saying that most Universal Language Actions presented thus far in the book help support vocabulary development. For example, as we have noted previously, Action 1.1 *Using gestures, facial expressions, images, pictures, drawings, objects, and manipulation materials* is an effective way to help students understand the overall message, but it can also be used to teach specific vocabulary. Likewise, teachers will indirectly assess vocabulary knowledge and need to fill in vocabulary gaps when using Action 1.4 *Assessing the extent of prior knowledge and filling in any major gaps.*

The ULAs presented in this chapter address particular learner needs with respect to understanding, developing, and expanding vocabulary. To build such vocabulary knowledge, students need to know the words, their meanings, and how these words operate in the world around us (how they fit in different contexts and settings). We know that if learners are to continue developing proficiency in a target language, their knowledge of vocabulary needs to keep expanding to encompass new topics—almost like a ripple effect in water.

Initially, beginning language learners will acquire basic vocabulary related to familiar themes, personal experiences, and basic needs. To increase second language proficiency, they will need to acquire more sophisticated vocabulary related to a wide range of more complex topics. It has been estimated that students need to know between 5000 and 10 000 words to understand more academic texts.

At times, language learners may need additional support in understanding and using new vocabulary. In such cases, they may present some of the following characteristics:

- ❑ repeat the same words
- ❑ seem to have a hard time getting the words out
- ❑ cannot express ideas, feelings, opinions
- ❑ produce vague or unclear messages
- ❑ seem to be searching for the right words
- ❑ rely too heavily on their first language to communicate
- ❑ take a long time to produce
- ❑ need long pauses to come up with words
- ❑ get bogged down by content
- ❑ over-rely on basic and simple words
- ❑ seem lost with the material
- ❑ seem confused
- ❑ get discouraged

Basics of Vocabulary Instruction: What We Know

There are many great researchers who specialize in areas of vocabulary development and vocabulary teaching (e.g., Paul Nation, 2001, 2006; Avril Coxhead, 2000; Batia Laufer, 1998, 2006; Paul Meara, 2009, 2014; David Beglar, 2010; Marlise Horst, 2005, 2013; and Scott Douglas, 2013). Several research findings have highlighted conditions or principles that facilitate vocabulary acquisition. These include the following:

- Rich literacy environments: Vocabulary development occurs more effectively in literacy-rich environments, that is, environments that have word walls, listening centres, meaningful conversations, songs, lots of rich reading materials of different varieties, and writing exemplars on the walls. It has been reported that students can learn many new vocabulary words incidentally by being read to, by listening to books on audio files, and by participating in rich language experiences (Cunningham, 2005; Cunningham & Stanovich, 1998; Kamil & Hiebert, 2005).
- Explicit teaching: Vocabulary knowledge is increased when taught explicitly; we cannot trust that students will acquire vocabulary through uninstructed ways.

- A balanced approach: Vocabulary knowledge is strengthened when students are able to read the words, listen to the words, and use the words, that is, see them, hear them, and use them in context. Moreover, vocabulary teaching is best done (with better results) when using different approaches rather than one instructional method; for ways to vary instruction, see the ULAs below.
- Lesson planning: Lessons that are planned with vocabulary development in mind make a difference because vocabulary becomes a lesson focus. The more students are exposed to words throughout the lesson, the more automatic their usage becomes.

What is perhaps most interwoven in these principles of vocabulary acquisition is the need for repeated exposure to new vocabulary. Language learners need multiple exposures to words orally and in writing. Words need to be taught, seen, and revisited in context, through meaningful oral contexts and in written texts. Gone are the days when vocabulary was taught in isolation through drills and random weekly lists. Learners need to actively engage with new vocabulary: they need to use words, think about their meanings, and make connections between and among words.

For suggestions on how to re-expose learners to new material (in this case, vocabulary), you may want to refer to Action 1.7 *Reusing and recycling pedagogical materials* in Chapter 5.

Universal Language Actions That Support Vocabulary Development

We have identified five ULAs designed to support language learners in developing and expanding their vocabulary. Actions 4.1 to 4.5 are outlined in Figure 8.1.

Figure 8.1

Universal Language Actions That Facilitate Learner Development and Expansion of Vocabulary

Action 4.1 Identifying and presenting required language at the outset of a lesson or activity

Action 4.2 Capitalizing on the use of word walls and word maps

Action 4.3 Accessing the senses to facilitate vocabulary acquisition

Action 4.4 Using role-play and games to present or reinforce new vocabulary

Action 4.5 Explaining vocabulary using examples, synonyms, antonyms, cognates, and teacher/learner definitions

Several ULAs can be used for different purposes. Many of the actions found in Chapters 5, 6, and 7 can also help support learners in developing and understanding new vocabulary. These can include, but are not limited to, Action 1.1 *Using gestures, facial expressions, images, pictures, drawings, objects, and manipulation materials*; Action 1.4 *Assessing the extent of prior knowledge and filling in any major gaps*; Action 2.3 *Creating and displaying linguistic supports around the classroom*; and Action 2.5 *Using pedagogical and language production routines.*

This ULA can be used

- ✓ **When teacher is presenting content and/or language**
- ✓ **When learners are engaged in a learning task**
- ✓ **When learners are demonstrating learning and understanding**

ACTION 4.1 Identifying and presenting required language at the outset of a lesson or activity

Because we work with second language learners, *all* of our lessons are language lessons—it makes no difference what class we teach. As a result, new or lesser-known vocabulary is embedded in all of our lessons.

When working with second language learners, we know that an important aspect of lesson planning is identifying the language students will need in order to

- understand and explain concepts
- accomplish a given task
- work cooperatively with others

Let's consider the following example. The focus of an upcoming lesson is plant growth. What is the required language or vocabulary that students need in order to be able to *understand* and *explain* the life cycle of a plant, as illustrated in Figure 8.2?

Figure 8.2: The Life Cycle of a Plant

At first thought, we might think of the following words: *soil*, *seed*, *stem*, *leaf*, *flower*, *water*, and *sun*. However, students need a lot more vocabulary than that if they are to understand and be able to explain this concept. They need other types of words such as these:

- verbs: growing, planting, producing, releasing, falling, developing, germinating, flowering, pouring, burying
- connector words: first, second, after, as a result, because, consequently
- adjectives and adverbs: sunny, cloudy, windy, loosely, sandy, rocky, humid, dry, slowly, gently, gradually

Planning lessons for second language learners requires a careful assessment of what vocabulary students will need to fully participate in the lesson. This ULA ensures that students have the necessary vocabulary to understand and communicate more effectively in the target language. Language learners are not as able to draw on context to figure out the meaning of unknown words, which is another reason why explicit attention to vocabulary is required.

Once the teacher has identified the required vocabulary needed for the lesson, he or she can proceed to explicitly teach this vocabulary in context at the beginning of the lesson or before students undertake a task. The teaching of this vocabulary can be done in conjunction with other ULAs presented in this chapter: these include using word walls and word maps (4.2), the five senses (4.3), role-play and games (4.4), and examples, synonyms, antonyms, cognates, and teacher/learner definitions (4.5). Once the required vocabulary has been presented, it is important to review it often throughout the lesson and subsequent lessons.

REFLECTION ON PRACTICE

- To what extent do I see my lessons as also being language learning lessons?
- When planning my lesson, to what extent do I consider the vocabulary words my students will need to know to accomplish a task or an activity?
- When I think about a particular concept I teach, what vocabulary words come to mind? What types of words are these?
- How can I present and teach vocabulary words of different types?
- How can I give more importance to all the required language my students need in order to explain or describe a concept or articulate their ideas?

BROADENING ACCESS

- To build learner autonomy, could I share with my learners the value of this action so that they, in turn, use the different types of words to help them express themselves orally and in writing?
- With respect to targeted support (e.g., Response to Intervention), are there any specific language learners in my class who could benefit from this action?

Action 4.1 in Action!

I teach mathematics and I typically have a space in my room where I post vocabulary words related to the mathematical concepts being studied. I must admit that previously, I used to display more nouns than other types of words. Students understood those nouns, but I realized they didn't have the vocabulary to "talk" about these mathematical concepts—all the supporting language they need to explain concepts. Before I start a unit, I consider the nouns, adjectives, adverbs, verbs, language functions, and connector words my students need to have to explain (in writing or orally) these concepts.

Fractions Example

• multiply by	• equivalent to	• in this image
• as a result	• part	• a whole
• the numerator	• a whole	• a portion
• the denominator	• because	• larger
• equal	• a unit	• smaller
• for example	• a section	• this demonstrates
• according to the picture	• same	• this shows that
• quarter	• simplifying	• third
	• reducing	• different than

Probability Example

• probability	• absolutely	• contrary to
• chance	• possibly	• even though
• a number	• probable	• among
• an amount	• improbable	• between
• a percentage	• if	• must be
• never	• it's possible that	• could be
• maybe	• likely	• only
	• unlikely	

I present these words throughout the unit, as they would naturally come up. I've noticed my students turning their heads toward the words when they write and when they talk. I've also seen that students then use the target language more. They rely less on their first language.

—S. Jones

I do something similar in my language class. We talk a lot about the weather in my class so I decided to provide my students with the language required to talk about the weather. I provide them with the beginning of sentence structures they need to formulate their thoughts. I also provide them with many other types of words not related to the weather, but rather words they need to describe the weather. Here are a few examples:

• Outside I see	• I also notice	• windy
• It feels like	• sunny	• cloudy
• I think	• It might	• It could
• I observe that	• This means that	• chilly
• In my opinion	• There is a chance that	• in addition
• There is a possibility that	• also	• therefore

I've noticed that all students use different words—it pushes some to use more advanced vocabulary. With these examples, students can push themselves a bit further in describing or explaining the weather because I've provided ways for them to be able to talk about the weather.

—M. Paulin

ACTION 4.2 Capitalizing on the use of word walls and word maps

Word walls and word maps are used by inclusive teachers to present, display, and revisit important vocabulary. When thinking of word walls and word maps, we need to consider important differences between high-frequency and low-frequency words, and the ways in which we teach these words.

In the reading literature, for example, *high-frequency words* refer to the words most often found in children's books. There are approximately 200 high-frequency words that have been identified as the words students need to know to help them move toward more complex reading. Of course, the importance of being able to recognize, read, and spell these high-frequency words is well documented in research (e.g., Clay, 1993, 2003; Fountas & Pinnell, 2001; Giasson, & Theriault, 1983).

As a result, high-frequency words should have a prominent place in literacy classrooms, particularly when students are still acquiring the foundations of a second language (at least two years). Typically, to build a high-frequency word wall, a handful of high-frequency words are chosen and presented every week (see Figure 8.3). Teachers display these words in alphabetical order because it is easier for students to retrieve the words they need. Throughout subsequent lessons, students should review and work with these words to attain a certain level of mastery at reading and spelling the words, as well as using them in conversation.

Figure 8.3: Word Wall

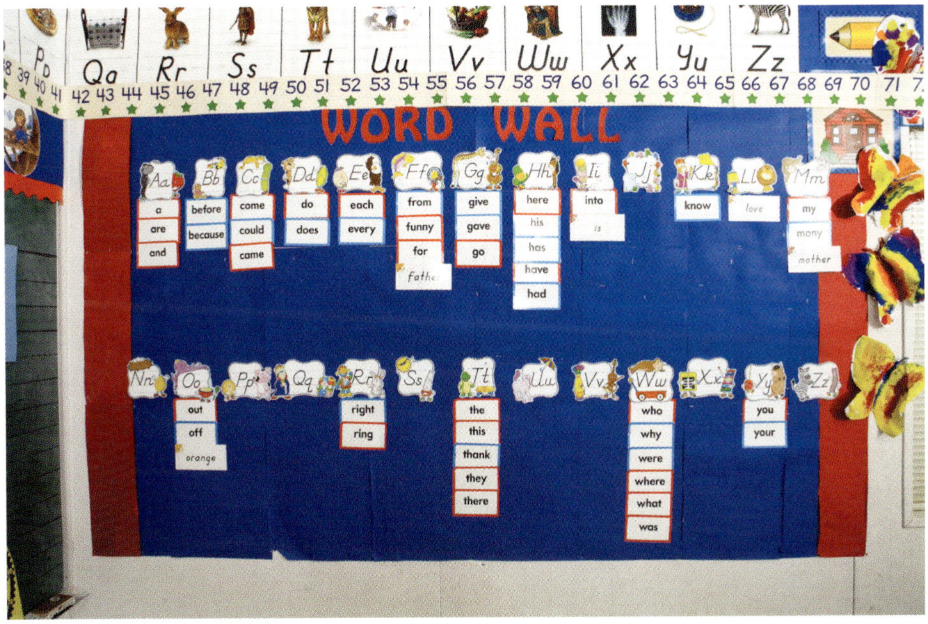

This ULA can be used

- ✓ **When teacher is presenting content and/or language**
- ✓ **When learners are engaged in a learning task**
- ✓ **When learners are demonstrating learning and understanding**

For lists of high-frequency words, see the *Access for Success* website.

Along with high-frequency words found in children's literature, students need a lot of exposure to words most often related to the theme, concept, or content being studied. These are the words students will encounter most often as they learn about a concept or a theme. This is where the previous action, Action 4.1 *Identifying and presenting required language at the outset of a lesson or activity*, more likely will come into play.

Once students have a large enough vocabulary base, the focus can start shifting to lower-frequency words—words that are context specific, words that are more specialized, words that students are less exposed to. Thematic or content-specific words can be presented and displayed in several ways, including word maps, such as the one in Figure 8.4.

Figure 8.4: Word Map

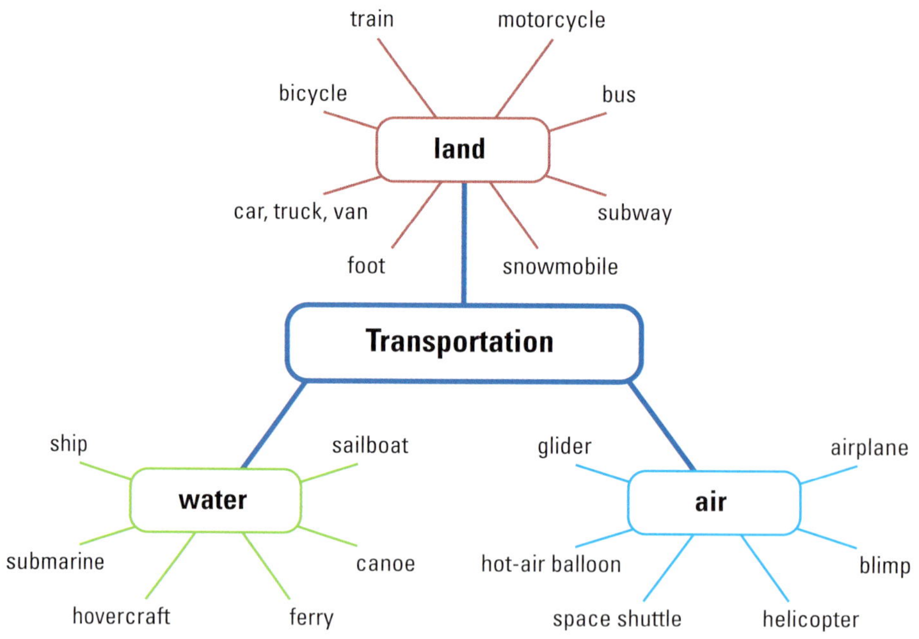

Word maps are a great way to classify and visualize words that are generated through discussions, brainstorming, reading, or listening activities. In fact, research has found that word maps are very effective in helping students understand and recall complex concepts (Cunningham, 2005; Farrand, Hussain, & Hennessy, 2002).

High-frequency word walls and thematic word maps are easily accessible because they are displayed in class, or possibly shared electronically with students, so they provide great visual supports for second language learners. These resources are very much linguistic tools that can help learners communicate more easily when speaking and writing.

Notice that this action focuses on capitalizing on rather than creating word walls and word maps. Students must be able to work with these word walls and maps as often as possible. Here are a few examples of ways to exploit word walls and maps:

- using word games, word searches, and word classification activities
- finding or creating word families
- finding words that rhyme, that have similar sounds, or that share similar characteristics
- creating sentences with the words
- finding words in reading passages
- working on prefixes and suffixes

By practising and reviewing (that is, using and reusing) vocabulary words that are displayed in the classroom, we ensure that students are actively working with vocabulary, rather than simply being exposed to language.

REFLECTION ON PRACTICE

High-Frequency Words

- How well are my students able to recognize, read, and write high-frequency words?
- What can I do to help my students master high-frequency words?
- What types of words are currently displayed in my classroom? Do I have verbs, adjectives, nouns, connector words, adverbs? (See Action 4.1.)

Word Maps, Webs, and Walls

- How often do I create word maps and webs with my students? When do I do so? Is it before a unit of study, before a lesson, before reading a text?
- How often do I revisit my thematic word walls or maps with my students?
- What are some of the ways I use my word walls or maps in class?
- What activities could I do to further exploit the value of my word walls or maps on an ongoing basis?
- Do I remind my students to use the thematic word walls and maps before they undertake an oral or written task? Do I remind them that these are great resources?

BROADENING ACCESS

- To build learner autonomy, could I share with my learners the value of this action so that they, in turn, use word walls and word maps to help them learn?
- With respect to targeted support (e.g., Response to Intervention), are there any specific language learners in my class who could benefit from this action?

Teachers at the secondary level may want to move this action to an electronic format, in that the "board" could be an online shared document that the whole class can access.

Action 4.2 in Action!

I decided to use presentation boards in my class as my word walls. I teach different groups of students and I teach different subjects and grade levels, so wall space in my classroom is somewhat limited. As a result, each group of students has their own presentation boards with vocabulary related to the themes we're studying.

At first, the boards are blank with the exception of a picture and the name of the theme. I present key vocabulary (Action 4.1 regarding required language) to the students, and we add the words to the presentation board. At the end of each subsequent lesson, I take five minutes and we talk about new words that we may want to add to the presentation board. Because students read, listen to, and talk about the theme, they're exposed to new vocabulary each day. Together, we decide what words are essential to add to our presentation board. We build our vocabulary word wall together, bit by bit, throughout the unit.

One day, students were leaving my class to go to another one of their classes and they asked me if they could bring their presentation board with them. They said, "We're working on a similar topic in our next class and these words would be helpful to have." I was really impressed that first, they valued the presentation board as a resource; second, they recognized its utility and application in another context; and third, they took ownership of their own learning by asking for the board. It was really nice to see this from a group of middle school students.

—J. Beyea

ACTION 4.3 Accessing the senses to facilitate vocabulary acquisition

This ULA can be used

✓ When teacher is presenting content and/ or language

✓ When learners are engaged in a learning task

✓ When learners are demonstrating learning and understanding

This ULA calls for using sounds, smells, taste, touch, and sight to learn and experience new vocabulary. Activating the senses can be done through pictures, drawings, real objects (realia), and movements. In particular, movements whereby students respond with whole-body actions are a great way for learners to quickly recognize meaning in the language being presented (see work done on total physical response by Asher, 1969). We can also activate the senses by creating for students experiences where they need to use their senses to experience the moment. These are all great ways to help clearly illustrate the meanings of words. Further, it has been shown that when students experience vocabulary through different means, it enhances memory.

In Action 1.1, we noted the importance of using pictures and real objects to help learners comprehend messages, but pictures and objects can also be used to help students learn and understand key vocabulary words. By looking at pictures or examining real objects, students can create mental images for new vocabulary quickly. The more quickly students can do this for new vocabulary and understand the key vocabulary of a lesson, the more quickly teachers can dive into deeper learning.

When using pictures and real objects to teach vocabulary, we need to remember to show different representations of the word. Let's consider the example of a teacher wanting to teach students the word *bear*. When using pictures with second language learners, it would be important to show pictures of different types of bears: polar bear, black bear, grizzly bear, teddy bear. We don't want learners to think that *bear* is synonymous only with the one picture shown. We want students to associate the word with more than one visual representation.

Pictures can be more difficult to use to teach more abstract words such as adverbs, verbs, and adjectives. If a teacher shows a picture of a boy riding his bike to teach the word *riding*, students could misinterpret the word *riding* to mean the bike, the backdrop, or even the boy. It would be better for students to see the verb in action through physical movement, short video clips, for example, or a few drawings depicting the different parts of the action (e.g., boy getting on bike, boy starting to pedal, boy pedalling faster).

Older learners who may be resistant to "acting out" language may be more willing to use sign language to associate words with meanings. There are various resources online for learning signs for certain words.

In the case of verbs, adjectives, and adverbs, it may be better to activate other senses such as touching, smelling, tasting, and listening to real objects. If students experience touching honey, for example, they can create an instant mental representation of the adjective *sticky*. Here are a few other examples of when students could use their senses to understand abstract concepts: a *soft* surface, a *rigid* material, a *porous* sponge, *sandy* soil, a *juicy* fruit, a *sour* juice, a *loud* noise, a *delicious* smell, a *salty* taste, *slowly* walking, a *stunning* sunset, a *conscious* breath, a *huge* building, a *famous* person.

BROADENING ACCESS

- To build learner autonomy, could I share with my learners the value of this action so that they, in turn, use pictures, objects, movements, and drawings to help their classmates understand words?
- With respect to targeted support (e.g., Response to Intervention), are there any specific language learners in my class who could benefit from this action?

REFLECTION ON PRACTICE

- What are some of the different ways I could teach the words *short* and *tall*? How could I help my students make instant visual representations of these two words?
- How do I illustrate new vocabulary to my students?
- To what extent do I get my students to experience new or key vocabulary by using their senses?
- Do I activate different senses to teach concrete words as opposed to more abstract words (e.g., verbs, adjectives, adverbs)?
- When teaching a word that can have different representations (e.g., *bear, bag, building*), to what extent do I provide different pictures to illustrate the different meanings of the word?

Action 4.3 in Action!

In December, we were about to start a new unit of study in my class related to winter. Of course, students needed to acquire new vocabulary (nouns, adjectives, adverbs, verbs) related to winter. I watched the weather and waited a few days for the first snowfall. When we had our first snowfall, the students were excited because it was starting to *look* a lot different outside, but I wanted to have them pay attention to the other four senses—the different feelings winter brought.

I took some time that morning to teach about the five senses. What does winter smell like? What does it feel like? What comes to mind when we think of winter and the foods we eat? What does it sound like? I really wanted to build students' vocabulary knowledge of winter. After teaching about noticing our five senses, we went outside to experience winter and the winter weather. After, we came back in and the students had so many ideas that I could use to illustrate and provide meaning to new words—the smell of the crisp air, the wetness of the snow on our cheeks, the sounds of cracking branches, the sounds of the wind, the warmth of our breath underneath our scarves. It was an awesome way to start building our thematic word wall.

—A. Manderson

One of the ways I use to expand my students' vocabulary is to explore a text more in depth using our five senses. For example, let's say we're reading a text about the Roman Empire. Of course, we'll read the text to learn about the Roman Empire, but I'll also use the text as a springboard for vocabulary development. Once we've discussed the content of the text, I'll ask my students questions about the five senses: What could we have possibly seen at the Coliseum? What do you think we would have heard in the marketplace? What would their housing material possibly

continued

have felt like? What about the food? What would it have tasted like (remembering notions about food preparation in this time period)? What would public steam baths have been like? What would we have heard as we walked through an ancient Roman city (cobblestone, aqueducts, animals, etc.)? I find that these types of questions are a great way to build and teach vocabulary, but also a great way to reinforce concepts being studied. I keep track of this vocabulary by writing it on my board. When students write in their learning journals, they tend to refer to the board and use the new vocabulary.

—C. Phillips

ACTION 4.4 Using role-play and games to present or reinforce new vocabulary

Another great ULA to help second language learners acquire and use new vocabulary is through role-play and games. More specifically, role-plays and games are filled with visual, sensory, kinesthetic, and repetitive elements, making them all very beneficial for language learners (Snow, 1989).

Role-play, an important component in second language teaching, is particularly effective for illustrating the meanings of new words or concepts for language learners who may need additional support in this area. Associating role-play with learning new words means that students embody or personify the words. For example, beginning second language learners may curl up in a little ball to represent *small* and may stand on tiptoe with arms up high to represent *tall*; students learning more advanced vocabulary may form societal groups (e.g., poor, poor working class, working class, upper middle class, upper class) to represent social hierarchy and learn about the meaning of each of these terms.

Games are a great way to get language learners to use and reuse new vocabulary. Games should be designed or chosen with pedagogical value in mind so that students do, indeed, use language and reuse vocabulary. Elimination games should be avoided because as students get eliminated, they are no longer involved in the learning activity, and games that have timed elements disadvantage students who have slower processing rates.

When choosing which games to use in the classroom, consider the following questions:

- Are the students hearing key vocabulary associated with what is being studied?
- Are they using this key vocabulary throughout the game in meaningful ways?

This ULA can be used

- ✓ **When teacher is presenting content and/or language**
- ✓ **When learners are engaged in a learning task**
- ✓ **When learners are demonstrating learning and understanding**

- Do the students reuse the language in a way that's authentic for life outside the classroom?
- When a game is reused several times, is it still linguistically challenging enough?
- Does the game involve the students in reading or writing key words?

Games offer students the chance to play with language in a lower-stakes way, which can encourage learning. Games as learning activities should not be the primary form of instruction.

If the answer is *yes* to one or more of these questions, then the game has pedagogical value. Examples of games that have lots of pedagogical potential for vocabulary development include well-developed bingo games, matching games, Jeopardy, charades, group Pictionary, rhyming word relays, trivia games, and memory games (e.g., students examine a scene, a group of objects, a line of students, or a picture for a few minutes, then close their eyes and remember things about the visual). Again, it is important to maximize students' language production and vocabulary acquisition when developing these types of activities.

During games and role-play activities, students may not be actively aware of the extent to which they are learning because there is a sense that they are playing. However, a lot of learning occurs through play, and enjoying an activity, having fun, and laughing while learning are all elements indicative of motivation and engagement. At the end of a game or role-play activity, though, it is important to recap with students the learning that occurred during that time.

BROADENING ACCESS

- To build learner autonomy, could I share with my learners the value of this action so that they, in turn, create their own language- or vocabulary-learning games?
- With respect to targeted support (e.g., Response to Intervention), are there any specific language learners in my class who could benefit from this action?

REFLECTION ON PRACTICE

- What concepts or words do I teach that would lend themselves well to role-play (where students could embody the concepts or words)?
- What value do I place on the role of games in my classroom? Can I see the pedagogical value of games and role-play activities?
- How do I use games as a way for my students to review and reuse key vocabulary?
- What do I keep in mind when designing or choosing games for my students? Are they helping my students learn and use the target language? How do I ensure that students are included throughout the game?
- How can I enhance the learning experience (or vocabulary value) of the games I use in my classroom?
- Can my students complete the following sentence starter: "Playing this game is helping me learn ..."?
- Do I explain the value or purpose of the game at some point during the lesson?

Action 4.4 in Action!

To reinforce words related to place (*under, over, next to, beside, to the left, to the right, above, near, far, close*), I get six or seven students to line up in front of the class. We take a minute or so to try to remember the placement of each student. Then I get the rest of the class to turn around so they can't see the lineup anymore. I then ask questions, such as "Who was next to Julie? Who is near Fred?" In groups of two, students discuss the possibilities. My students really enjoy this type of memory game—I've used it to teach vocabulary relating to clothing, colours, and physical characteristics. It's a great way for students to listen to these words and further understand their meanings.

—J. Dickson

I use games in my content-area classes. I do a lot of Jeopardy-type and question-and-answer games. To reinforce concepts and newly acquired vocabulary, I take out my pocket chart and give each of my students an index card. Some cards are blue, some are yellow, some are green, and some are red. Each colour has a different point value attributed to it (for example, blue = 20 points). I don't tell students right away the point value of each colour.

On one side of the index card, they have to write out a question. They will write something about what they have learned throughout the week, for example. I give them time to review their notes. Then they'll come up with a question such as "What is a carnivore?" (in my science class) or "What is an equivalent fraction?" (in my math class).

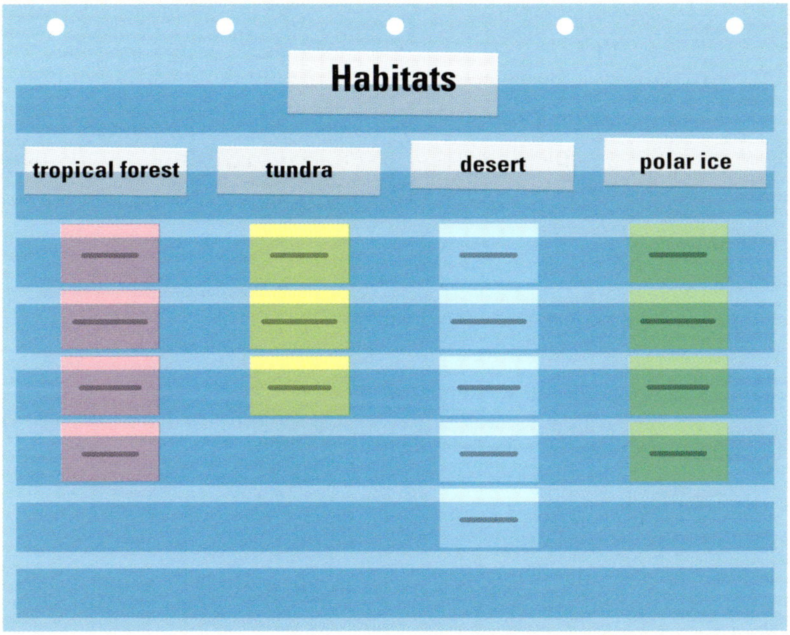

continued

On the other side of their index card, they need to provide an explanation or answer for their question. Once all students have completed their cards, I organize them by colour in the pocket chart. Then I group the students in pairs (partner 1 and partner 2).

I choose the questions randomly, using a colour pointer. Then I read the explanation on one of the cards (an animal who eats meat). Partner 1 from each pair will try to figure out the question, for example, "What is a carnivore?" If partner 1 succeeds, he or she gets the points for this category. We then move on to another index card for partner 2. The goal of the game is to gain more points than your partner.

Students really enjoy playing these types of games. They serve as a great review tool; students get more exposure to the vocabulary we're studying.

—F. Sheranko

This ULA can be used

- ✓ **When teacher is presenting content and/or language**
- ✓ **When learners are engaged in a learning task**
- ✓ **When learners are demonstrating learning and understanding**

ACTION 4.5 Explaining vocabulary using examples, synonyms, antonyms, cognates, and teacher/learner definitions

One challenge second language learners face when learning new vocabulary is to understand the meanings of words. More specifically, sometimes the definition of a word can be just as complicated as the word itself. A dictionary definition, for example, may be filled with additional vocabulary second language learners may not know. Therefore, a dictionary is not always the most useful resource when trying to get at the meaning of a word. Moreover, we need to consider the amount of time learners spend at trying to find the meaning of a word when there are easier and quicker ways to explain what the word means to the student.

There is a delicate balance between teaching vocabulary to students and getting students to learn what new words mean themselves. The latter requires students to have quite a bit of language proficiency in the target language. In the meantime, learners who are still acquiring a strong vocabulary knowledge base need easy and effective ways to quickly access the meaning of a word. We don't want students to get bogged down trying to work out the meaning of a word in a text when we could be quickly teaching them its meaning by using examples, synonyms, antonyms, cognates, and simplified teacher definitions.

For any number of words, teachers could use or provide the following:

Examples and Counter-examples	Synonyms and Antonyms
• For the word *country*, the teacher could say: "Canada, Mexico, France, Morocco, Japan, and China are all countries" and "Toronto, Calgary, and Paris are not countries, but cities."	• For the word *skyscraper*, the teacher could say, "Oh, this word is another word for a tower or high-rise building." • For the word *huge*, the teacher could say, "This word means not small."
Cognates: Words that look similar in students' first language	**Simplified Definitions**
• For the word *gigantic*, the teacher could say, "This word looks similar to a word you may know in French, *gigantesque*." However, it is important to explain to students that while some words do look similar in both languages, they can have quite different meanings. These are referred to as *faux amis*.	• Teachers could provide their own simplified definitions that are language appropriate for their students. Using simplified language helps students remember definitions.
Prefixes and Suffixes	
• Prefixes and suffixes provide clues to understanding certain words. For example: – The prefix *chron–* means "related to time," as in *chronology*, *chronometer*, *chronicle*, and *chronic*. – The suffix *–ant* means "a person who," as in *immigrant*, *applicant*, and *servant*.	

Interestingly, not all languages have synonyms and antonyms to the same degree as English and French. Both of these languages are very "deep," meaning they have a large vocabularies.

The more quickly students acquire a strong vocabulary base, the easier and quicker it will be for them to dive into more complex topics with more sophisticated vocabulary.

REFLECTION ON PRACTICE

- How do I teach my class what certain words mean before a listening or reading task?
- What are some of the ways I use to quickly provide the meanings of specific words during a listening or reading activity?
- What kind of balance do I have between teaching the meaning of the word and having students find the meaning of the word?
- What role do cognates play in my classroom? How do I explain this concept to my students?
- How do I provide my teacher definitions to my students? Do I say the definitions out loud? Do I write them on the board? Do I get my students to record them in a personal dictionary?
- Are my students at the stage where they could learn what certain prefixes and suffixes mean?

BROADENING ACCESS

- To build learner autonomy, could I share with my learners the value of this action so that they, in turn, ask for synonyms, antonyms, or examples of this word?
- With respect to targeted support (e.g., Response to Intervention), are there any specific language learners in my class who could benefit from this action?

Action 4.5 in Action!

Some of my students have home languages in which synonyms and antonyms really do not exist; in their languages, there is just one way to express a particular idea. So, for them, working with synonyms and antonyms in this language is actually more of a challenge. During a lesson, I have to deliberately plan or otherwise think about which synonyms or antonyms I will use to help develop a concept further. For example, we recently did some lessons about the fish and other water creatures in our local rivers and lakes. In a few activities, we needed to compare the creatures to each other, which ended up being a really good time to work with the synonyms and antonyms linked to size. I made a series of picture cards to post in the room, to help show them the difference. Before I posted the pictures, we discussed how they showed the synonyms and antonyms.

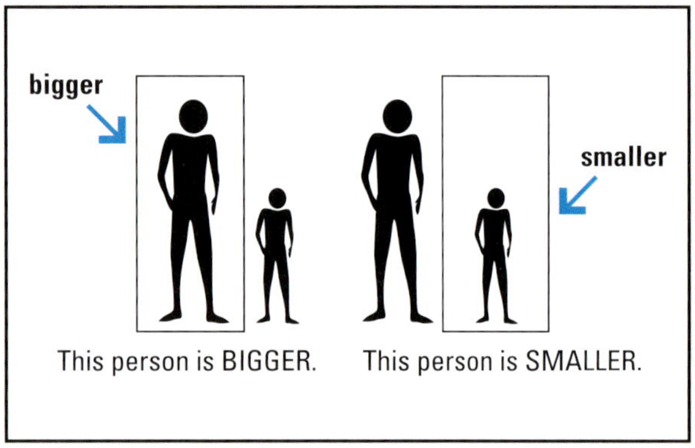

—B. Chaves

At the start of every major unit, I provide my students with a list of the key vocabulary words we'll encounter. I ask the students to go through the list and highlight, in yellow, all of the words they know and can use well in a sentence. Then, I have them highlight in pink the words that they think they know or that look like other words they already know. Once they do that, I ask students to share the words that have not been highlighted on their pages. I make a list of these words on the board (knowing that some of these words may be known by some students already). Once the list is complete, I divide the class into groups of three. Each group is assigned a portion of the list to look up in dictionaries (bilingual and unilingual), thesauruses, or other resources to help build the meaning. They create their own definitions of the terms from the resources they consult. Then, after they confirm with me that their definitions work for our purposes in the lesson, they prepare posters showing those definitions. The groups present their definitions, and the rest of the class is responsible for noting the definitions of any terms that were also not highlighted on their original list. Inviting the students to create their own learner definitions has definitely helped with student engagement with vocabulary, and we also spend the time focusing on the words they really do not know.

—E. Khan

Closing Thoughts

Besides the chapter activity ideas and suggestions for varying the ULAs, we want you to take away these key points about helping students' vocabulary development:

1. Vocabulary does not develop automatically. You need to be intentional in how you help students expand their vocabulary.
2. Vocabulary development is ongoing and takes time. It is not about doing one activity to help the students learn words they are going to use and then giving them a quiz later. Rather, it is about using and reusing the words in context, over and over again, so that the students understand how the words fit into the broader language. To use the vocabulary in a meaningful way, the students need to be accountable for more than just knowing the definition.
3. We have to be intentional and deliberate in how we use images, videos, and other means to help make the meaning of a term apparent to students. Not all images clearly convey the concept, or perhaps the image could be interpreted in many different ways. Avoid using the same image to represent multiple concepts.
4. Be mindful of the general language patterns you have as the teacher. We have seen students get stalled on words that have no meaning, such as *um* and *uh*.

As you reflect on the contents of the chapter, consider the following questions:

- Which of these actions represents an extension of something that I'm already doing in class?
- What are the key vocabulary terms of the current unit? Which terms are more concrete? Which abstract terms deserve particular attention? Which terms could be key to unlocking student understanding of the concept?
- How can I capitalize on resources such as word banks, word walls, and concept maps?
- With whom could I work to create an image bank for use in lessons?
- How can I involve students more in using and expanding their vocabulary?
- Are there certain key vocabulary words from previous units that I need to revisit, to ensure that students really know the terms?

CHAPTER 9

Differentiation to Facilitate Access

As we shared in the introduction to Access Point 3, differentiation is about providing students with a variety of access points into and through a learning activity; students pursue the learning path (either by their choice or the teacher's) that aligns with their current needs, interests, or readiness. This chapter will explore ways in which differentiated activities and differentiated instruction can be implemented to support inclusive language education.

This chapter is organized to consider differentiation in four ways: (1) how it intersects with the notion of linguistic complexity, (2) how activities and instruction can be differentiated to support varied student needs, (3) how differentiation can intersect with the Universal Language Actions (ULAs) as presented in Chapters 5 to 8, and (4) how differentiation intersects with assessment.

Differentiation by linguistic complexity, or DLC, was proposed by Katy in *Languages for All* to show how students can access a topic or concept by working with content aligned with their current skills in the language (see Arnett, 2013c). DLC requires teachers to attend to students' language (both the input and the output) as something that can vary according to learner needs, interests, or readiness. Next, we apply the more traditional application of differentiation proposed by Tomlinson (1999, 2001) and extended by others (Heacox, 2002; Hume, 2009) to offer ideas for differentiated activities where students can select (or are assigned to) a specific path that responds to their needs, interests, or readiness for a task. These tasks are designed to foster understanding, production, attention, and vocabulary development. Then, we explore how the ULAs and differentiation can intersect in a classroom setting by returning to several Action in Action vignettes from Chapters 5 to 8 and offering ideas on how those actions could morph into activities that are differentiated to support student learning needs and learner traits. Often, these three aspects of differentiation intersect with one another, so as you progress through or skip around the chapter, you will see various examples of how they can be combined. Finally, we get a jump-start on Chapter 10 and explore specific issues of assessment as they intersect with differentiation, including the big question of how to assess students' learning when they are all doing different activities.

To begin the chapter, we will review some baseline premises of differentiation. Doing so will allow us to contextualize the practical suggestions that follow.

Getting Started with Differentiation

Using differentiation effectively in the classroom requires agreement about a few basic concepts (beyond the definitions shared in the Access Point 3 introduction).

Activity Versus Task

Though the terms are sometimes used interchangeably within broader discussions of pedagogical practice, in the world of differentiation, there is a distinction between an activity and a task. Broadly, an activity is the targeted learning goal, or outcome, whereas a task is the actual learning event, or what the students do in order to arrive at the learning goal. The tasks themselves are the different options for the activity; the activity is differentiated through its offering of various task options. For example, the learning activity is "constructing good descriptions of food," but the task options might be reading and annotating menus to show examples of descriptions; writing an entry for a food blog about what you ate over the weekend; and given a mix of foods, creating sketch notes that offer descriptions of those foods.

Student Grouping

In the world of differentiation, exchanges about grouping students do not mean that the activities are either collaborative or cooperative. Rather, grouping is about the decisions involved in ensuring that the students are following the learning path aligned to their needs, interests, or readiness; this decision can be made by the teacher, but leaving it with the student is often preferred (Tomlinson, 1999). These groupings are intended to be flexible; the students needing support or challenge on their paths will vary according to the learning goals, expected previous knowledge, and skill.

The conceptions of need, interest, and readiness that we apply in this book are presented in Figure 9.1 below.

Figure 9.1: Student Need, Interest, and Readiness

Need	Interest	Readiness
The student's approach to learning requires a support or way of doing that is embedded into one of the task options.	The student has a personal curiosity or preference for a particular path.	The student is ready to work with a particular element or thinking pattern available on a path; this would be typically viewed as a growth opportunity for the student's learning.

Considerations for Student Grouping

- Student interest can be explored in relation to a task topic, a task procedure, or a task mode.
- If a teacher makes the decision about which learning path a student pursues or otherwise suggests to a student to change a path, the teacher should be doing so using evidence from previous student work (e.g., assessment).
- Students should be told about the path options for an activity and invited to participate in the decision making as much as possible. Doing this supports learner autonomy and encourages motivation in the classroom.
- If a student selects a particular path in the belief that he or she is ready for the challenge that's there, but has difficulty with the task, the teacher may want to give the student the option of switching paths, particularly if the task is linked to developing a better understanding of a key concept. However, student struggle is not always a bad thing—it can motivate students, too.
- Students can be given the responsibility of managing their paths if differentiated activities are regularly used. To ensure that students have a balance of experiences, teachers can set the expectation that students vary the paths they take. Not doing the same types of tasks repeatedly can be helpful for preparing students to take on the more challenging tasks.

Differentiation by Linguistic Complexity

At its core, DLC is about reworking vocabulary choices and language structures to ensure that students can more easily grasp the ideas and content being presented to them. DLC is a dynamic process, marked by interactions between the teacher and student that allow the teacher to calibrate choice of language for the student's current level and needs. Given that background knowledge, prior experiences, and first language skills (among other factors, as we learned from Chapter 2) will influence a language learner's ability to decode a message and find meaning, DLC requires teachers to be open to probing a student's language skills with each new text or learning event. Some students may be able to manage more complex questions in a discussion about modes of transportation because of a keen personal interest in the topic, but struggle to navigate activities that are focused on sports because of a lack of familiarity with sports. The teacher should be prepared to help the student jump around the language paths as the situation allows.

DLC engages all four dimensions of language learning we targeted in the ULAs: understanding, production, attention, and vocabulary. Providing access to the kinds of language texts, prompts, and questions most aligned with students' current level of proficiency in the target language is critical to gauging student skill with the content. Offering students questions and prompts well outside their linguistic reach adds to both teacher and student frustration and gives the impression that the student is not learning much of anything.

Although DLC and Action 1.3 *Adjusting the complexity of oral and/ or written language* are seemingly addressing the same construct, we consider them to be two different dimensions of support. If a teacher is using DLC, all students are being offered distinctly different learning paths that are shaped by their proficiency needs. On the other hand, when a teacher adjusts the complexity of the language at a more general level to support all students, the teacher is said to be using the ULA.

DLC takes time. First, it takes time to become adept at knowing what students' language skills can do at certain levels. Next, it takes time (especially at the beginning) to formulate prompts and adjust the texts to align with students' proficiency levels. We urge you to persevere with it. Of the many ideas shared in this book, DLC is one of the best ways of providing access to language learners, and many of the ULAs will not be as effective in the classroom if the students are working with materials or language worlds away from their current skills.

To get you started with DLC, we are going to offer two key supports. First, the next section will present a series of prompt tables for two general types of learning events in a classroom where teacher questions are critical to student learning: (1) exploring an information text (e.g., teacher talk, non-fiction text, skill demonstration) and (2) exploring a narrative or fictional text. We offer the stems, or prompts, as jump-starts to your own question tables and acknowledge the work of Hill and Flynn (2008) and Fairbairn and Jones-Vo (2010) in inspiring this organizational approach to DLC. Second, in the subsequent section, we offer examples of how you can apply DLC to a prepared text to be more accessible to a student in class without necessarily having to locate or write a separate text.

Prompts to Support Differentiation by Linguistic Complexity

The following pair of tables (Figure 9.2 and Figure 9.3) provide question stems to help students navigate a particular text or learning event at a level consistent with their language skills. The idea is that students are assigned the readiness level that aligns with their language skills. This assignment can look like you, as the teacher, asking these questions directly of the student or it can embed the questions into activities to ensure that the student can contribute throughout the lesson. Students should be given access to the questions they can currently manage; a student at Level 2 in the proficiency development process should not be working with questions at Level 4.

To review the stages of second language acquisition, you can refer back to pages 30 to 32 in Chapter 2.

These tables juxtapose the levels with the most recent version of Benjamin Bloom's taxonomy (Bloom & Krathwohl, 1956; Anderson & Krathwohl, 2001) for cognitive challenge. As pointed out by Hill and Flynn (2008), higher order thinking is possible for students who are learning a second language; the challenge is that we (as teachers) are often thinking about cognitive challenge through the lens of the first language. What is cognitively easy for a student operating in the first language can be very cognitively demanding for a language learner. Therefore, the tables that follow may first read to you as misclassifications of the actions as certain levels of cognitive challenge. However, keeping in mind the way in which learning a language demands certain kinds of thinking, these charts are consistent with what is reasonable to ask of students developing proficiency in another language.

In the tables that follow, the questions or prompts typically assume that the students have been working with the content or concept to some degree already, and that these prompts or questions are there to help assess and expand understanding. Though the prompts or questions could be used to assess prior knowledge at the start of a lesson, you may need to use more ULAs to ensure that students understand what is being asked of them.

In the chart that follows, we use "the plant" generically to refer to the topic of the question or prompt.

Figure 9.2: DLC Prompts for Exploring Information Texts

	Level 1 (non-verbal response to high-frequency, single-word responses)	Level 2 (two-word response to short phrases with prompts)	Level 3 (simple sentences with some errors)	Level 4 (multiple sentences with some variation in structure)	Level 5 (varied-length responses resembling work of proficient students)
Creating	Show me three pictures of the plant.	Tell me three words I said.	What are three key words about the presentation?	What is the main point of what I said?	Write about four questions about the presentation.
Evaluating	Point to the white plant; the bigger plant.	Y/N: Does *tree* mean *plant*?	How are plants related to our previous topic of the water cycle?	Which is the best example of a house plant? Why?	Compare and contrast the poinsettia plant and the hosta plant.
Analyzing	Draw the groups of plants.	What plants are in this group? (Show picture of lots of different trees, plants, and flowers.)	What are the parts of a plant?	What is a problem with plants?	Why do these changes to plants matter?
Applying	Y/N: Are you a plant?	Do you agree with the author that plants are pretty?	Do you agree with the author that everyone should own plants? Why or why not?	What is your opinion of plants?	How can you use information about plants in your life?
Understanding	Show a picture of a plant. Ask student to confirm: "Is this a plant?"	What two words describe the plant? (Give options.)	Give me three words to describe a plant.	What is another example of a plant?	Write a sentence that describes a plant.
Remembering	Point to a plant. (Provide picture prompts.)	Y/N: Is this a plant?	Where is the plant?	Explain how a plant is different from a tree.	What did you know about plants before? What do you know now?

In the chart below, we use "the character" to generically refer to the topic of the question or prompt.

Figure 9.3: DLC Prompts for Exploring Narrative or Fictional Texts

	Level 1 (non-verbal response to high-frequency, single-word responses)	Level 2 (two-word response to short phrases with prompts)	Level 3 (simple sentences with some errors)	Level 4 (multiple sentences with some variation in structure)	Level 5 (varied-length responses resembling work of proficient students)
Creating	Show me the character on each page.	What does the character like and do?	What do you think the character will do next?	Tell me the story in your own words.	Write a new ending for the story.
Evaluating	Is this the character? (Show picture of wrong item.)	Is the character good or bad? (Idea is to have students make a choice.)	How is the character different from Y?	Would you do what the character did? Why or why not?	Did the character make a good decision? Why or why not?

continued

	Level 1 (non-verbal response to high-frequency, single-word responses)	Level 2 (two-word response to short phrases with prompts)	Level 3 (simple sentences with some errors)	Level 4 (multiple sentences with some variation in structure)	Level 5 (varied-length responses resembling work of proficient students)
Analyzing	Find the character in the group.	Y/N: Is this a part of the character?	Describe the character.	What is the main idea?	How would the story change if the character did this?
Applying	Draw the character.	Do you have the character at your house?	Why do you like the character?	What do you think the character should do?	How are you like the character?
Understanding	Circle the character. (Give two visual options.)	What is the character?	What did the character do?	Why did the character do that?	What are the reasons that the character did that?
Remembering	Point to the character. (Provide picture prompts.)	Y/N: Is this the character?	Where is the character?	What does the character do?	Tell me everything you know about the character.

Adjusting Texts to Support Differentiation by Linguistic Complexity

For adaptable templates, see the *Access for Success* website.

There are two types of texts to consider for differentiation by linguistic complexity: (1) texts that students listen to or read to gain information about a topic and (2) texts that students work with (e.g., worksheets, activity guides) to convey their understanding of a topic. Both require some time on the part of the teacher to create or adapt, but once you gain experience with a few templates, the investment in time should lessen.

DLC for Spoken/Written Texts for Gathering Information

Ideally, there would be a variety of language levels reflected in the texts (audio, visual, or print) that students use in class to learn about a particular topic or concept; however, it is not often feasible (or possible) to locate such texts, let alone create them. Thus, the focus of DLC for a premade text (by the teacher or others) is how to streamline the text to make it more accessible to a student's language level; these streamlines relate to several ULAs.

Figure 9.4 explores how DLC can be used when working with premade texts, as DLC looks different according to the text type and language skills of the student. For DLC to be evident, all three types of language learners would have access to their particular path when working with a text; if one path is made available to the group of students with those particular language skills, that's an example of using Action 1.3 *Adjusting the complexity of oral and/or written language*, making it an accommodation. In general, DLC of premade texts is focused on injecting other modes of language expression into the presentation of text to support learners' language development.

Figure 9.4: Differentiation by Linguistic Complexity and Premade Texts

	Audio-Only Texts	Print Texts
For students with minimal skills in the target language	Identify one or two key words. Before playing audio, work with students on pronunciation and meaning of words (e.g., with pictures). Students listen for recognition of terms. Stop text frequently to confirm instances of terms.	Identify one or two key words. Highlight or circle all instances of key word(s) in text in student's copy. Emphasize key word(s) in any read-aloud of text.
For students with some skills in the target language	The text is divided into several sections, and in advance of listening, students are presented with the meaning or message of each section. Students listen to the text in chunks, possibly confirming key terms and phrases for meaning.	Underline several key phrases or sentences that convey the main idea.
For students with extensive skills in the target language	Students are given the meaning of the text in advance; when listening, without pause, they focus on words and phrases that support the main idea.	Underline the key phrases and sentences that convey main idea and supporting detail.

DLC for Student Activity Guides and Worksheets

If DLC is embedded, typically it means that students choose the amount of language they need to navigate and produce to build and convey their understanding. Figure 9.5 is an example of worksheets designed for an early English language classroom:

Figure 9.5: Activity Sheets Differentiated by Linguistic Complexity

Option A

Building Materials

Circle the correct answers.

The tower/lighthouse is made of concrete/glass.

The house/doghouse is made of wood/brick.

The house/doghouse is made of brick/glass.

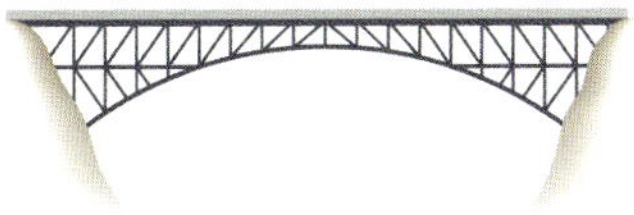

The lighthouse/bridge is made of metal/brick.

Option B

Building Materials

Structures	Materials
house	concrete
doghouse	wood
lighthouse	brick
bridge	metal
tower	glass

Add the missing words.

The ______________ is made of ______________.

The ______________ is made of ______________.

The ______________ is made of ______________.

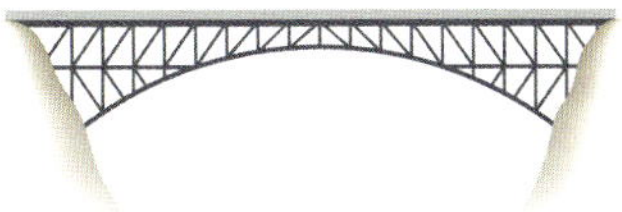

The ______________ is made of ______________.

As you can see, the version on the left requires students to circle the correct term, while the option on the right expects students to use a word bank to complete the sentences. Option A is considered to have a lower level of linguistic complexity since the students simply read and circle the relevant language. Option B expects students to produce language (though with the help of a word bank). There is a lot more language (and thinking) for the student to manage, which therefore makes option B the most complex of the two. If you have a student in the class who has even more basic proficiency than what could support option A, you could consider having the student match the term for the type of building to the corresponding image.

Differentiated Activities to Support Understanding, Production, Attention, and Vocabulary

For language learners, and in a setting where you are trying to facilitate language development and possibly content knowledge, the ideas presented here show how integrating many familiar learning tools (e.g., graphic organizers and concept maps) into task options creates meaningful differentiated activities in support of the four key areas of learning that are of importance to language learners—understanding, production, attention, and vocabulary. It could be the case that on Monday a teacher would use a concept map to help the students navigate the lesson, but on Tuesday would feature a note-taking outline. While the variety is something to appreciate, for a class with varying levels of language proficiency, it may not serve to improve student access to the learning. It would be more efficient—from a learning standpoint—to integrate the concept map and the outline as options for the students each day. Because each learning tool has its own language demands and required learning behaviours, offering both tools allows students to more readily align their skills with the task.

The activity suggestions that follow thus show various combinations of learning actions and tools that can support a range of language proficiencies in the classroom. These activity ideas also show how the different strands of focus—understanding, production, attention, and vocabulary—can work with each other to further support student learning.

IDEA NO. 1 What Does That Mean?

SUPPORTED TYPES OF DIFFERENTIATION:

Linguistic Complexity

Process

Product

PRIMARY SUPPORT FOCUS:

Understanding

Production

Attention

▶ Vocabulary

Activity Goal

- To help students define concepts

Activity Materials

- Bilingual and monolingual dictionaries
- Paper, markers

Guidelines for Differentiating

1. Select 10 to 12 terms that students will be using to explore a text or complete an activity.
2. As part of a pre-reading or pre-exploration exercise, students prepare a dictionary of the terms. This dictionary can be presented as a part of the preparation and could also serve as an assessment of background knowledge.

It is important to keep in mind that at this point students in the lower levels of proficiency cannot be expected to learn all of the terms. They should be expected to work only with the terms they have been assigned. Students who are at the more intermediate levels can be expected to work with the terms assigned to the students with lower proficiency and their terms. They should also be at least exposed to the terms assigned to the most proficient students.

Sample Paths for Students

Path A: *Captioned Images*	**Path B:** *Illustrated Concept Map*	**Path C:** *Extended Entry*
Students are provided with a term. Perhaps accessing a bilingual dictionary or other first language support, students create an image or graphic that conveys the meaning of the term. The image is captioned with the term.	Students are provided with a selected term, and then using the format of an illustrated concept map, they list and illustrate other terms that are associated with the targeted term. For example, if the term is *arachnid*, the students can create concept maps featuring *spider*, *web*, and *black*, illustrating those terms as well.	Students are provided with the selected term, and to accompany an illustration or graphic they create, they write two or three sentences to explain the term in their own words. They can consult dictionaries or other resources to support the activity.

Possible Grouping Strategy for Students

Current language production level (Level 1 and Level 2 students complete Path A; Level 3+ students complete Path B; most proficient students complete Path C.)

IDEA NO. 2 Listening for Your Word

SUPPORTED TYPES OF DIFFERENTIATION:

Linguistic Complexity

Process

PRIMARY SUPPORT FOCUS:

Understanding

Production

Attention

▶ Vocabulary

Activity Goal

- To promote word recognition in spoken language

Activity Material

- An audio or video clip

Guidelines for Differentiating

1. This activity can work with any text that is presented to students aurally or even through something like a video.
2. This activity should be used after students have listened to or viewed the text a few times to enable it to be used as a comprehension check.
3. Students can be asked to raise their hands when they hear their terms, or they can be asked to write down the terms and concepts as they are presented.

Sample Task Directions for Students

Path A: *The Key Word*	**Path B:** *Detail Words*	**Path C:** *Specialist Words*
Student listens for highest-frequency word or key word that is the central concept of the text. For example, if a text is about types of rocks, the student would listen for the word *rock*.	Student listens for words that are closely associated with the key word, but also add some detail. Continuing the example about types of rocks, the student would listen for *igneous*, *sedimentary*, and *metamorphic* or adjectives that may be used in the text to describe the rocks (e.g., *hard*, *sharp*, *heavy*).	Student listens for words in the text that are the most technical or academic and prepares to explain their meaning as presented in the text. Continuing the example about types of rocks, the student would listen for *igneous*, *sedimentary*, and *metamorphic* and be expected to explain how the text defines and depicts those terms.

Possible Grouping Strategy for Students

Current language production level (Level 1 and Level 2 students complete Path A; Level 3 and Level 4 students complete Path B; Level 5 and most proficient students complete Path C.)

IDEA NO. 3 Deconstructing the Text

SUPPORTED TYPES OF DIFFERENTIATION:

Linguistic Complexity

Process

Product

PRIMARY SUPPORT FOCUS:

▶ Understanding

Production

Attention

Vocabulary

Activity Goal

- To help students identify key ideas and details from a text

Activity Materials

- Question/statement prompts about the text
- Graphic organizers
- Recording devices

Guidelines for Differentiating

1. Following a presentation or review of a text, students complete a task that allows them to convey their current understanding of the ideas presented in the text.
2. Any combination of summarizing types of activities work; the options offered here play up the differences in format as a way of varying the support for understanding.

Sample Task Directions for Students

Path A: *A Conversation or a Monologue*	**Path B:** *Written Responses to Questions*	**Path C:** *A Form Poem*
Using a recording device, a student individually reports his/her understanding of the text, perhaps a string of key words recalled or a detailed summary. Or, with a partner, students could talk about the ideas presented in the reading. Questions or sentence prompts could be provided to guide the discussion.	Individually or in pairs, students respond to direct questions about the content. The questions can be closed-response (one right answer) or open-ended. There can be a mix of prepared questions, and depending on student language skills, certain mixes would be distributed.	Form poems are a type of writing in which students write a description of an object in the shape of that object. Many times, the poem is not very poetic, but it is an opportunity for students to use really descriptive language and to write in a less traditional way.

Possible Grouping Strategy for Students

Because the type of output for this activity is somewhat dependent on the question prompts students are given, students can select the output option they like the best first, and then they can be provided with question supports aligned to their proficiency.

IDEA NO. 4 This Is How You Do It

SUPPORTED TYPES OF DIFFERENTIATION:

Linguistic Complexity

Process

Product

PRIMARY SUPPORT FOCUS:

▶ Understanding

Production

Attention

Vocabulary

Activity Goal

- To help students develop familiarity or skill with executing a particular process or procedure

Activity Materials

- Directions for the process, cut into individual steps
- Devices that students can use to film

Guidelines for Differentiating

1. Following a presentation or review of a process or procedure, students complete a task that allows them to convey their understanding of that process or procedure.
2. Any combination of summarizing types of activities work; the options offered here play up the differences in format as a way of varying the support for understanding.

Sample Task Directions for Students

Path A: *Out of Order*	**Path B:** *Paired Protocol*	**Path C:** *Video Replay*
Students are provided with the steps for the process, cut into individual strips. Students put the strips in the correct order, without consulting the original text. To add challenge, a step could be missing, and the students would need to provide that step at the end.	Two students are each provided with half of the steps of the process (on those strips). Working only through conversation, they need to sequence the process using the provided strips.	Students create a short film showing how to do the process/procedure. They narrate their actions as they are working.

Possible Grouping Strategy for Students

Because the type of output for this activity is somewhat dependent on the question prompts students are given, students can select the output option they like the best first, and then they can be provided with question supports aligned to their proficiency.

IDEA NO. 5 Picture Envelopes

SUPPORTED TYPES OF DIFFERENTIATION:

Linguistic Complexity

PRIMARY SUPPORT FOCUS:

Understanding

▶ Production

Attention

Vocabulary

Activity Goal

- To give students practice building sentences or expressions with certain terms

Activity Materials

- Picture cards related to featured concepts (e.g., sports & activities, types of flowers), possibly several sets
- Direction slips with sentence frames or sentence starters that can be added into envelopes or glued on their fronts.

Guidelines for Differentiating

1. Select 12 to 20 terms or concepts that students have been already working with as part of a learning segment.
2. Locate images that represent those terms and concepts, and prepare picture cards accordingly. Sort the images into three groups, considering the cognate relationships between the target language and home language (if applicable), or at least the frequency of the terms as they have been used in class. The number of cards in each group can vary, assuming that students with lower proficiency will be working with the most frequent words or cognates, but can also have fewer cards to work with.
3. Prepare sentence frames or sentence starters that students can use to build sentences using a selected image.
4. Prepare several envelopes with the picture groups and frames. Consider marking the envelopes with a different symbol for each path, to allow for smoother management of the activity.

Keep in mind that students in the lower levels of proficiency cannot yet be expected to learn all of the terms. They should be expected to work only with the images and concepts they have been assigned.

Sample Paths for Students		
Path A Student envelopes contain images of words that have a strong cognate relationship to first language or high frequency; sentence frames and starters with this envelope are simple. In relation to other envelopes, there may also be fewer images. Students will select an image from the envelope, and using the provided prompt, create a statement or a question that incorporates that image.	**Path B** Student envelopes contain images of words that mix cognate and high-frequency words with less common or less obvious terms. The sentence frames and starters with this envelope are more complex. There may be more images in the envelope than for Path A. Students will select an image from the envelope and, using the provided prompt, create a statement or a question that incorporates that image.	**Path C** Student envelopes contain images of words that are less common or represent new ways to discuss targeted concepts. The sentence frames and starters with this envelope are more complex. There may be more images in the envelope than for Path A. Students will select an image from the envelope and, using the provided prompt, create a statement or a question that incorporates that image.

Possible Grouping Strategy for Students

Path A can be for pairs of students with Level 1 or Level 2 proficiency.

Path B is recommended for pairs of students with Level 3 or Level 4 proficiency.

Path C is recommended for students who are Level 5 and beyond.

IDEA NO. 6 QR Talking Circuit

SUPPORTED TYPES OF DIFFERENTIATION:

Linguistic Complexity

Content

PRIMARY SUPPORT FOCUS:

Understanding

▶ Production

Attention

Vocabulary

Activity Goals

- To help students talk about ideas and respond to questions about a task. This activity structure allows for students to talk about a topic consistent with their proficiency level.

Activity Materials

- Software for creating QR codes and a site for hosting the questions students will discuss (The QR code quiz at the classtools.net site will create the codes and host the questions.)
- Mobile devices for reading QR codes
- Questions about a topic or concept, written at various levels of linguistic complexity

Guidelines for Differentiating

1. Prepare a set of questions for reviewing a topic or a text with which students are already familiar.
2. Using QR code software, load the questions to generate QR codes.
3. Print the QR codes for each path option on different-coloured paper. Assign the students the coloured path that best matches their proficiency needs.
4. Post QR codes around the room and allow student pairs or trios to navigate through the path using the mobile devices. (*The path of questions does not need to be sequential, so students can start anywhere on the path to allow for easier management of student movement for the whole class.*)
5. As students move through the classroom, you can use an observation checklist to do any sort of assessment of their speaking.

This activity can also be adapted to allow students to complete the work individually, and to write their responses rather than speak.

Sample Paths for Students		
Path A Students working with Level 1 and Level 2 questions (They may have fewer questions to answer.)	**Path B** Students working with Level 3 and Level 4 questions	**Path C** Students working with Level 4 and Level 5 questions (Level 4 students can be split between this path and Path B.)

Possible Grouping Strategy for Students

Language skills/question type

It is also possible to have each path focus on a different group of questions. For example, students on Path A could work with one theme or concept, students on Path B, another theme or concept, and so forth.

IDEA NO. 7 WebQuest

SUPPORTED TYPES OF DIFFERENTIATION:

Process

Content

PRIMARY SUPPORT FOCUS:

Understanding

Production

► Attention

Vocabulary

Activity Goal

- To explore a concept in greater depth to allow for application, analysis, evaluation, or synthesis of key ideas

Activity Material

- A WebQuest (WQ) with multiple pages/tangents to allow for an in-depth inquiry into a topic. It can be a WQ you have made, or a WQ you have located.

Guidelines for Differentiating

1. Locate or develop a WQ on topic. The WQ should offer a mix of texts for students to explore, such as print articles, videos, visuals, and podcasts.
2. Determine how the texts work with each other and allow for certain ideas to be explored together. Group the texts accordingly, and determine an appropriate summarizing task for the WQ, if one is not already provided.

Sample Paths for Students

Path A	Path B	Path C
Student watches video A online. Student reads article A online. Student responds to questions that address content in both the video and the article. Student completes an online task (like creating a presentation) that involves summarizing key points.	Student reviews video A and video B online and completes a comparison of the ideas from each video. From a list of possible resources, student selects a third text to review about the topic; the student can choose an article, another video, or a podcast. Student then completes an online task (like creating a presentation) that involves summarizing key points.	Student reviews video A and video B and completes a comparison of the ideas from each video in the form of a presentation that summarizes the key points.

For more information about WebQuests, including how to create one, see the *Access for Success* website.

Possible Grouping Strategy for Students

Student readiness, based on text type

If the summary tasks for the WQ vary, that could also be a way to differentiate through student interest in the topic.

IDEA NO. 8 Jigsaw Exploration

Activity Goals

- To identify details within a text
- To synthesize information across a text or a series of texts
- To exchange information with peers

Activity Materials

- A group of texts on the same topic, offering different information and ideas and reflecting different reading levels
- A graphic organizer or some sort of table where students can record information from their text and from those read by their peers

Guidelines for Differentiating

How differentiation is applied in this activity will depend on the types of texts selected, as well as the overall topic.

1. Review the texts and generate a list of questions that are answered within and across texts. Not all questions need to be answerable across every text, but it is helpful to have most questions overlap across texts. This ensures that the students will have to talk to one another to complete the graphic organizer.
2. Create groups the size of the number of texts available. For example, five texts means a group of five, which is about the largest effective size. There can be some deliberation in the group configurations as well as which texts are assigned to which students. Text topics and language complexity can inform the differentiation here.
3. Allow students time to explore the texts individually and complete their section of the organizer; then, group students to share the information from their sections.
4. As is recommended, provide a follow-up activity that will allow students to use the collectively gained information in a new way.

Note: This activity can also work for dividing up a single text among a group of students.

Possible Grouping Strategy for Students

Linguistic complexity

Content

SUPPORTED TYPES OF DIFFERENTIATION:

Content

PRIMARY SUPPORT FOCUS:

Understanding

Production

▶ Attention

Vocabulary

For a sample organizer that can be used with the Jigsaw Exploration, see the *Access for Success* website.

Universal Language Actions in Support of Differentiation

This section offers ideas on how to deploy some of the ULAs in a differentiated way. These ideas are tied to the Action in Action experiences shared in Chapters 5 to 8, the chapters on ULAs for understanding, production, attention, and vocabulary. The suggestions show how the support offered by the ULA can be extended into different directions to create a differentiated learning opportunity.

UNDERSTANDING		
Universal Language Action	**Action in Action Synopsis**	**How to Use Differentiation to Maximize the ULA**
1.1 *Using gestures, facial expressions, images, pictures, drawings, objects, and manipulation materials*	K. Hennessey: Creating a support to provide students with images will help them understand the meaning of each paragraph. (p. 97)	Give students options for how the images are accessed and used in the class: 1. Group A is provided the visual support, but must add key words to each section of the image as or after they read. 2. Group B is expected to draw an image conveying their understanding as or after they read. 3. Group C is expected to match provided images to the paragraphs as or after they read.
1.4 *Assessing the extent of prior knowledge and filling in any major gaps*	T. Gauvin: Students are helped to understand features of urban life in advance of a unit on sustainability. (p. 103)	Set up a series of learning centres. (*Note:* If you're working with middle and high-school students, call them *stations* and put them in different corners of the room.) At the centres, students complete short tasks focused on urban life: 1. Describing what they see in the live feed of a street-view camera 2. Watching a short video about transportation in an urban setting 3. Comparing maps of a few different urban areas to see common features in cities 4. Participating in a Skype chat with members of a class in an urban setting Students could either visit one or several stations, depending on their background knowledge.

continued

1.5 *Providing wait time when presenting new information, after asking a question, or before inviting learners to start a task*	P. Manson: The teacher gives students time to process a question before calling on students to respond. (p. 105)	Consider providing different questions to different students. For students who may need more time to process the question and develop a response, give more direct, close-ended questions, but students who work with language more quickly or have more proficiency may be able to tackle open-ended questions in the same time. The questions could be given to students on separate cards.
1.7 *Reusing and recycling pedagogical materials*	M. Carmel: Various tools and activities can be completed by students about the topic (in this case, the zoo). (p. 112)	Set up a 3 x 3 table (a tic-tac-toe board), and write an activity option in each cell. Give the boards to students, and guide them to complete a row, column, or diagonal of activities to explore the content.

PRODUCTION		
Universal Language Action	**Action in Action Synopsis**	**How to Use Differentiation to Maximize the ULA**
2.2 *Using graphic organizers to support oral and written production*	S. Arsenault: Students use graphic organizers to help structure small-group discussions. (pp. 123–124)	Pre-select a group of organizers focused on different ways to structure content. Group students based on a language skill they need to develop. For example, one group could use an organizer focused on sequencing, while another group may work with main ideas and supporting details.
2.3 *Creating and displaying linguistic supports around the classroom*	M. Dunbar: Students exchange certain words for others, so as to have more varied language in their output. Visual references help with the exchanges. (p. 126)	At the start of a class, present students with a group of terms relevant to the day's lesson. Colour-code the terms according to complexity or familiarity to the students, and post them in a space where all can see. As students arrive in class, give them a chip or card that represents the colour of the terms they need to follow. As they work through the class, those terms will need to be featured in their responses.
2.5 *Using pedagogical and language production routines*	A. Johnson: Students talk about their weekend every Monday, and student production is supported with different thinking tools. (p. 130)	Create a tic-tac-toe or similar choice board from which students can pick other topics. Make several different choice boards, so that the boards can be rotated among students and add to variety in their discussions. One way to structure this is to include questions in each cell that the students need to answer about their weekends; each cell would have questions varying in complexity. The complexity would also vary across the cards.

ATTENTION		
Universal Language Action	**Action in Action Synopsis**	**How to Use Differentiation to Maximize the ULA**
3.1 *Providing specific listening and reading intentions*	S. Jenkins: Students are provided with purposes and intentions for reading to help focus attention. (p. 141)	Develop a bank of reading intentions and use them to personalize students' approach to a text. Write reading intentions on index cards or make a table in a Word document with slips of various reading intentions. Keep them in an envelope or cup, and distribute them to students in advance of reading a text.
3.3 *Incorporating discourse markers to oral and written texts*	K. Kertson: The teacher uses discourse markers while speaking in class. (p. 147)	Use the activity structure shared in this chapter, "Listening for your word," to provide scaffolded and structured attention to the various discourse markers used in class.
3.4 *Providing explicit cues to refocus learners' attention*	D. Crawford: Slides are embedded into presentations to refocus or cue learner attention to specific content. (p. 149)	At the start of a lesson, group students into "focus areas" for the lesson. These students will listen or read for specific details and ideas over the course of the lesson and will be positioned as the experts for that area. At different points of the lesson, use the slides to cue students in the various groups to their attention areas; later, the students can be asked specific questions about this part of the content.
3.7 *Summarizing key points of lessons, activities, and reading passages*	B. Kane: A poster and sticky notes are used to track ideas shared over the course of a lesson. (p. 155)	Generate a list of possible ways for students to summarize content (e.g., quick sketch, a tweet, a sentence). At various points in the lesson where a summary could be helpful, have students use one of two options of summary strategies you give; then, invite students to share some of their ideas.

VOCABULARY		
Universal Language Action	**Action in Action Synopsis**	**How to Use Differentiation to Maximize the ULA**
4.1 *Identifying and presenting required language at the outset of a lesson or activity*	M. Paulin: A word wall focused on weather terms can support students' daily conversations about the weather. (p. 162)	Assign values to the terms. For example, *sunny* could be worth a nickle, while *It appears to me* could be worth a dime. Distribute fake coins to the students, paying attention to students who may need support with certain language or who need to expand their phrasing. They must use terms corresponding to the values they have been given in any contributions they make to the discussion.

continued

4.4 *Using role-play and games to present or reinforce new vocabulary*	J. Dickson: A memory game about where students are positioned in relation to each other serves to promote vocabulary. (p. 171)	In advance, prepare index cards with several different question types. Some cards have questions about the positions and space relationships, while others have questions about clothing, appearance, or something else that can be observed in the group of students. Use different cards with different students to alter the focus to something that either needs further reinforcement or adds complexity.
4.5 *Explaining vocabulary using examples, synonyms, antonyms, cognates, and teacher/learner definitions*	E. Khan: Student groups create their own definitions based on resources and share their definitions with the class. (p. 174)	Be strategic as to how students are grouped and which terms are given to which groups to generate the definitions. This can allow for linguistic complexity and some process differentiation.

Assessment and Differentiation

Although we have a whole chapter focused on the role of assessment in inclusive language education (Chapter 10), we decided that the intersection of assessment and differentiation should be included here because of concerns we have regularly encountered in our work with teachers.

Assessment to Create Student Groupings

As mentioned previously, student grouping means something different in the differentiated classroom than it means elsewhere. In the differentiated classroom it does *not* mean that the students are expected to work in groups to complete differentiated activities. It simply refers to the organization of students into their respective learning paths. There are two general ways to use assessment to inform such student grouping.

The first way to use assessment to inform student grouping is student self-assessment. Students can be asked to think about the task options that have been presented and select the option that interests them the most or that they believe addresses their learning needs or readiness needs the best. This approach can result in students sometimes selecting a path that is not the best fit for their work in relation to the learning goal. Depending on the class or the student, it may be useful to establish a teacher reset option which would be exercised when you recognize a detrimental mismatch between the activity and the student. However, if the student wants to persist with an activity, that should be respected. This approach promotes learner autonomy.

For more information on grouping students and the use of assessment tools in differentiated instruction, see pages 221 to 223 in Chapter 10.

The second way to use assessment to inform student grouping is teacher controlled and requires you to use student performance on previous tasks or quick diagnostic assessments to guide students to a particular path. For example, in a lesson where the students are going to learn more about the *Titanic* and its sinking off the Newfoundland coast, the lesson begins with a six-question warm-up, designed to help determine what the students already know about the *Titanic*. After a few minutes, the answers are revealed, students score their responses, and then based on the results they are informed of the path to take in the lesson. Here's one way to present the directions to the students after they do the pre-assessment.

If you got 0, 1, or 2 questions correct, today you will	If you got 3 or 4 questions correct, today you will	If you got 5 or 6 questions correct, today you will
1. Watch the video about the *Titanic* and its sinking. 2. While watching the video, complete a note-taking guide on yellow paper. I will ask questions about the video as we watch. 3. After the video, you have the choice to learn more about one of two topics: • the route of the *Titanic* across the Atlantic (using maps) • what the ship looked like (using pictures of the ship)	1. Watch the video about the *Titanic* and its sinking. 2. While watching the video, complete a note-taking guide on blue paper. I will ask questions about the video as we watch. 3. After the video, you have the choice to learn more about one of two topics: • the passengers (using texts that talk about who they were) • the rescue operation (using stories from people who helped the survivors)	1. Watch the video about the *Titanic* and its sinking. 2. Take notes about what is in the video on your own paper. I will ask questions about the video as we watch. 3. After the video ends, spend a few minutes adding in details (in a different colour of pen) of what else you know about the *Titanic*. 4. Next, decide on a topic you want to learn more about in relation to the *Titanic*. Review your notes and identify three areas where you think you could learn more. Possible topics include the food on the ship; the sister ships of the *Titanic*—the *Olympic* and the *Britannic*; how historians determine if an item is actually from the *Titanic*; and the lives of the survivors. Share your choice with me, and I will give you the tools for your exploration.

When thinking about inclusive environments, our goal is to facilitate learning opportunities that are fair, which means that students get access to what they need. This means that students are not supported *equally*, but rather, *equitably*.

Students may be nervous about moving around to pick up materials aligned with a particular path because they are worried about how their peers will respond. To allay such concerns, be sure to consistently convey the message that differentiation is used to support everyone and everyone's differences should be respected. It is also worth noting that, in a good differentiated learning experience, the students who need the most help to do an activity will end up changing depending on the demands and experiences in the class. The only exception to this may be allophone newcomers to Canada who have limited cultural and language proficiency.

Assessing and Evaluating Student Work from Differentiated Activities

Let us address the biggest concern we most often hear from teachers: that they believe they need as many scoring tools as there are task options within the learning activity. **To assess a differentiated learning experience, you do *not* need to have as many scoring tools as there are task options. In fact, you can often use the *same* scoring tool for *all* of the tasks.** Why? Well, simply stated, assessment or evaluation is focused on the learning goal. When you are focusing on the learning goal—and recognize that nearly all differentiated learning experiences are simply providing divergent paths to the same learning—it is possible to use the same assessment tool to gauge student work. If there are some differences across the task options within an activity, there can be slight variations in the tool, but really, it comes down to good assessment design. In this section, we focus on building good rubrics, which are a go-to assessment and scoring tool for differentiated activities (as well as for other learning activities).

Wiggins and McTighe (2005), the proponents of backward design and strong links between learning objectives and student assessment, point out that rubrics are most efficient and most effective when the criteria are limited, specific, and clearly stated. Assessment and scoring tools that are excessively detailed become cumbersome for the teacher to use and are often overwhelming for the student. We need our assessment tools to make good, informed, but quick decisions, and any rubrics we use to make those decisions should be efficiently organized and offer clear signposts about levels of student success in relation to the goal. Scoring tools should have no more than five criteria to manage.

W. James Popham (2016) has regularly tackled the issue of wording in rubrics, pointing out that clarity in how the criteria are described is at the heart of good assessment. According to Popham, there are three general approaches to writing a rubric description: (1) making it general in such a way as to allow for as many different interpretations as possible, (2) making it task specific, so that students can see the exact steps they need to do to complete the task to a certain level, and (3) making it skill specific, to enable students to focus on the learning goal, not the activity, as the central part of the learning experience. This latter type of focus allows teachers to construct rubrics that work effectively with differentiated activities and lessons.

Combining these two schools of advice, we have become experienced in preparing scoring tools to assess the different tasks. Over the next few pages, we will review those tips in relation to rubrics (one of the go-to scoring tools of the criterion-referenced assessment toolkit) and offer examples of these tools that can be used in support of differentiated learning activities. We will also explore how these tips can be applied to other types of scoring tools, such as scoring guides and observation checklists.

Rubrics for Differentiated Activities

There are three key ideas to keep in mind about building rubrics for assessment purposes in a differentiated classroom:

1. Rubrics are a part of criterion-referenced assessment. They allow student performance to be compared to stated criteria. They do not technically allow teachers to compare students to each other like a multiple-choice test would, for example.
2. Rubrics require a particular set-up if you want to use them to record a mark that students can understand.
3. Rubrics, as assessment tools, are most effective when being used at the end of a learning experience to determine a student's achievement in relation to standards. They are not effective tools, necessarily, for formative assessment (Wiliam & Leahy, 2015).

Making a Good Rubric

To build a good rubric, you begin by thinking about four dimensions: (1) the learning goal, (2) what the students do within the learning activity, (3) the skills that are involved in the activity, and (4) how the activity will be differentiated. Here is a sample:

Learning Goals	What do the students do?	What skills are involved in this activity?	How is this task differentiated?
• To analyze a text in order to locate points of support and disagreement with a particular position • To orally and visually present a concise overview of the analyzed text	The students will read or listen to their text. They prepare a response to a series of questions or prompts about the text as a PowerPoint. They create a recording delivering their PowerPoint.	• Following directions (because the activity requires specific components in the analysis) • Reading for meaning (understanding the content) • Identifying the relevant details • Preparing an organized presentation • Delivering the presentation • Using academic language	Students can select the text they want to analyze, which allows for differentiation of content and most likely linguistic complexity.

Framed another way, the skills required to complete a learning activity are the success criteria of the task. For more details about the role of success criteria in the classroom, see Chapter 4, page 68, and Chapter 10, page 211.

Next, look at the skills and determine how they could possibly be grouped or combined to allow for criteria headings in the rubric. Remember that there should be no more than five criteria. The criteria can look exactly like the skills, or they can be worded in a slightly different way. Possible criteria for the above skill set include the following:

- completeness of the submission (Are all prompts addressed?)
- demonstrated understanding of content
- visual layout and organization of PowerPoint
- effectiveness of communication (How easily was the message understood?)
- mechanics of language used to convey ideas

When creating a rubric, keep in mind the need to use criteria that aligns with your district's expectations. For example, some districts may want assessment rubrics to feature criteria that are directly tied to the curriculum and its wording.

Then, it is important to revisit the type of differentiation being used in the activity and think about its influence on the task. For the example we are using here, the students choose a text to respond to the first learning goal: the text analysis. So text content will vary, and it could be that the format of the texts will vary as well (audio, print, video). Both the content and the format of the text could influence how well the student does the task. If the concept or the language is hard to follow in the selected text and format, it will show in the final product, when the student is presenting the details about the text. That sort of difference is not necessarily something that will influence the assessment, but it would be something to keep in mind about future activities that use this sort of format. The student may need to be directed to a different text type to maximize his or her skill with the analysis.

The other learning goal for this activity is to have students concisely present oral and visual information. The products the student creates—the PowerPoint and filmed presentation—are not differentiated components. If the students present in real time, rather than on film, the goal is not affected. However, if the products created are changed in such a way that the student cannot meet the learning goals as they were identified, then a different activity has been created altogether, and that would require a new rubric.

Finally, it is time to start building the rubric by thinking about the actual descriptions in the rubric cells. Here's where the advice from Popham (2016) to be skill focused comes into play; you need to think about what the skill looks like in action. If you are familiar with the idea of success criteria, this is where you offer elaborations of the success criteria: where you explain what the students do with the skill to achieve a particular level. Figure 9.6 explains how to build the rubric in a broader way, while also thinking about how to assign point values to particular levels, if you are going for a mark.

Four-level rubrics tend to allow for the right amount of detail for shaping degrees of student success. Three-level rubrics make it difficult to separate the really strong performers from the solid performers, for example. Five-level rubrics also tend to create too many details to manage to identify the different levels.

Figure 9.6: Building a Four-Level Rubric

	Criterion 1	Criterion 2	Criterion 3	Criterion 4
Level 4	This level of success or mastery is likely to be attained by students who need challenge and prefer to go above and beyond target expectations. Here, we often describe how Level 4 is distinguished from Level 3, usually by beginning with "Everything from Level 3 plus," or if Level 3 allows for a few errors in some areas, Level 4 is for the near-perfect submission. In creating a rubric, this is the third level we write.			
Level 3	This is the *targeted* level of mastery or success with the criteria. Be specific about all of the components that are evidence of success (framed as Can-Do statements). This level is the first we write, since it is the target.			
Level 2	Level 2 typically describes the level of mastery or success as about halfway there in that the student has gotten the good general skills down, but there are various details or components where the student is either incorrect or the work is incomplete. This is the last level we write.			
Level 1	Level 1 typically tries to give the student a starting point for the most basic evidence of progress with the targeted criteria. It can allow for many errors and problems, but works to acknowledge that the student is starting somewhere. This level is the second we write, since it is the baseline expectation.			

The rubric in Figure 9.7 is designed for older learners. For a rubric for younger learners, see the *Access for Success* website.

At this point, you may be interested to see what this looks like in practice. Let's take a look at Figure 9.7 which offers a rubric that could be used in support of the aforementioned activity where students are analyzing a text.

General tip for criterion-based assessment tools: Be careful not to let student scores straddle levels. If the student satisfied the criteria for Level 3 only partially, for example, the student should be scored at a 2, even if the student work does not entirely resemble the description of what is in the Level 2 box. In these situations, particularly if the rubric is being used to assign a mark as well as assess, be sure to explain the scoring to the student.

Applying These Ideas to Other Criterion-Referenced Assessment Tools

For examples of scoring tools, see the *Access for Success* website.

No matter the criterion-referenced assessment tool (e.g., observation checklist, scoring guide, checklist), the same rules and processes we outlined for creating rubrics for differentiated activities apply here. The major variation tends to occur when figuring out the scale you are going to use to judge the students' work against the criteria. Not all scales need to be a number value, as in the rubric. Figure 9.8 offers some ideas.

Figure 9.7: Rubric for a Text Analysis

Level	Coverage of Required Components	Organization of the PPT	Demonstrated Understanding/ Mastery of the Content	Delivery of the PPT
4	• At least one more detail beyond the elements has been added to enhance the presentation.	• In addition to Level 3 components, animations, interesting layout, or other features are added to the presentation to add visual intrigue.	• Student conveys a very strong grasp of the material, and is well-versed in all details.	• Student's use of tone, intonation, rhythm, and pacing creates a consistent and very engaging delivery.
3	• All required elements are present.	• Slides balance colour, font size, background, images, and layout and work consistently together to help convey an organized presentation.	• Student conveys a strong grasp of the material, but may not be well-versed in all details.	• Student consistently speaks clearly and smoothly; this can consider student use of rhythm, intonation, pacing, and some pauses.
2	• One required element is missing or is not completely addressed.	• Most of the slides balance colour, font size, background, images, and layout to help convey an organized presentation.	• Student conveys a general understanding of the material, but may have missed several important details.	• Student speaks clearly and smoothly most of the time; this can consider student use of rhythm, intonation, pacing, and some pauses.
1	• Multiple elements are missing or are not completely addressed.	• A few of the slides balance colour, font size, background, images, and layout to help convey an organized presentation.	• Student conveys a limited understanding of the material, evidenced by either omissions or errors.	• For only a small part of the presentation, student speaks clearly and smoothly; this can consider student use of rhythm, intonation, pacing, and some pauses.

Figure 9.8: Examples of Scoring Tools and Scales

Scoring Tool	When to Use	Options for Scales to Use with These Scoring Tools
Scoring guide or scale	• Students complete an activity where you want to look at their work on a scale in relation to criteria, but may not need a full rubric to gauge success.	• Number scale (1, 2, 3; 1, 2, 3, 4, 5), with the ability to mark between numbers • STC: Support-Target-Challenge (Indicate if students required **S**upport or **C**hallenge to navigate the task; students are on **T**arget if they complete the task as designed.) • Mark the box: Arrows denote if student is approaching, on, or beyond target with the task. ↗ Approaching ↑ Beyond →→ On Note: We suggest avoiding use of symbols such as check marks, +, and –, since they tend to be understood by students if they happen to see notes we are trying to keep private.
Observation checklist	• Observing student independent work • Observing student pairs during speaking activities • Observing student work in centres or learning stations	

Closing Thoughts

Differentiation is a powerful way to build on the strengths your learners are bringing to the classroom experience. It acknowledges and promotes the idea that every learner has the opportunity to reach a learning goal in a way that supports the individual's needs, interests, and overall readiness. Although building up a repertoire of differentiated activities and lessons may take time, it is well worth the energy: students appreciate opportunities aligned with their individuality.

As you consider ways to use differentiation to support inclusive language education, we offer some reflection questions to help you with those ponderings:

- In what ways are you already using differentiation in your classroom?
- Why do you think differentiation supports inclusive language teaching?
- Which of the presented practical ideas for differentiation in support of inclusive language teaching most closely aligns with what you are already doing in the classroom? How can you build on your practice using the ideas shared here?
- What does a more complex or less complex language system look like in your classroom? Are there standard directions or activities for which you can create variations and reuse them as needed?
- In the near future, what lessons are you teaching where it would be helpful to offer different paths to reach the learning goals? What could those paths look like, using resources and materials you already have?

> ACCESS POINT 4

Assessment and Decision Making in Support of Inclusive Language Education

This last access point for facilitating inclusive language education considers how we acquire, process, analyze, and draw conclusions about how to support our students. We are considering this process in two ways:

1. How to incorporate assessment into the classroom experience so as to know which Universal Language Actions are appropriate and when or how to differentiate a learning activity or a lesson to respond to particular learner needs
2. How to structure discussions across a school or community about ways to best support learners and the development of an inclusive classroom for language learners. These professional conversations could be related to
   - a student (or two, or three) who may be experiencing some difficulties

- students who may be doing well with class content, but are in need of additional supports
- students whose state of emotional and social well-being is having an influence on their learning such that teachers want to ensure that related needs are properly addressed within the classroom as much as reasonably possible

This process and these conversations require that you have good information—or dare we say, data—about your learners. We have found that acquiring good information is often about asking the right questions and analyzing that information, with as little bias as possible.

Being an inclusive educator means being a *strategic* collector and consumer of information about our students and accepting that we will always be making decisions with what could be called "incomplete knowledge." We can expect to do the best with the information we have at our disposal at that time, so long as we are confident about the value and merits of the information we have.

As discussed in other chapters of this book, developing proficiency in another language is a complicated experience. Individual differences among our students, the curriculum, and our own teaching personalities and approaches create a highly complicated matrix of factors to consider (and we know there are still others) when making instructional and programming decisions for students.

Sometimes, it can be hard to figure out which factor or factors should guide what we end up doing in the classroom to facilitate inclusion. Chapter 10 discusses the role of classroom assessments in helping us determine progress, areas of growth, and possible areas needing support. Assessment for the benefit of student learning and instructional decisions is a perpetual endeavour; hence, there are important considerations in the ways you construct students' assignments and then interpret their work to ensure that you are facilitating inclusive language education.

In Chapter 11, we look at the processes involved in taking the conversation about inclusive language education within and beyond the classroom. The teacher is still at the centre of this decision-making process, and we focus on the interplay between teaching techniques and actions and student needs. Further, we explore how to bring in other perspectives to support the students' needs, with some consideration of leadership and productive discussions about student needs. Bringing multiple perspectives together can be incredibly beneficial for figuring out paths forward, but the process is complicated if some of the stakeholders are not familiar with how learning a language shapes the overall learning experience.

For both Chapters 10 and 11, we believe strongly that the best decisions are made when working with the information we have in hand. We cannot make solid decisions if we are making conjectures to fill in what we don't actually know. This understanding is particularly relevant when you are working with students who have incomplete educational histories, limited experiences with the target language, or general difficulty with learning.

For a glossary of some of the terms used in this book, see the *Access for Success* website.

Further, the absence of information is *not* evidence or a justification to think that a deficit exists. It simply means we do not have this information. We may rely on our previous experiences as teachers, our own biases, and our knowledge of learners' first-language backgrounds to guide our decisions. No doubt, yes, our previous experiences and personal knowledge are important tools for problem solving in the classroom, but they do not form the complete picture. Only good data collection and information gathering can do this for us. And we need to be aware of that potential when we have the power to make a decision that will have a key influence on what happens on a student's educational journey.

CHAPTER 10

The Role and Place of Assessment in Inclusive Language Education

Even though this chapter is the next-to-last chapter in the book, assessment is not an afterthought in inclusive language education; in fact, it's central to using best practices. Throughout the chapters earlier in this book, principles and applications of assessment have been interwoven into many of the explorations, including how to get to know your learners (Chapter 3), how to help learners leverage metacognitive thinking in the classroom and develop their autonomy there (Chapter 4), and, of course, how to apply all of those Universal Language Actions (ULAs) and differentiation ideas across Chapters 5 to 9.

This chapter considers how assessment practices within the classroom can be used to support inclusive language teaching. We will be revisiting some themes and suggestions from earlier access points to show how these are relevant to good assessment before, during, and after instruction, so be prepared for lots of margin notes directing you back to certain areas of the book.

This chapter highlights key understandings of assessment in inclusive second language education, including the following:

- knowing our students
- formative and summative assessments
- the role of teacher questioning
- oral corrective feedback
- activity goals—What are we really asking learners to do?
- assessing in the differentiated classroom
- technology and assessment in the L2 classroom

We close out the chapter by providing assessment ideas for the second language classroom.

Key L2 Assessment Principle: Knowing Our Students

As we shared in Access Point 2, knowing our students beyond their personalities, interests, and class performance is critical to meaningful language education. To the extent possible, having a sense of students' educational histories, language experiences, and personal cultural contexts will help ensure that your assessments of their work—whether for formative or summative reasons—are relative to their backgrounds.

Although there is value in judging a student's progress or mastery in relation to a curricular standard or other larger learning goal, there also needs to be recognition of how language proficiency can filter the extent to which a student makes progress or shows mastery. Moreover, in Access Point 1, we talked about how second language learners are not necessarily comparable to other learners. Thus, assessments should not include comparisons across students as ways to determine if instruction has worked. We cannot assume that students who do not adhere to the trend are underperforming or overperforming relative to their peers. We need to dig deeper into individual student performance to see why a given student is achieving at that particular level or in this particular way.

Key L2 Assessment Principle: Formative and Summative Assessments

We consider assessment in the same way that it was considered in *Languages for All* (Arnett, 2013c): as a continuous, iterative process guided by information from a variety of sources. Assessment is used to determine the extent to which students are on track to meet learning goals/outcomes (assessment *for* learning), the extent to which they meet or have met those goals/outcomes (assessment *of* learning), and what the students think about their learning in relation to those goals/outcomes (assessment *as* learning). These three functions of assessment work together to allow you to gather information at any stage of the learning experience and make good decisions about the trajectory of the lesson or the student's work. Figure 10.1 summarizes key features of each type of assessment practice.

Figure 10.1: Types of Assessment in the Second Language Classroom

Type of Assessment Practice	What is it?	How does it support language learners?	What are some considerations when using it with language learners?
Assessment *for* Learning (AFL)	Formative check-ins to determine students' progress in relation to learning goals/outcomes.	By monitoring student progress in an ongoing manner, it is easier to see when or where students may have difficulty when understanding language in relation to content, and thus make revisions to lessons to maximize comprehensibility.	Language proficiency develops in a fluid way; sometimes words or ideas come easily, but other times, words are hard to recall. Thus, make adjustments based on AFL moments only if events happen on multiple occasions; an adjustment based on a one-time event may be less effective.
Assessment *of* Learning (AOL)	Summative/evaluative check-ins to determine the extent to which a student's work meets a particular goal/outcome.	By looking at student work at specific points or intervals, it is easier to establish trends in their growth over time. This can be helpful in determining how their skills with language are evolving, particularly if copies of AOL activities are kept for reference.	When judging students' work in relation to criteria, it is important to consider the content mastery or understanding as a function of a student's proficiency, particularly for newer learners. Students should not be penalized for their lower proficiency level.
Assessment *as* Learning (AAL)	Reflective/metacognitive moments that allow learners to make connections in their learning, set goals, and otherwise consider their progress or skills; this is sometimes considered to be a type of formative assessment.	Because prior experiences and prior first language knowledge will shape how second language skills are developed, asking students to reflect on those connections, make goals about their learning, and otherwise think about their thinking will help them bridge the two languages.	Teachers should demonstrate the value of self-assessment and metacognitive thinking by using the information shared in those reflections to better support student learning experiences. The goal-setting dimension of AAL is critical to developing student autonomy. As shared in Access Point 2, this is a key goal of language education.

Assessment for learning considers what we do to ensure that our students are on the best path for their learning needs at a given point. It can involve pulling information from diagnostic tools (like a pre-reading brainstorm about a topic), in-lesson tools (e.g., questions that are asked as students read a text), or post-hoc tools (e.g., a consolidation at the end of a lesson). Thus, assessment for learning is really formative assessment. Data from this type of assessment can enable us to tweak a lesson or an activity, change the path a student is following, or otherwise confirm that the current approach to learning is the best for meeting a student's needs and the learning goals. Colby-Kelly and Turner (2007) describe assessment for learning in the language classroom as an interactive and dynamic experience.

Assessment of learning is synonymous with evaluation (e.g., assigning a mark, making a judgment about the quality of a student's work in relation to criteria or standards). These assessments are used to confirm the degree to which students have learned (or not) particular content; in this way, assessment of learning is regarded as summative assessment. When we work with language learners, summative assessments can be a bit tricky to navigate because we have to account for their proficiency in relation to the content and ensure that any judgments about their work quality and mastery are cognizant of their proficiency relative to the task. To do this well requires sharing learning goals with students and co-constructing success criteria, which we have mentioned elsewhere in this book.

Assessment as learning is a critical tool for language learners, in particular. It encompasses metacognitive thinking that supports learner autonomy: students are asked to reflect on their progress, establish learning goals, and make their own connections between previous and new learning. Students can be asked to think about how the language they have recently learned allows them to express new ideas and understandings. Assessments as learning, therefore, enable students to see the growth in their language proficiency and recognize their role as active participants in the learning experience. As we showed in Chapter 4, this kind of metacognitive engagement is a real asset to language development. It is worth noting that this type of assessment has been identified as a type of formative assessment and, in some circles, is viewed as a sub-component of assessment for learning (Black, 2009).

In a seminal literature review of more than 500 studies, Black and Wiliam (1998) found that formative assessment and self-assessments were the most critical forms of assessment to advancing student learning. Their review found that learning activities and processes that allowed the teacher to frequently gauge learners' progress toward learning goals and skill mastery, as well as provide feedback to learners about this progress, had more of an impact on student learning than summative assessments. The Black and Wiliam (1998) review has been foundational in subsequent research on formative assessment, as it has allowed researchers to use the premise of its effectiveness in student learning as a starting point. You might also want to refer to other works in this field, including Black (2009), Jiang (2014), Klein (2007), Lee (2007), and Leung (2004).

Key L2 Assessment Principle: The Role of Teacher Questioning

From our experiences, we have found that there are assessment opportunities that can sometimes be missed or otherwise underdeveloped during teacher (oral) questions.

In terms of teacher questions, we are talking about the types of questions a teacher uses in the classroom to monitor student learning, as well as the teacher feedback to those questions. There are patterns to the types of questions teachers tend to ask in the classroom, as well as patterns in how teachers respond to student answers, and those patterns have implications for learning. As questions are often one of the least planned elements of classroom instruction (Orlich, Harder, Callahan, Trevisan, & Brown, 2012), tuning in to better questioning techniques will have positive impacts on student learning.

Mehan (1979) first brought our attention to the IRE/IRF (teacher Initiate-student Respond-teacher Evaluation/Feedback) pattern that exists in most teacher–student question exchanges in the classroom. These exchanges typically allow the teacher to confirm a student's knowledge of a particular idea; thus, they tend not to move beyond the initial levels of Bloom's taxonomy of cognitive challenge. Most of the time, teacher questions focus on recall of key details and information from class or texts; sometimes, the questions test understanding of a concept or its application to another context. Few questions address aspects of analysis, evaluation, or synthesis (Orlich et al., 2012).

Open-ended questions are divergent questions because they allow for multiple possible responses. For more information about teacher questions, see Chapter 6, Action 2.7 *Asking questions that encourage learners to elaborate.*

Richards and Lockhart (1994) classify further teacher questions in the classroom according to the content of the question: procedural (e.g., questions about classroom events and activities) or convergent/divergent (e.g., questions with either one right answer or multiple possible responses). Jiang (2014) considered teacher question patterns too, and found that the majority of questions asked were convergent questions that focused on material presented in classroom texts.

Connecting Points: See pages 181 and 182, where you will find two tables (Figure 9.2 and Figure 9.3) that offer ideas for varying linguistic complexity. Analyze those question stems. Which are convergent, and which are divergent? How does convergence/divergence in questions relate to student proficiency, as you see it in the table? Consider reviewing pages 133 and 134 as well, where we offer ideas on elaboration techniques to use in the classroom.

While there is nothing wrong with a teacher confirming the extent to which students grasped the basic knowledge of the content under study, these questions limit opportunities for language growth. As Jiang (2014) saw in her research, many convergent questions had easily accessible answers for students, which meant that language-wise students were repeating or reading aloud language that had already been provided to them. There was limited opportunity for students to create their own language. Linguistically speaking, they could manage the demands of spontaneous language.

While convergent, accessible-answer questions are good for language learners with beginning and basic proficiencies, there is a need to transition to divergent questions as students become more skilled with the language. Extrapolating findings from other research (e.g., Black, 2009; Black & Wiliam, 2009), Jiang also found that the use of divergent questions with these more proficient users of the language help advance their understanding of content.

Another dimension to consider is how we, as teachers, respond to the student response. In other words, how do we provide feedback during interactions? Many teachers have come to repeat the pattern that they learned as students: to offer praise or a correction of the student answer as the extent of the feedback/evaluation. Once the teacher has identified the response as good or bad, he/she then moves on to question another student (Long & Sato, 1983). However, various studies (e.g., Jordan, Lindsay, & Stanovich, 1997; Orlich et al., 2012) have shown the benefit of the teacher continuing the exchange with the student, using the initial response to launch into another round of questions and probing. The feedback/evaluation spins into other questions because the teacher works with the answer the student has provided to probe the different dimensions of understanding. Figure 10.2 contrasts these two exchange patterns more concretely.

Figure 10.2: Teacher–Student Exchanges

	Typical Teacher–Student Exchange	Enhanced Teacher–Student Exchange
Example A	T: What is the definition of *circumference*? S: The circumference is the edge or boundary of a round shape, like a circle. T: Correct! Moving on to the next question …	T: What is the definition of *circumference*? S: The circumference is the edge or boundary of a round shape, like a circle. T: Good, now can you say that another way? S: It is the distance around something. T: Nice. Is it possible to measure the circumference of a box? S: Yes. T: Are you sure? Is it round? S: No! You can't measure the circumference of a box. T: Right. For a box, you need to measure the perimeter. Let's move on.
Example B	T: What is the weather today? S: It is sunny. T: Yes. It is sunny.	T: What is the weather today? S: It is sunny. T: Yes. It is sunny. Is it warm or cold today? S: It is cold. T: Is it cloudy? S: No, it is not cloudy. T: Okay, can you describe today's weather with all three of the words? Start with the phrase "Today's weather is …" S: Today's weather is sunny, cold, and not cloudy. T: Nicely done.

Black, Harrison, Lee, Marshall, and Wiliam (2003) posit that good formative assessment questions focus on developing student understanding of the content. In the classroom, however, teachers seemingly mistake conceptual and language understanding for recall of those ideas and relevant language. Let's explore the two examples from the previous table for how they move the exchange beyond recall or rote response and deepen conceptual and language understanding.

Example A, on the previous page, resembles an exchange that could occur in a language classroom with a content focus, such as an immersion classroom. The traditional exchange is seeking to confirm the student's understanding of the concept of circumference. Using synonymous terms to describe the circumference conveys that understanding. The teacher confirms the response, and that's the end. In the enhanced exchange, we can see how continued questioning allowed the teacher to see how much of the concept of circumference was known to the student. The exchange could have been extended further, to include questions about formulas that require knowledge of the circumference or other terms relevant to circumference (e.g., diameter, radius), but it is still clear with the offered exchange that the student can do more than simply recall the definition of circumference. Here, the teacher is able to gauge how the student places circumference among other measurement concepts.

Example B resembles an exchange that would occur in a language classroom where the students are focused on learning how to communicate in the language (e.g., a Core language classroom). In this exchange, the conceptual focus is describing weather. In the traditional exchange, the student offers just one way to talk about the day's weather. The teacher accepts the response and moves on. Conversely, in the enhanced exchange, we see how the teacher elicits additional description about the weather, even asking questions in other ways (giving the student two possible terms for one type of description, then asking the student to confirm a description offered). In this exchange, we see not only that the student is able to offer a richer description of the day's weather, but that the student can interpret different wording patterns to add to that description.

> **Research to Practice:** See pages 112 and 113, where we provide the overview of how the ULAs for understanding can be used to monitor understanding. How can any of those actions be incorporated into exchanges with students in your classes?

The one caution we want to offer here relates to research that has focused on inclusive teaching practices in regular education classrooms: teachers who hold beliefs that students with special needs are not capable of the academic work or do not belong in the setting are less likely to engage in academic exchanges with these students (Jordan, Lindsay, & Stanovich, 1997; Jordan & Stanovich, 2001). Thus, we have to be mindful of how our value systems as teachers influence how we may unconsciously select students to respond to our questions. As you may recall from Chapter 1, we talked about the overall paradigm of inclusive education and the philosophies it embeds. Here, we can see a link between philosophy and practice.

Key L2 Assessment Principle: Oral Corrective Feedback

Because we're working with language learners, we also have to consider the way a teacher responds to the interaction when the student response is incorrect either linguistically or conceptually. In other words, what kind of corrective feedback will help our learners further develop their language skills?

Roy Lyster and Leila Ranta published a study in 1997 that sought to determine which mechanisms of teacher corrective feedback enabled language learners (in this case, students in an immersion setting) to self-repair their responses, leading to more grammatically sound or linguistically clear responses. We should note that while many language teachers can often understand the content or conceptual message learners are trying to convey—even if it has several errors—teachers should still be working to help the student make a more precise response to foster language proficiency. Further, it is sometimes hard for the teacher to separate a conceptual misunderstanding from a language error—particularly when the student has a limited vocabulary—making teacher feedback even more critical to gauging understanding and promoting language learning.

The Lyster and Ranta (1997) study offered two key contributions to our understanding of corrective feedback of oral language and learner response to the feedback: a taxonomy for classifying the forms of teacher corrective feedback and the idea of *uptake*, which they define as the student's immediate response to the teacher feedback that somehow conveys an awareness of the correction (1997, p. 49). The following table summarizes the taxonomy they created and offers classroom examples of the feedback forms. We have chosen to offer an example in Figure 10.3 that straddles the form/meaning issue, showing how incorrect word choice is both a language and a content issue requiring correction.

Figure 10.3: Types of Corrective Feedback

Type of Corrective Feedback	Definition	Example
Clarification request	The teacher conveys that the message has not been understood and uses phrases like "I don't understand" or "Excuse me?" to prompt the student to either repeat or revise the statement.	S: (pointing to a rectangle) This is a square. T: Excuse me? Are you sure? S: No, it is a rectangle.
Elicitation	There are three ways in which a teacher can elicit the correct form: 1. Asking the student to finish the teacher's prompt (Example: "This is a ...") 2. Asking questions about the correct form (Example: "How do you say it in English?") 3. Asking the student to restate the response *All of these questions require the student to give more than a yes or no as a response to the prompt.*	S: (pointing to a rectangle) This is a square. T: No, it is a r ... S: R ... rectangle!
Explicit correction	The teacher directly tells the student that the answer is incorrect and provides the correct form.	S: (pointing to a rectangle) This is a square. T: No, it is a rectangle.
Metalinguistic feedback	The teacher does not tell the student the correct form for the answer, but instead asks questions like these: "Is that how you say it in English?" "Do we say ...?"	S: (pointing to a rectangle) This is a square. T: Do we really call that a square? S: No. It is a rectangle.
Recast	The teacher provides the student with the correct form of the response, without offering any direct indication of the error.	S: (pointing to a rectangle) This is a square. T: (pointing to a rectangle) This is a rectangle.
Repetition	The teacher repeats the student's error and uses his/her voice to draw attention to the problem area in the response.	S: (pointing to a rectangle) This is a square. T: (with intonation rising on *square*) This is a *square*? S: Oh. This is a rectangle.

In their study, Lyster and Ranta (1997) found that the most common form of corrective feedback—the recast—was not effective in causing students to self-repair their language. The most effective method they noted was elicitation, followed by metalinguistic feedback. These findings are logical, given that the goal was to determine which method allowed the *student* to make the correction.

Lyster expanded on this research with Saito in 2010 by completing a meta-analysis of research of other studies that had looked at patterns of corrective feedback in language classrooms; this analysis was important because it was the first to identify which types of corrective feedback are most effective in a classroom environment. Specifically, they looked at recasts, explicit corrections, and prompts (elicitation). Various statistical tests later, they found that all three types of corrective feedback had a positive influence on students' language skills, but they caution that the effectiveness is increased when the corrective style is more pedagogical than conversational (Lyster & Saito, 2010, p. 290). As a feedback mechanism, then, elicitation is more effective than recasts, but explicit correction is neither more nor less effective than the other two methods. Lyster and Saito hypothesize that the limited effectiveness of explicit correction could be tied into the fact that the learner is told the answer is wrong—the emotional side of learning may be at play here. Another finding to note is that corrective feedback was found to have more of an impact on younger learners than older learners, regardless of the learning environment. The reasons for those differences require additional exploration.

This section had a lot of information, so we're offering the summary table in Figure 10.4 for quick reference to help you better use questions as formative assessment tools in your classroom.

Figure 10.4: Key Ideas for Using Formative Assessment to Support Student Learning

What kinds of questions help students advance their learning?	How should a teacher respond to the student answer?	What kind of corrective feedback should a teacher offer?
For students who are early in their proficiency, convergent questions (e.g., questions with one right answer) are reasonable; as proficiency builds, use divergent questions (e.g., questions with multiple possible answers) to allow them more chances to use language. For all students, plan questions for the class that move beyond the initial levels of Bloom's taxonomy. The tables in Chapter 9 show you how to vary linguistic complexity at the various levels of the taxonomy to support the different proficiencies.	Do more than just tell the student if the answer was right or wrong. Probe the concept further; ask follow-up questions that allow you to confirm the student's understanding. Keep in mind that a challenge with the language could overshadow what they know about the concept, which is why the additional probes are important.	For students to be able to correct their own responses, elicitation, or prompting, works best. Elicitation/prompting is most effective for helping students advance their language skills overall. Recasts are not effective; explicit correction has a neutral influence.

Key L2 Assessment Principle: Activity Goals—What Are We Really Asking Learners to Do?

In terms of activity goals, we are referring to an awareness of the actual skills and language demands that are embedded in an activity. We have seen plenty of activities used in classroom settings where the teacher has misidentified the learning emphasis of the activity and, consequently, misinterpreted student performance during the activity. Thus, drawing on the research, we will explore the ways in which teacher questions and activity goals can be better framed as assessment tools in order to support student learning.

If you want to know how tall you are, you don't stand on a bathroom scale. You'll use the scale for your weight, but not for any other measurement purpose. Similarly, you can't presume that all you need to know about your health is captured by the weight showing on the bathroom scale. You may get a sense that your weight could be a sign of other issues, but you lack definitive information—you would have to consult other sources.

We talk about the bathroom scale and what it does and does not measure to draw your attention to the importance of ensuring that the tools used to gauge student learning are aligned with the learning goals. What's more, you need to recognize that nearly all the tools you use for assessment are giving a snapshot of a particular skill at a particular time. We have seen (and heard of) plenty of situations in classrooms where language learners' progress is misunderstood or misjudged because of a mismatch between the learning tool and the learning goal or a failure to recognize the scope of the assessment tool. The next several subsections will explore common problem areas and offer advice on how to navigate these potential pitfalls in your classroom.

Form and Function of Language in the Activity

In language education, one of the most prevalent dichotomies is that of form versus function. By *form*, we are referring to the grammar, spelling, and precise delivery of the language, whereas *function* is concerned with the message the language is trying to convey or capture. As discussed to some degree in the previous section, problems with the language form can impede the clarity of the intended message. The message being conveyed could also be hampered by misunderstandings of the language being used.

Though teachers should be concerned with both, a decision sometimes needs to be made as to which construct will get more attention in the learning activity; otherwise, it is entirely possible that teachers will become overwhelmed trying to address all of the elements which, in turn, will overwhelm the learner. When arriving at a moment when you want to use formative assessment, we advise, take a critical eye to the learning activity and determine which construct—form or function—is going to get most of your attention. Base your decision on the learning goal of the activity as it relates to the overall learning goal of the unit of instruction.

Figure 10.5 offers an example, including variations of the activity according to the proficiency level of the students.

If you need a refresher as to the language skills aligned with a level, consult pages 30 to 32 in Chapter 2.

Figure 10.5: Distinguishing Form and Function in Learning Activities

Learning Goals for Instructional Segment	Current Learning Goal	Learning Activity for Formative Assessment	Teacher Look-For
Students can explain how the water cycle supports life on Earth. Students can propose a method for better water conservation to respond to needs in drought-prone areas of the world.	Students can construct a sequential narrative that describes the water cycle. (function)	Students will draw a visual of the water cycle, annotating each step to explain its role in the process. *Variation for Level 1 student:* Student sorts pictures showing stages of water cycle into correct order. *Variation for Level 2 student:* In addition to Level 1 task, student also matches labels of each stage name to the pictures. *Variation for Level 3 student:* Student has access to a word and phrase bank to help with the descriptions.	This goal/activity is focused on the sequence, so the activity should be reviewed to see how the student managed the function of sequencing. Content details need to align with each step; language errors can be tolerated. Draw student attention to misspellings.
Students can explain how the water cycle supports life on Earth. Students can propose a method for better water conservation to respond to needs in drought-prone areas of the world.	Students can describe the difference between a *deluge* and a *flood* when talking about water-related weather events. (form)	Students write a series of statements using the targeted words in context. (exit slip) *Variation for Level 1 student:* Student matches pictures depicting each event with the term. *Variation for Level 2 student:* Student writes the appropriate term next to an image. *Variation for Level 3 student:* Provide a sentence starter.	Because this learning goal is concerned with a subtle difference in two terms, the attention should be on the form of the words that are used in the sentences to explain the terms.

continued

Learning Goals for Instructional Segment	Current Learning Goal	Learning Activity for Formative Assessment	Teacher Look-For
Students can describe food preferences. Students can describe dietary restrictions. Students can place an order for food items at a restaurant.	Students can ask and answer questions about food preferences (function)	Students participate in an Inside-Outside circle, where they alternate asking and answering questions about the foods they like and don't like. *Variation for Level 1 student:* Student uses pictures and possibly question and sentence starters to help construct the questions and responses. *Variation for Level 2 student:* Student uses question and sentence starters to ask and answer the questions. *Variation for Level 3 student:* Provide a question or a sentence starter.	Teacher would listen for students' question techniques, possibly noting who needed support or prompting to frame or respond to the questions.
Students can describe food preferences. Students can describe dietary restrictions. Students can place an order for food items at a restaurant.	Students can use appropriate expressions of formality to place an order. (form)	Students complete a role-play where they incorporate particular terms or phrases that show formality (e.g., in French, "s'il vous plaît," "vous," "je voudrais"). *Variation for Level 1 student:* Student possibly re-enacts a previously viewed or shared role-play and reuses the language *Variation for Level 2 student:* Student uses question and sentence starters to participate in the role-play, ensuring that specific terms are included in the starters.	Teacher listens for and notes instances where students effectively used the terms for formality and where they missed opportunities to do so.

The True Meaning of the Verbs in Learning Goals

When talking about language functions, we must consider the meaning of the academic terms that describe what students are expected to do during learning; in other words, we need to pay attention to the verbs we are using in our learning goals. As various language researchers and practitioners have shown (e.g., Echevarria, Vogt, & Short, 2016; Zweirs, 2014), the demands of academic language are sometimes underappreciated when assessing students in the classroom because we have not considered the language expectations embedded in the verbs of the learning goals.

For example, in English, there is a difference between *describe* and *explain*. Sometimes, these terms are used interchangeably when giving students directions about learning activities; "describe the character's actions" is close to the direction "explain what the character did." However, as an action, describing is different than explaining. A description typically conveys how something is perceived by any one of the five senses, while an explanation typically conveys *why* something is the way it is. These differences are so subtle and abstract for many young and early language learners that they cannot be understood through context or repeated use of the terms. Consequently, students may have an incomplete understanding of the language demands of the learning activities in the classroom, and we may realize it only at the moment of assessment.

Connecting Points: Review the various ULAs that support vocabulary development in Chapter 8 for ideas as to how to help increase student understanding and use of key terms. In particular, you may want to review Action 4.1 *Identifying and presenting required language at the outset of a lesson or activity.*

As part of the supports you offer to students during instruction, you should include time to deconstruct the verbs at the centre of the learning activity. Doing so will permit the students to be aware of the learning expectations ahead of them. Consider creating posters or reference guides that students can use to know which verbs, sentence stems, and language structures support a particular function in the classroom. There are numerous examples of these guides online in English, and they can provide a good starting point.

Practical Issues in Implementing Assessment: Assessing in the Differentiated Classroom

As was established in Access Point 3, good assessment practices are central to differentiated instruction. In order to know which learning paths are best suited to students' needs or readiness, teachers need strong formative tools, deployed as pre-lesson and pre-unit diagnostic assessments, post-lesson and post-unit assessments, or assessments in between.

In Chapter 9, we address how to assess or evaluate student learning when students complete differentiated tasks. Though the topic fits with this chapter, we included it in the differentiation chapter to allow you to see more easily the match between the differentiated activity and the assessment tool.

Pre- and post-assessments should clearly focus on the targeted concepts and skills for the unit of study in one of two ways. First, you can use direct questions that are readily scorable, either because they are closed response (one right answer) or their open-ended nature permits the creation of an efficient rubric (as in the main idea was identified clearly, and the student offered two accurate supporting details). Second, if you are looking for opportunities to promote learner autonomy and student engagement, student self-assessment (assessment as learning) can be used as part of the diagnostic; students can be invited to think about their facility with a particular skill to help guide decisions about the task options to pursue. Either way, analyzing the results of the assessment allows you to determine the differentiated paths. Figure 10.6 captures some of the ways students can be grouped according to the results of an assessment tool in support of differentiated instruction; these groupings apply to the need/readiness dimensions explored in Chapter 9.

Figure 10.6: Grouping Students

Possible Ways to Group Students According to Need or Readiness for Differentiated Activities	
Groups of two possible paths	• Students who have prior knowledge of concept and students who have minimal or no prior knowledge • Students who need additional time with current skill and students who are ready to add a new dimension to a skill • Students who need to work with current knowledge using resources that revisit or re-explain the concept and students who are ready to work with current knowledge using resources that add new details to the concept • Students who would like to continue with current skill and students who would like to extend their skill (if self-assessment is used as part of diagnostic)
Groups of three possible paths	• Students who have a lot of prior knowledge of concept, students who have some prior knowledge, and students who have minimal or no prior knowledge • Students who need additional time with current skill, students who are ready to add a new dimension to a skill, and students who need to revisit a prior skill to help enhance the current skill • Students who need to work with current knowledge using resources that revisit or re-explain the concept, students who are ready to work with current knowledge using resources that add new details to the concept, and students who need to work with current knowledge using resources that apply the concept in a new way • Students who clearly grasp and are skilled with the current concept, students who are on solid ground with the current concept but would benefit from additional exploration, and students who need more time to develop understanding of the key concept • Students who would like to continue with current skill, students who would like to extend their skill, and students who overall would like to try a new skill (if self-assessment is used as part of diagnostic)

continued

Groups of four possible paths	• Students who have a lot of prior knowledge of concept, students who have some prior knowledge, students who have minimal prior knowledge, and students who have no prior knowledge • Students who need additional time with current skill, students who are ready to add a new dimension to a skill, students who need to revisit a prior skill to help enhance the current skill, and students who are ready to connect current skill with another separate skill • Students who need to work with current knowledge using resources that revisit or re-explain the concept, students who are ready to work with current knowledge using resources that add new details to the concept, students who need to work with current knowledge using resources that apply the concept in a new way, and students who could create new resources for applying or demonstrating the concept • Students who clearly grasp and are skilled with the current concept and can link it to another concept, students who are on solid ground with the current concept but would benefit from additional exploration with the concept as they know it, students who are in need of additional time to develop understanding of the key concept, and students who grasp and are skilled with the current concept and can deepen their knowledge of that particular concept • Students who would like to continue with the current skill, students who would like to extend their skill, students who would like to try to combine two skills in a new way, and students who would like to develop a new skill (if self-assessment is used as part of diagnostic)

Examples of differentiated activities for these groupings can be found on the *Access for Success* website.

Extending Your Learning: In order for assessment in support of differentiation to be an efficient enterprise, the tools we use to create the student learning paths need to be similarly efficient. W. James Popham is one of the most respected authors about classroom assessment practices, and his books offer clear advice on how to design effective multiple-choice, short answer, and extended response questions (among other structures).

Practical Issues in Implementing Assessment: Technology in the L2 Classroom

The rise of technology-based and mobile-supported student learning has vastly expanded the tools available to teachers to engage students and assess learning. No longer do teachers need to reserve a language lab or a computer lab and schedule specific activities during those windows. Thanks to mobile devices and web-based platforms for student learning, it is now easier than ever for students to listen to texts in the target language, record their own audio or video responses, collaborate through document sharing, locate age- and/or language-appropriate authentic texts, find content-based resources in the target language, and create new narratives with animations and illustrations. We'll talk about some of those opportunities later.

The rise of these technology-based and mobile-supported assessment tools (e.g., student response systems, apps that allow students to complete quizzes online, apps that allow students to type, create, or record content showing mastery) has been a boon to student engagement and, in many cases, has led to a more efficient system for marking, when possible. However, as with any educational tool, there are some cautions about using these tools for assessment purposes in the classroom.

First, there needs to be consideration of the role of time in the tool. Student response systems, such as Turning Point and SMART, and quiz apps, like Kahoot! or GoSoapBox, often use structures that can reward fast response times. While many of those settings can be turned off, if they are used in an activity, the likelihood is strong that language learners will not fare as well in those activities or that the activities will be dominated by those students whose brains process language quickly. In general, when working with language learners, activities that embed time as a marker of success should be avoided or at least strongly minimized. These activities end up measuring how quickly students can process the language, rather than how well they can process it. Sometimes, we have mistaken a fast processing time with evidence of students knowing the material, which can lead to later misunderstandings or ill-informed decisions about instructional support or even student learning in the language.

Second, it is worth noting that competition, which often happens with these response systems and apps, is not always culturally understood by newcomers in the classroom setting. Though many of these apps and platforms can be positioned as a game within the lesson, be aware that some students may not engage with the task because they do not see it as a part of the learning experience. In these cases, students need to be directly taught about these learning activities as part of the education tradition here (in terms of knowing that they are a part of the learning), or you may need to prepare students for the competitive element.

Finally, though access to mobile devices has increased and students today are generally regarded as technology savvy, this is not a universal truth. Be sure to provide lesson time for students to learn how to use the technology tools that will be pertinent to any later assessments. You can thereby avoid situations where a limited technology literacy, rather than language skill, frames the assessment experience.

For more information on technology-based tools for the L2 classroom, see the *Access for Success* website.

Those caveats aside, we can now offer some ways in which technology-based tools can be used to create new opportunities for assessing student learning and in how we actually assess student learning.

Cloud-Based Documents

In recent years, most educators have become familiar with the suite of tools in Google Apps for Education. The core tools that allow for documents, forms, and presentations to be created have embedded features whereby the texts can be shared across multiple devices, enabling students to co-construct such texts together (using different colours to convey different collaborators, perhaps) and enabling teachers to view and comment on their work.

One potential downside to these cloud-based tools is that they do not always easily show the history of specific changes to the documents, which could be important if you are trying to quickly determine how students did or did not respond to feedback. This can be easily remedied by directing students to have multiple versions of the text within the same document. Each time students are expected to revise or edit their work, require them to make a copy of the previous version and paste it below *in a different colour* (or in another tab) of the same file. In keeping the various drafts and final copies together, it is also possible (and possibly easier) for students to self-assess their progress and set goals for later learning. Highlighting and commenting tools within these apps can be used as a part of this process, to really draw attention to changes that occurred from one version to another.

Beyond the Google Apps web-suite, there are increasing numbers of apps that have platforms that enable sharing of student responses with the teacher. For example, Classkick allows teachers to create virtual classroom spaces that are housed on individual iPads. Teachers can "push" questions or prompts to the students, and the students can respond individually. Teachers can view the students' work and instantly comment on what they see (a stylus helps do this job somewhat neatly). From their side, students can "raise a hand" to get the teacher's attention (which then pops an alert on the teacher side of the app) and ask a question on their page, and they can immediately address the feedback the teacher offers. This app makes it possible for the students to work independently and the teacher to respond easily to the students who are asking for help.

Recording Responses

Between the old cassette tapes and the more modern voice-recording software in mobile devices and computers, students may be able to create asynchronous presentations or recordings of their spoken language skills. No matter the platform you use, try to keep multiple examples of students' spoken language over the course of the year. Students can be asked to review their recordings and self-assess what they hear, either setting goals for next time or talking about their growth. As teachers, we can review their recordings over a period of time to also monitor for growth. Bear in mind that when reviewing student work outside of class—particularly with spoken language—it is sometimes easier to provide more constructive feedback because the presentation can be stopped and replayed as needed.

Another platform for recording to consider is the screencast. Generally available on computer, either as a downloadable software or a web-based tool, screencasts allow students to record their delivery of a presentation or demonstration in support of images, graphics, and texts on the screen (like a PowerPoint). This can be a great way to also help students develop focus and pacing within a presentation, as several of the free versions of such software (e.g., Jing) have a time limit on the recording that can be made. Screencasts can also be a way to provide student feedback, as they allow us to narrate any student work we may be viewing on a screen.

Hope (2011) found that students preferred screencasts to written feedback about lab reports because they felt that the instructor had looked at the assignment with more attention to detail and that the format was more accessible than written comments. Some students noted that screencasts could be difficult to use for locating a particular piece of feedback to address in revisions or future assignments. Hope concluded that screencasts were a viable feedback mechanism because of the students' positive response and because they were less time-consuming for the instructor to create than written comments. Further, Séror (2012) describes and reflects on his use of Jing screencasts to provide focused feedback on discrete and global issues in students' writing. Séror points to the perceived emotional benefits from his end: he is able to produce feedback that is "more conversational in nature" and "allows for a greater degree of personalization and subtlety" because, for example, he can use the tone of his voice to convey "true sincerity when praise is offered or genuine confusion [in reacting to a section that is difficult to understand]" (p. 111).

Practical Issues in Implementing Assessment: Structures for Facilitating Assessment in the Classroom

Since any learning activity has the potential to be an assessment event, Figure 10.7 offers ideas on how to manage or structure certain learning events to allow you to more easily collect and assess the evidence about students' learning.

Figure 10.7: Ideas for Structuring Assessment in the Language Classroom

You want students to ...	Consider setting up the assessment as ...	So you can ...
Ask and answer questions in an oral interaction	1. Inside-Outside circle or line dance 2. Carousel activity	1. Circulate around the students easily and take notes about their performance on an observation checklist. 2. Set up at one of the spots on the carousel and observe the interactions as students rotate through.
Prepare and deliver an oral presentation about a topic	1. A screencast presentation or other recording 2. One of several activities students do over the course of class so that the presentation is made either to you or to a small group of students 3. A recording created by using an app or other tech tool, to be sent to or shared with you	1. Review the presentations outside of class time. 2. Provide individual feedback to students as they present; this set-up can also help manage student anxiety about presenting in class. 3. Review the presentation outside of class time.
Respond to questions about a text (in writing)	1. A list of 10 to 12 questions from which you can select subsets or individual questions for students, depending on proficiency. Activity structures can support this (see "Dice Questions/ Questions in a Cup" in Arnett (2013c), *Languages for All*). 2. Carousel activity: put the questions on various pages, and have students rotate to various questions.	1. Review student work outside of class time. 2. In class, ask students to sign their names to their responses. Circulate as they are writing or discussing and make any notations about responses in an observation chart. Follow up with clarification or support to the whole group.
Summarize a key idea or text	1. Jigsaw: assign students certain sections or texts to summarize. 2. A series of blog posts, tweets, or other electronic messages	1. If used in a discussion format, summaries can be observed. 2. On a class website or other tech forum, these can be reviewed as students post.
Explain a process	1. A written narrative 2. An audio or video recording 3. A flow chart to be completed from a template 4. A flow chart created and narrated by the student	All of these can be reviewed outside of class using a rubric.

continued

You want students to ...	Consider setting up the assessment as ...	So you can ...
Apply a skill	1. Use a choice board, RAFT structure, or other differentiated task framework to give students various options for how to apply the skill. 2. Do an in-class demonstration to a small group of peers—perhaps on a learning centre rotation or in a Carousel activity.	1. Depending on the activity structure and task options, review student work in or outside of class. 2. Review work in real time, using a rubric.

Closing Thoughts

Good assessment practices are not an afterthought or something to do toward the end of your planning. The *what* and the *how* of the information you need to collect about your students' learning is central to the early stages of your planning; you plan your assessment(s) as you establish your learning goal. Assessment is at the heart of good decision making, and your decisions are only as good as the information you have gathered about or from your learners.

As you reflect on the contents of the chapter, consider the following questions:

- How do I already use AFL, AAL, and AOL in my teaching?
- How could I expand or revise my use of AFL, AAL, or AOL in my teaching?
- What are my go-to methods for interpreting student learning: looking at their answers, observing their behaviours, a mix?
- How do I use assessment on a daily basis?
- Do I value the language skills comparably in my assessment practices, or do I skew toward one or two in particular?
- What do I expect learners to do when I ask them to describe, explain, show, and so on?

CHAPTER 11

Bringing It All Together: Protocols and Processes in Support of Inclusive Language Education

As we mentioned in the Introduction, we first began working together in 2012 as part of a couple of research projects and initiatives examining ways by which to make immersion classrooms more inclusive. We came together as members of a larger conversation about how inclusion and second language learning could better coexist. Part of this conversation resulted in teachers identifying a need for a more robust, systematic problem solving that could document and address specific learner challenges and needs. From this work, we developed the Cycle of Support for Inclusive Language Education, or COSFILE, protocol—a tool to help teachers navigate situations where there was a need or interest in providing a more structured system of support to a student. As noted, this protocol was based on research with a group of teachers and a review of literature on interventions. This decision-making protocol includes a collection of inventories, reflection tools, and guiding principles designed to help stakeholders facilitate conversations that can lead to more inclusive classroom experiences. We have worked with the COSFILE protocol further, aiming to make it relevant to various second-language education contexts.

The COSFILE protocol is available on the *Access for Success* website. It is downloadable and editable for personalization to your context. Additional information about the protocol is also available on the website.

This chapter describes how various components of the protocol inform good decision making in support of inclusive language teaching: reflection on and analysis of our own practice; detailed considerations of learner needs, inviting input from others; targeted teaching practice; and monitoring and analysis.

A secondary goal of the initial protocol was to reduce the number of students leaving French immersion because of a belief that their learning needs could not be met in the program. As mentioned in Chapter 1, there has been a history of questioning which learners should pursue French immersion study based on their learning profiles or educational histories (e.g., see Mannavarayan, 2003, for a review of this literature). Further, there is still evidence of students with particular learning challenges being counselled out of immersion or otherwise denied access to the program (Wise & Chen, 2010). Some of those decisions are seemingly informed by misconceptions about how support can be structured (and that it can be cross-linguistic support!) or that the student's challenges would disappear or be minimized moving into English. The hope was that the protocol would either be implemented if a request to transfer out of immersion was filed or that it would be used as part of any decision-making process about supports. The protocol is never structured or framed to justify decisions to exclude or remove a learner from the immersion classroom. The whole purpose of the protocol is to facilitate a targeted consideration of a learner's needs in relation to classroom practice.

The Structure and Key Concepts of the COSFILE Protocol

The following are the components of the protocol—they are individual processes implicated in inclusive second language education. **The protocol is structured in such a way as to allow stakeholders to complete several steps in their choice of sequence and/or marry different components to existing district or school protocols.** Figure 11.1 summarizes the phases of the protocol, demonstrates how different components are grouped, and indicates where there is flexibility within the protocol.

Figure 11.1: Phases of the COSFILE Protocol

Phase 1 of the Protocol ***Reflecting on current techniques and student needs***	**Phase 2 of the Protocol** ***Giving focused attention to and use of inclusive supports***	**Floating Components of the Protocol** ***Involving stakeholders***
• Complete the Teacher Inventory of Baseline Techniques (TIB-T). • Prepare a student learning profile (SLP). • Analyze patterns and information within and across both documents.	• Complete analysis of and reflection on Universal Language and Differentiation Actions (ULDAs). • Implement and monitor use of selected ULDAs over a specific period. • Analyze results of ULA and differentiation use.	• Involve parents or guardians of learner in providing information about their child. • Collaborate with other colleagues to seek insight about the student.

Though the various components of the protocol can be reordered to reflect school and district practices, we do suggest keeping, in separate phases, the TIB-T and the frequency analysis of ULDAs. Doing so ensures that there is an awareness of the good, general second-language teaching practice that is needed to undergird inclusive practice in the language classroom.

Key Terms in the Protocol

Though we have defined and used these terms in other parts of the book, we have collated their definitions here to help frame some of the aspects of the COSFILE protocol. Some of these terms are not directly implicated in the protocol, but we offer them here as a way for you to better understand what the protocol directly addresses.

Pedagogy: Globally, this refers to how teachers deliver daily instruction, elicit information and language from students, and otherwise engage with a resource in the classroom for teaching the content or language.

Baseline Technique: Within the context of the language classroom, baseline techniques are the teaching techniques that are supported by research as being integral to meaningful support and progress within second language learning. These techniques have been alluded to throughout the earlier chapters of this book as integral to inclusive language education. Some of these teaching moves may be directly tied to student learning in the classroom; others are tied to how we reflect on our teaching.

Generally speaking, a technique is usually synonymous with an action. Techniques and actions are concrete components of a lesson designed to support instructional delivery or exploration (e.g., brainstorming, making concept maps, activating prior knowledge, writing key terms and concepts on the board for student reference).

Universal Language Actions (ULAs): Aligned with the principles of Universal Design for Learning, these more than thirty teacher actions allow students to more easily understand, express, and be motivated to use the target language. Further, these actions, proposed earlier in this book, adhere to the principles of Universal Design for Learning in that they are to be proactively selected to support student learning. They provide students with support to understand, produce, or be otherwise engaged with the content.

Teaching Practice: This term applies to any specific sequence of teacher-led moves that allow students to work through the content in a specific way. Some examples include modelled writing, guided reading, shared reading, inquiry, hypothesis-testing, read-alouds, and guided math.

Strategies: Strategies are conscious actions that students can use or call upon to complete a task, with a particular focus on the language skills required therein. Examples include reading strategies (e.g., asking yourself questions as you read, using context clues to find meaning, sounding out words, looking at text features) and oral communication strategies (e.g., taking turns, providing peer feedback).

Phase 1: Reflecting on Current Techniques and Student Needs

Protocol Component: The Teacher Inventory of Baseline Techniques (TIB-T)

Good teaching requires us to regularly consider our own practice through reflection. Though the learner is at the centre of our efforts to be inclusive, inclusive teaching begins, develops, and is implemented by us as the teachers. Research shared in Chapter 2 demonstrated how teaching methods and techniques do lead to different types of student success (Erlam, 2005), and sometimes the mismatch between student needs and teaching techniques is left under-explored or not considered at all. Consequently, the first step in the COSFILE protocol is to reflect on your own pedagogy.

The TIB-T (Figure 11.2) asks you to consider the extent to which you are already using certain techniques as a part of your pedagogy; *the techniques in the TIB-T provide a starting point for good second language teaching.*

The elements found within the TIB-T link directly to the content in Chapters 1 through 4.

The TIB-T is not designed to imply that there is a mismatch between your teaching and the needs of the students; it is meant to remind you of the importance of considering specific elements of your pedagogy in relation to the students' evidenced needs. The TIB-T is not an evaluative tool. The absence or limited application of some of these baseline techniques could have an influence on the current challenge facing the student, but at the same time their regular use in the classroom is not a guarantee that students are immune to difficulty.

Admittedly, self-reporting has been linked to the halo effect or incorrect, inflated reporting on the part of the person completing an assessment tool. Thus, when completing the TIB-T, it is important to carefully take stock of our daily practices—even if we think we fall short of being as inclusive as we want to be. To avoid misreporting, consider filming yourself for a day or two and then rating yourself while you watch the video.

Figure 11.2: The Teacher Inventory of Baseline Techniques

	Always (100%)	Most of the Time (90%)	Usually (75%)	Often (50%)	Sometimes (25%)	Never
Knowledge of Principles of Second Language Learning						
I am aware of and value the silent period for new language learners.						
I acknowledge the interrelated relationships of languages.						
I recognize that in a second (or any additional) language learning environment, progress is individual. Student progress or success is not comparable.						
I know that multiple factors contribute to individual student gains in a language.						
Planning						
I consider the linguistic demands of the lesson.						
I consider the language backgrounds of my students.						
I consider the cultural backgrounds of my students.						
I consider affective and socio-affective factors that could influence student participation.						
I consider the learning needs and experiences of my students when selecting in-class activities.						
I select instructional materials that reflect my students' lives and language needs.						
Instructional Delivery and Assessment						
I establish and promote a positive classroom environment.						
I exclusively use the target language to deliver instruction.						
I provide praise and positive responses to student use of the target language.						
I limit use of home language in the classroom in a way that does not punish or penalize students or otherwise create negative emotions toward the target language.						

continued

	Always (100%)	Most of the Time (90%)	Usually (75%)	Often (50%)	Sometimes (25%)	Never
I provide formal instruction, where needed, in grammatical and linguistic elements of the target language to support accurate language production.						
I provide multiple opportunities a day to every student to produce sustained **spoken** output, consistent with the student's current level of proficiency.						
I provide models or sample responses for students to use as a reference for producing spoken output.						
I provide multiple opportunities a day to every student to produce sustained **written** output, consistent with the student's current level of proficiency.						
I provide models or sample responses for students to use as a reference for producing written output.						
I clearly articulate learning goals to students.						
I work with students to co-construct success criteria for key learning activities.						
I provide targeted and descriptive feedback to student work.						
I explicitly teach the learning strategies I expect students to use to complete activities (e.g., reading strategies, cooperative learning strategies).						
I facilitate student-to-student interaction within academic tasks (e.g., collaborative or cooperative learning).						
I vary the way in which students are expected to engage with different aspects of the concept or language points over the course of the lesson.						
Metacognitive Support						
I identify with—and share with students—my experiences as a language learner.						
I encourage learners to reflect on their own identity or identities as part of their learning experience.						
I facilitate individual goal-setting to promote learner autonomy.						
I provide students with opportunities to monitor and reflect on their own progress.						

If you are interested in adapting the TIB-T content, or are intrigued by the idea of baseline techniques that best support student learning and growth in the language classroom, consider reviewing the *Teacher Effectiveness for Language Learning Framework*, available at www.tellproject.org. Developed by a group of world language educators in the United States, with input from scholars and researchers in language education, this framework, the centrepiece of the TELL Project, seeks to articulate, in a clearly organized schema, the research-based teaching behaviours that support effective language education. The forty-two behaviours are organized into seven domains: environment, the learning experience, collaboration, planning, performance and feedback, professionalism, and learning tools. The framework supports efforts in the United States to ensure that pre-service candidates, as well as experienced teachers in world languages, meet a variety of professional standards that are used within the field. We were inspired by the TELL Project to thematically organize the baseline techniques.

Protocol Component: Develop a Student Learning Profile (SLP)

Once you have had a chance to reflect on your own teaching, it is time to develop a more detailed SLP; as we outlined in Chapter 3, the profile is a critical element to determining how to facilitate inclusive language education. It needs to be created after the TIB-T so that your responses to the TIB-T are not coloured by what you have written about the student in the SLP.

The SLP can be created individually or in a team setting, whatever the problem-solving protocol is at your school site. Though the document includes many prompts that are focused on typical areas of concern about a student's performance, teachers are also prompted at different points within the document to think about the student's strengths and positive traits. The profile has also been constructed to somewhat mirror the behaviours that are included in the TIB-T, so as to facilitate reflection about possible overlaps that could create support.

Not only is a strengths-based framework helpful to use when considering instructional interventions for a student, it is also consistent with the Can-Do framework of the Common European Framework of Reference.

Depending on the educational history of your language learners, you may not have the answers to some of the questions in the profile. If so, leave them blank. These could be areas where you seek help from family members or others who could have this information.

For the student learning profile to use at this point of the protocol, see Chapter 3, pages 60 to 61. There is here, in this chapter, a small addendum to the learning profile step that allows feedback on the student's strengths and that needs to be solicited from other teachers.

For a downloadable version of the student learning profile, see the *Access for Success* website.

Student Learning Across the Classes

The next parts of the protocol document, presented below in Figure 11.3, are specific to different classes. Though you may be teaching the student in several content areas, this part of the document has been separated from the rest in the event it needs to be circulated; a separate page is used for each content area. Do not repeat what you have written so far in the SLP to make sure that the teachers are not influenced by what you have written. Include a note to explain that with this form you are trying to figure out other ways to help this student. The form could be managed by resource personnel in your building, too.

If, after gathering the results, you find that the student challenges are consistent across various classes, consider involving resource teachers and school leaders in discussions about stronger interventions. Be sure to consult parents at this point, too, if they have not yet been a part of the discussion.

If challenges are isolated to certain areas, talk to teachers who see most of the student's strengths on a consistent basis to see whether there are other strategies you could introduce in your class. You may wish to share your concerns with resource teachers, school leaders, and parents, perhaps to brainstorm other possible ways to respond to the student's needs in the class.

Figure 11.3: Individual Content-Area Assessment

Student: ______________________________

Teacher: ______________________________

Subject: ______________________________

Time of day/class period: ______________________________

Please describe the following:

Student Strengths	**Areas of Challenge/Difficulty**

continued

In relation to grade-level expectations, how would you describe the student's performance in class?

Consistent and under-performing	*Inconsis-tent and mostly underper-forming*	*Consis-tent and on-target*	*Inconsis-tent, but mostly on-target*	*Consistent and above-target*	*Inconsis-tent, but mostly above-target*

Analyze the TIB-T and SLP Together

The purpose of this step in the protocol is to provide guidelines and suggestions for interpreting the information captured in the TIB-T and SLP. This step is intended to promote focused reflection rather than advocate for a line-by-line data analysis, in order to inform decision making about a new practice to support the student. We recommend that you write the answers instead of simply thinking about the student in order to ensure that the details about the overlap areas are captured; such documentation may help with later problem solving, too.

1. Begin by reviewing the student's strengths and positive traits as identified in the SLP. Once those traits are identified, consider which teaching techniques in the TIB-T maximize those strengths. Are those practices being used as much as possible? How could helping the student take his/her strengths to a new level address some of the challenges?
2. What are some of the identified challenge areas? How do those challenge areas align with TIB-T techniques that are either used a lot or very little in the classroom? Could any of those challenge areas possibly be better supported if you were to adjust the frequency of the technique's use?
3. In reflecting on your responses to the first two questions, if you have determined that students could be better supported through increased use of certain baseline techniques, develop a plan to increase your use of up to three techniques (maximum) over the course of several weeks. As it takes time to develop new teaching habits and see evidence of how the general techniques support students, not implementing too many techniques at once is important. The techniques need to be used consistently to show benefit.
4. After four weeks (two weeks at the secondary level), if student challenges are continuing, move on to phase 2 of the protocol unless it is clear that you need to further bolster baseline techniques in the classroom. If that's the case, do another TIB-T, and follow the steps outlined in this shaded box.

Phase 2: Focused Attention to and Use of Inclusive Supports

Universal Language and Differentiation Actions: Frequency Analysis and Reflection

Phase 2 of the protocol begins with considering your current use of ULDAs. Again, you are asked to reflect on the extent of your use of certain actions already in your teaching. The actions in the ULDA inventory that follows in Figure 11.4 are designed to help you transition from being a good second language educator (what is covered in the TIB-T) to a good *inclusive* second language educator. Phase 2 of the protocol does assume that good, underlying second language pedagogy is being employed in the classroom.

After completing the inventory, be sure to revisit the SLP and reflect on your student's strengths and learning needs. To what extent are you using ULDAs that leverage the strengths and respond to the learning needs? Which ULDAs (at most three) could you possibly use more frequently in your teaching to provide targeted support to this student? Could any of those ULDAs also be of help to other students in the class or otherwise help foster a more inclusive classroom environment? Keep these ULDAs in mind as you move to the next step of the protocol.

Selection and Targeted Monitoring of a New *Inclusive* Action

Now that you have reflected on the frequency of your use of certain ULDAs and the learning strengths and needs in your classes, it is time to select and implement one or two of those actions in your classroom for the benefit of your students.

From research about language learners, as well as research about intervention protocols, we know that a practice or action is not necessarily going to have an immediate influence on the student's learning; it takes time for a student to become familiar with a new practice or action and use it to personal benefit in a learning experience (Chamot, Barnhardt, El-Dinary, & Robbins, 1999; Fuchs & Fuchs, 2006).

Figure 11.4: Inventory of Universal Language and Differentiation Actions

Universal Language Actions	Several Times a Day	Once a Day	A Few Times a Week	Once a Week	Once or Twice a Month	Never (No Need)
ULAs to Support Learner Understanding						
Using gestures, facial expressions, images, pictures, drawings, objects, and manipulation materials						
Playing with expression and voice intonation, and pacing rate of speech						
Adjusting the complexity of oral and/or written language						
Assessing the extent of prior knowledge and filling in any major gaps						
Providing wait time when presenting new information, after asking a question, or before inviting learners to start a task						
Repeating or reformulating oral and written language						
Reusing and recycling pedagogical materials						
ULAs to Support Learner Language Production						
Providing many exemplars of oral and written tasks						
Using graphic organizers to support oral and written production						
Creating and displaying linguistic supports around the classroom						
Offering planning strategies for learners to use before starting a task						
Using pedagogical and language production routines						
Choosing grouping arrangements that favour peer communication						
Asking questions that encourage learners to elaborate						

continued

Universal Language Actions	Several Times a Day	Once a Day	A Few Times a Week	Once a Week	Once or Twice a Month	Never (No Need)
ULAs to Support Student Attention						
Providing specific listening and reading intentions						
Dividing lessons, activities, and tasks into many small steps						
Incorporating discourse markers to oral and written texts						
Providing explicit cues to refocus learners' attention						
Using different modalities when presenting material						
Explaining the relevance of what is being taught						
Summarizing key points of lessons, activities, and reading passages						
ULAs to Support Vocabulary Development						
Identifying and presenting required language at the outset of a lesson or activity						
Capitalizing on the use of word walls and mind maps						
Accessing the senses to facilitate vocabulary acquisition						
Using role-play and games to present or reinforce new vocabulary						
Explaining vocabulary using examples, synonyms, antonyms, cognates, and teacher/learner definitions						
Differentiation Actions						
Differentiate activities by linguistic complexity						
Differentiate activities by product						
Differentiate activities by process						
Differentiate activities by content						
Grouping students based on interests						
Grouping students based on needs						
Grouping students based on readiness						
Use differentiated instruction over the course of a full lesson						

The purpose of this phase of the protocol is to capture some of the details involved in the decision making about the targeted ULAs or differentiation actions and to provide some general guidance about the implementation and assessment of the actions' effectiveness. Figure 11.5 provides a frame for recording decisions about selecting and implementing an inclusive action. Beyond that, there is a separate tracking sheet for monitoring the action's effectiveness (Figure 11.6) and a chart offering guidance on how to interpret the results of the tracking (Figure 11.7).

Figure 11.5: Selecting and Monitoring an Inclusive Action

Student: ______________________________ Current grade: __________

Action to be targeted: ______________________________

____

Rationale for selecting this action: ______________________________

____

Timeline for implementing action (see below): ______________________________

____

Class(es) where action will be implemented: ______________________________

____

Important Considerations for This Phase

1. It is best to focus on a single action at a time. In that way, you can avoid overwhelming yourself and the student. Taking this kind of focus also makes it easier to determine the impact of the action. However, if you do decide to use a second action, make sure that you track each action's use separately.
2. An action takes time to show an impact. At the elementary level, try the action for at least six weeks before determining next steps; at the intermediate level (even for late immersion students), four weeks; and at the secondary level, three weeks.

   Note: If a student is working with multiple teachers who have noticed the same issue, consider applying the actions in as many classes where it could be relevant to the student.
3. There is a separate sheet for tracking the action use and success (Figure 11.6).

continued

4. Please model and explain the action to the student before beginning its use. Doing so will allow you to ask the student to share perceptions about the effectiveness of the action for his or her learning.
5. You can interpret the results of your experience with the action by using Figure 11.7.

Figure 11.6: Targeted Action Tracking Sheet

Targeted Action Tracking Sheet

Student: ______________________________

Targeted Action: ______________________________

How or When the Action Was Used (e.g., Monday during Math warm-up)	The student's work approached task expectations	The student's work met task expectations	The student's work surpassed task expectations	Was the student's work on this task an improvement over his/her work on similar tasks done earlier?	
				Yes	No

Figure 11.7: Guidance for Interpreting the Results of the Implemented ULDA

After you have tried and tracked the action(s) for the suggested time period, look for the overall trend. Generally, here's how you can interpret the results.

If student's work **approached** task expectations most of the time	AND	Work was consistent with his/her skills and prior performance	THEN	Continue the action for three more weeks to determine if the student can eventually meet the task expectations.
If student's work **approached** task expectations most of the time	AND	Work was **not** consistent with his/her skills and prior performance	THEN	Try another action.
If student's work **met** task expectations most of the time	AND	Work was consistent with his/her skills and prior performance	THEN	Continue with this action in the classroom.
If student's work **met** task expectations most of the time	AND	Work was **not** consistent with his/her skills and prior performance, and it was a **decline** in quality	THEN	Try another action.
If student's work **met** task expectations most of the time	AND	Work was **not** consistent with his/her skills and prior performance, and it was an **increase** in quality	THEN	Continue with this action in the classroom.
If student's work **surpassed** task expectations most of the time	AND	Work was consistent with his/her skills and prior performance	THEN	This task may not have posed difficulty for the student in relation to the targeted challenge; the action impact was negligible.
If student's work **surpassed** task expectations most of the time	AND	Work was **not** consistent with his/her skills and prior performance, and it was a **decline** in quality	THEN	Change the action during this task; it could be that task familiarity limited impact of action.
If student's work **surpassed** task expectations most of the time	AND	Work was **not** consistent with his/her skills and prior performance, and it was an **increase** in quality	THEN	Keep up with this action! It's a clear benefit to the student.

→ If the targeted action did **not** have a favourable impact on student success, choose one more action and monitor for the recommended time period. You may also want to begin other parts of the protocol if a student's work continues to decline.

→ If the targeted action **did** have a favourable impact, continue its use and continue to monitor student progress.

Flexible Parts of the Protocol

These other elements of the protocol can appear in either phase 1 or phase 2, or you can choose to include them as a separate phase 3. This flexibility has been built in to respect individual school and district protocols related to supporting students in need of additional focus. No matter the phase in which they appear, these elements become further data points to consider when making decisions about which techniques to use more frequently in class or which ULAs and differentiation actions to implement in a targeted way.

Seek Information from Parents/Guardians

The purpose of this part of the protocol is to gain some information from parents or guardians in a non-alarming way to help frame support and be more aware of how the home environment may or may not be supporting language education. (Remember from Chapter 1 that it's not critical that parents be speakers of the target language to be able to support the language learning!)

For translations of this document, see the *Access for Success* website.

It is recommended that teachers and schools make this document more "personal," so that it looks less like an official questionnaire for the parents; we have also underlined areas of this inventory that we believe should be edited to reflect the language of study. This inventory could be a good one to send home with all students mid-year or every quarter as a way to keep up with how the home supports language education. Of course, these questions can also be used to guide a parent conference or sent home as email.

Figure 11.8: Parent/Guardian Inventory

Student: ________________________________

Home language(s): ________________________________

Please take a bit of time to respond to the questions and prompts provided here. The information you share will help the teacher know your child better.

Does anyone in the home speak or use <u>*the target language*</u> *with your child?*

(Y/N): ________

(For immersion/elective programs) *Why did you enrol your child in this program?*

____

____

____

continued

What are three adjectives that come to mind when describing your child?

____

What does your child like to do outside of school?

____

____

____

In general, what does your child do well?

____

____

____

In general, what does your child have difficulty doing?

____

____

____

Describe, briefly, what you know about your child's current performance in the language program:

____

____

____

What do you do in the home to support your child's work in the language program?

____

____

____

Describe what you have noticed when your child is doing homework in the target language:

____

____

____

What do you think is easy for your child to do in the target language? (For example: to read, to write)

____

____

____

What do you think is hard for your child to do in the target language? (For example: to read, to write)

____

____

____

continued

In regard to your child's work in the language program, what else do you think the teacher should know about your child?

____

____

____

Parent/Guardian signature: ____________________ Date: __________

Facilitate Collaboration with Other Colleagues

The purpose of this part of the protocol is to guide a dialogue with other colleagues who may be able to help you determine better supports for the student. These colleagues may be other language teachers, resource teachers familiar with special education needs, reading/literacy specialists, or board consultants or supervisors for language education. Each colleague should be given a copy of the student's learning profile before a visit or meeting.

This part of the protocol sets up and debriefs a visit to your classroom focused on observing the challenges in action (see Figure 11.9, which is in two parts). The visit and debriefing can be completed before determining the practice or action you want to implement to help the student, or they can be completed after you have tried out a practice or action with no success and are looking for more ideas.

Figure 11.9: Collaborating in Aid of a Student Needing Better Supports

Part I: Context for the Classroom Visit

Student: ____________________

Briefly describe the strengths of this learner: ____________________

____

____

____

Briefly describe the challenge: ____________________

____

____

____

Identify the strategies that are a regular part of your teaching (based on the TIB-T).

____

____

____

continued

Possible "look-fors" during the observation that may be connected to the challenge (e.g., how the student responds to confusion, how long the student takes to start a task, how the teacher uses multiple modes to explain concepts):

After you have provided the context, arrange a time for the colleague to visit your classroom and observe. Give your colleague a copy of "Observation Notes" and a copy of the student's learning profile.

Part II: Observation Notes

Student: ______________________ Time/Date of observation: ___________________

Subject:

Describe what is happening in class:

What did you see the student do well or in a way that was positive?

In what ways did the student's struggles show through during the class?

Responses to the look-fors identified in Part I

General Notes/Suggestions:

Making Good Decisions Around the Table

We want to draw your attention to a point made by researchers Beth Harry and Janette Klingner (2014), who have considered why students of colour in the United States are over-represented in special education as a proportion of the total student population. In their work, Harry and Klingner found that before the various stakeholders met to address the learning needs of a child having difficulty in the classroom, those stakeholders had already reached a decision about what the learning needs were and what the supports should be. Meetings should not exist simply to confirm ideas—they are meant to *challenge* them. It is important to ensure that meetings are designed to discuss ideas and co-construct a plan—not confirm predetermined outcomes.

We raise this point because a similar risk exists with the COSFILE protocol. We know that many of us teach languages in contexts where we often face challenges.

- School administrators and leaders need to understand the current research about best practices in language education and recognize how their experiences may be shaping their beliefs and practices. Research has found that school administrators are one of the most influential factors in the success of second language programs within a school (Rehorick, 1995).
- For those of us teaching newcomers, there are limited resources (particularly in rural areas) for reaching out to newcomer families and helping them acclimate to Canadian schooling and cultural expectations about learning.
- Our capacities to meet the needs of students, particularly if those needs are unusual or particularly demanding, may be tested or strained.
- Some parents question the value of language study, and some parents select language programs to gain access to a particular school or avoid another learning setting.

All of these forces (and others) can cause us to settle on an opinion too early in a problem-solving situation; it's part of the we've-seen-it-before phenomenon. Looking at surface issues that look like all the other surface issues we've seen before limits our problem-solving skills. We think we are saving time because student A's challenges look much like student B's needs, and this is what we did for student A, so that's what student B must need.

Such an approach may have some basic face validity when you're working with learners in their first language, but it is a precarious mindset to use in a second-language learning context. Why? Remember the apple and pickup truck comparison in Chapter 2. That's why. Each learner needs to be considered relative to his/her own situation, not through any sort of outside standards or comparisons to other learners.

The following tips summarize some suggestions for making around-the-table discussions conducive to truly open discussion about the student's learning needs while using the COSFILE protocol.

Tips for Promoting Effective, Open Problem-Solving Discussions

- Identify a central question you want to answer through the discussion. Doing so allows the discussion to be focused and sets you up for a better outcome. For example, instead of saying that the goal of the discussion is "to help Amir," frame it to a specific need: "How can we help Amir become more confident about speaking in class?"
- Set an agenda for the meeting, in terms of knowing who is going to present what information.
- Bring student work samples. The work samples need to show what the student is doing well and where there are areas of challenge.
- Gather findings from inventories and observations done to this point and share copies with everyone present, so they see the same information you've been seeing. To the extent possible, make those notes available beforehand (though we recognize that if there is a language barrier with parents, this may not be easily achieved).
- At the start of the discussion, agree with those present that no comparisons will be made to other students and situations. If needed, explain why to any parents or guardians present.
- Don't simply talk about the documents and the observations. *Create* something as you are talking out the ideas. We have seen problem-solving situations change completely when the participants have co-constructed T-charts of strengths/challenges or techniques that have worked/techniques that haven't worked, made Venn diagrams comparing what happens in X class versus what happens in Y class, or consolidated findings from inventories and observations from across the school. Patterns are more recognizable—and participants have more time to gather their thoughts—if we take the time to record ideas or information in new ways.
- Set reasonable goals. While you may find it tempting to try to implement as many new initiatives as quickly as possible, that path can backfire quickly because there are too many variables to manage or the time window is unrealistic.

Leadership and Inclusive Language Education

It has been documented in research on inclusive classroom contexts that a teacher's pedagogy is more likely to be inclusive if the teacher holds beliefs that view disabilities and learning challenges as entities that can be shaped or addressed through teaching acts (Jordan, Kircaali-Iftar, & Diamond, 1993; Jordan, Lindsay, & Stanovich, 1997; Jordan & Stanovich, 2001). Further, research has found that a principal's views and beliefs about inclusion will shape the extent to which teachers in that school will hold similar beliefs and, consequently, engage in inclusive teaching practice (Stanovich & Jordan, 1998). Thus, we can extend this to say that the beliefs of those in school leadership roles (including those in district offices) can influence the extent to which inclusive learning contexts are facilitated and nurtured.

Within any organization, this leadership can take many forms. There are leaders who consider their power and authority absolute: they make decisions independently about the values and actions that will define their enterprise, and they may expect allegiance to those values and actions as a condition of membership. There are leaders who believe that they can and should make the "final call" in a situation or otherwise set the tone for a particular context, but they also invite differing perspectives and seek out information from various resources to make those decisions. There are leaders who view their role as that of a servant-leader, in that their primary power and authority is to do what will empower others in the setting to maximize their potential and do their best in their own jobs. There are leaders who view their primary role as that of a facilitator, helping others in the organization access resources and learning opportunities that allow them to independently problem-solve and reach new conclusions. There are leaders who combine several of the aforementioned qualities or introduce others. And, so far, there is no evidence to suggest that certain leadership styles are more likely than others to be tied to viewpoints that enable inclusive language education.

All of that said, how does leadership figure into our current efforts to make language education more inclusive? To answer that, we must think about the two likely populations reading this text. First, some of you reading this are in positions of leadership, and you want to increase efforts to support inclusive language education in your district or make it more of a reality, in general. Some of you, conversely, are individuals who want to help those in leadership positions better understand language education and how it can take place in an inclusive learning environment. Both groups of readers are likely confronting questions about how to engage reluctant personalities, how to articulate the importance of inclusive language education, and how to convince others to find the time in their already busy teaching lives to make this a priority.

Based on our experiences designing and leading professional learning experiences for teachers and school leaders about this topic, we have found that, really, leadership in support of inclusive language education is about asking questions and sparking discussions. It is not about creating policies and letting folks figure out how to implement them. It is not about stating views and convincing folks to jump on board. Really, it is about creating the space for a conversation, seeding that conversation with ideas and observations that are pertinent to the context, taking the time to listen and respond to the views shared, and working to find common ground. Although we don't have the empirical evidence to support the effectiveness of our experiences, anecdotal evidence has revealed shifts toward more inclusive teaching education by invoking the facilitating leadership style mentioned earlier. To that end, Figure 11.10 offers some conversation starters and jump-start actions for individuals who are leading "from the top" (who hold titular positions of power/authority within the education hierarchy and want to influence those who do not hold these positions) and individuals who are leading "from the bottom" (who do not hold titular positions of power/authority and want to influence those who do).

Figure 11.10: Facilitating Conversations and Actions in Support of Inclusive Language Education

Questions for Those Leading "from the Top"	Questions for Those Leading "from the Bottom"	Possible Follow-Up Actions
• What are some of the learning strengths and learning needs in your classes? • How have you leveraged those strengths or responded to those needs? • What supports and resources have you used to help your students? • What supports and resources do you think would be of additional help? • What do you want to know about or know how to do to better support the students in your class? • What questions about student needs or teaching would you like help answering? • Tell me about a success story with a student. What do you see as your role in facilitating that success? • When you encounter a student who is having difficulty in your class, what do you do?	• What were your experiences as a language learner or with language learning? How do those experiences inform what you do now? • Besides the actual words used to express ideas in another language, what do you believe is gained by studying another language? • In your view, how is teaching a language similar to or different from teaching any other content? • When students have challenges in a classroom, what sorts of supports have you recommended to teachers? (Once you have a reply, ask, "How do these recommendations overlap with what you think happens in a language classroom?") • What sort of information would you like to read or review to see how inclusive language education could be better supported here? • Would you like to visit my class and see how I work with all of these students?	• Form a book club using a professional learning text focused on inclusive language education. (We have a few suggestions!) • Locate additional readings to extend your learning in this area. • Reach out to local scholars and researchers and/or advocacy organizations and find out whether they would share their insights or experiences. • Engage in online discussions with learning communities about the topic. • Arrange classroom visits and debrief the visits over coffee. Make a visit less like a formal observation.

For further reading, consider seeking out an article that Katy wrote for a publication targeted to school principals (Arnett, 2013b). This article explores ways school leaders can facilitate dialogues in their learning communities that explore key tensions that often emerge when discussing inclusion. These tensions, when left unacknowledged or unexplored, can create frustration about including all students.

Closing Thoughts

In the Canadian educational landscape, we place a lot of value on collaborating, problem-solving for the benefit of the student, and working diligently to help students succeed to the greatest extent possible. As teachers, we want to ensure that we are using pedagogies that foster learning and promote student engagement, but sometimes our pedagogy and the needs of a student are misaligned. As members of a larger community of individuals invested in the success of language learners, we also want those who are similarly involved to be engaged, critical partners who allow us to dialogue in constructive ways.

As you reflect on the contents of the chapter, consider the following questions:

- How does the COSFILE protocol align or contrast with processes already in place at our school?
- At the school level, who should be involved with the COSFILE? Is this something to use with my grade-level team? with my department?
- How do I think the COSFILE or parts of it could be best used in support of language learners in my context?
- How would I sequence the COSFILE protocol for use in my school? In general, how can the COSFILE be adapted for our context?
- Are there other steps or stakeholders currently not in the protocol that I would be wise to include?
- In collaborative decision making, how can I work to avoid crystallizing my viewpoint before hearing the positions of others?

Conclusion

Throughout this book, we have highlighted the need for focus on four access points: access points that facilitate students' access to learning a second language or curriculum in a second language and that facilitate inclusionary practices designed to meet the various needs of our language learners. We see inclusion as an ongoing experience, not a finite goal of our teaching. To that end, we hope you have come to see this book as a resource to consult while you navigate your own path as an inclusive second language educator. We also hope that you continue to use this resource to help you in reorienting any socially and politically constructed ideas and practices that, at times, hinder access to second language learning.

We all need to continue striving to provide collective support for inclusion for all language learners who desire to learn an additional language. It is important to work together in continuing to shape attitudes toward second language learning. We all have the potential to promote and influence inclusionary practices for second language learners.

Graham Fraser (2012), Canada's former commissioner of official languages, said, "All Canadian children should have the opportunity to become bilingual" (p. 5). We agree with him, and we wish to extend this sentiment beyond Canada's borders in stating that no child *anywhere* should be left out of second language learning experiences, and, more important, every child should feel supported throughout his or her language learning journey.

Over the course of writing this book together (and working on the various projects that led to us writing this book), we have had numerous conversations about inclusion and how it can be put into use in language education contexts. We have talked at length with each other about what we did or would do differently now in our own language classrooms to facilitate inclusion. We have consulted with each other on the various inquiries we have had related to inclusive language education. We have discussed findings from empirical research and reviews of research literature. We have conducted action research projects, reviewed artifacts created during professional development sessions, and discussed their implications for practice. We have talked about how we facilitate inquiries of inclusion with teacher candidates and in-service teachers and administrators and how we answered the many questions we get during those sessions. We have compared notes on queries received from school districts, departments or ministries of education, and parents. We have talked to several other educators about inclusive language education, too.

No matter the conversation, we have always ended it with more ideas about how to help teachers facilitate more inclusive language classrooms. We hope that in this resource, you have found viable ideas for helping you make progress on your journey toward providing an inclusive second language classroom. Onward!

Katy   Renée

Chapter 2: 1. Breaking the Code, page 37

Decoding a language, letter by letter, symbol by symbol, word by word, is a time-consuming process. So much energy is focused on decoding the message that there is little energy or effort left to figure out the meaning of the message. Further, if you are listening to the language, you will likely miss a lot of content after the first phrases because you were so focused on what came first.

Chapter 2: 2. Putting Pieces Together, page 39

It's not uncommon for language learners to become frustrated, tired, or lose interest in a task if the language barrier is pretty high. Answering questions about a text (spoken or written) that they can partially decode is particularly challenging. As you are seeing now, just working through a few sentences takes a lot of focus to figure out the message, connect it to old knowledge, and keep track of it in your memory. Let's see how you've done once you go to answer the questions.

1. What are possible consequences of a high language barrier?
2. What requires a lot of focus?
3. How much did you have to reread these sentences to follow the message?

References

Anderson, L. W., & Krathwohl, D. R. (Eds.). (2001). *A taxonomy for learning, teaching, and assessing: A revision of Bloom's taxonomy of educational objectives.* Boston, MA: Allyn & Bacon.

Arnett, K. (2003). Teacher adaptations in Core French: A case study of one grade 9 class. *Canadian Modern Language Review, 60*(2), 173–198.

Arnett, K. (2008). Exploring the use of student perspectives to inform topics in teacher education: Issues in creating an inclusive Core French classroom. *Canadian Journal of Applied Linguistics, 11*, 63–81.

Arnett, K. (2010). Scaffolding inclusion in a grade 8 Core French classroom: An exploratory case study. *Canadian Modern Language Review, 66*(4), 603–628.

Arnett, K. (2013a). French second language exemptions: Should students with learning disabilities be excused from French class? *Education Canada, 53*(2). Retrieved from http://www.cea-ace.ca/fr/education-canada/article/french-second-languageexemptions

Arnett, K. (2013b). The genesis and perpetuation of exemptions and transfers from French second language programs for students with diverse learning needs: A preliminary examination and their link to inclusion. In K. Arnett & C. Mady (Eds.), *Minority populations in Canadian second language education* (pp. 103–117). Bristol, UK: Multilingual Matters.

Arnett, K. (2013c). *Languages for all: How to support and challenge students in a second language classroom.* Toronto, ON: Pearson Education Canada.

Arnett, K. (2014). Stakeholders' inquiries about the systemic inclusion of late adolescent newcomers to Canada: Moving from questions to understandings. *LEARNing Landscapes, 7*(2), 41–58.

Arries, J. F. (1999). Learning disabilities and foreign languages: A curriculum approach to the design of inclusive courses. *The Modern Language Journal, 83*(1), 98–110.

Asher, J. J. (1969). The total physical response approach to second language learning. *The Modern Language Journal, 53*(1), 3–17.

Ausubel, D. P. (1963). *The psychology of meaningful verbal learning.* New York, NY: Grune & Stratton.

Baker, C. (2011). *Foundations of bilingual education and bilingualism.* Bristol, UK: Multilingual Matters.

Bandura, A. (1982). Self-efficacy mechanism in human agency. *American Psychologist, 37*(2), 122–147.

Bandura, A. (1984). Recycling misconceptions of perceived self-efficacy. *Cognitive Therapy and Research, 8*(3), 231–255.

Bandura, A. (1986a). *Social foundations of thought and action: A social cognitive theory.* Englewood Cliffs, NJ: Prentice-Hall.

Bandura, A. (1986b). The explanatory and predictive scope of self-efficacy theory. *Journal of Clinical and Social Psychology, 4*(3), 359–373.

Bandura, A. (1988). Self-regulation of motivation and action through goal systems. In V. Hamilton, G. H. Bower, & N. H. Frijda (Eds.), *Cognitive perspectives on emotion and motivation* (pp. 37–61). Dordrecht, the Netherlands: Kluwer Academic.

Bear Nicholas, A. (2009). Reversing language shift through a native language immersion. In T. Skutnabb-Kangas, R. Phillipson, A. K. Mohanty, & M. Panda (Eds.), *Social justice through multilingual education* (pp. 220–237). Bristol, UK: Multilingual Matters.

Beglar, D. (2010). A research-based validation of the vocabulary size test. *Language Testing, 27*(1), 101–118.

Bialystok, E. (2001). *Bilingualism in development: Language, literacy, & cognition.* Cambridge, UK: Cambridge University Press.

Biggs, J. (1999). What the student does: Teaching for enhanced learning. *Higher Education Research & Development, 18*(1), 57–75.

Bild, E.R., & Swain, M. (1989). Minority language students in a French Immersion programme: Their French proficiency. *Journal of Multilingual and Multicultural Development, 10*(3), 255–274.

Birdsong, D., & Park, J. (2008). Second language acquisition and ultimate attainment. In B. Spolsky & F. Hult (Eds.), *The handbook of educational linguistics* (pp. 424–436). Malden, MA: Blackwell.

Black, P. (2009). Formative assessment issues across the curriculum: The theory and the practice. *TESOL Quarterly, 43*(3), 519–524.

Black, P., Harrison, C., Lee, C., Marshall, B., & Wiliam, D. (2003). *Assessment for learning: Putting it into practice.* Maidenhead, UK: Open University Press.

Black, P. J., & Wiliam, D. (1998). Assessment and classroom learning. *Assessment in Education: Principles, Policy & Practice, 5*(1), 7–73.

Black, P. J., & Wiliam, D. (2009). Developing the theory of formative assessment. *Educational Assessment, Evaluation and Accountability, 21*(1), 5–31.

Bloom, B. S., & Krathwohl, D. R. (1956). *Taxonomy of educational objectives: The classification of educational goals, by a committee of college and university examiners. Handbook I: Cognitive domain.* White Plains, NY: Longman.

Bourgoin, R. (2014). Inclusionary practices in French immersion: A need to link research to practice. *Canadian Journal for New Scholars in Education, 5*(1), 1–11.

Bourgoin, R. (2016). French immersion "So why would you do something like that to a child?": Issues of advocacy, accessibility, and inclusion. *International Journal of Bias, Identity and Diversities in Education, 1*(1), 42–58.

Bourgoin, R., & Dicks, J. (2013). Reading without borders: At risk students transitioning from L1 to L2 in French immersion. In K. Arnett & C. Mady (Eds.), *Minority populations in Canadian second language education* (pp. 118–134). Bristol, UK: Multilingual Matters.

Bourgoin, R., & Dicks, J. (in press). Learning to read in French and English: An exploration of allophone students' reading development in French immersion [Special issue]. *Language and Literacy.*

Bournot-Trites, M. (2008). *Fostering reading acquisition in French immersion.* Vancouver, BC: University of British Columbia, Department of Language and Literacy Education.

Brookhart, S. (2008). Feedback that fits. *Educational Leadership, 65*(4), 54–59.

Bruck, M. (1978). The suitability of early French immersion programs for the language disabled child. *Canadian Journal of Education, 3*(4), 51–72.

Bruck, M. (1982). Language impaired children's performance in an additive bilingual education program. *Applied Psycholinguistics, 3*(1), 45–60.

Bruner, J. (1996). *The culture of education.* Cambridge, MA: Harvard University Press.

Cenoz, J. (2003). The additive effect of bilingualism on third language acquisition: A review. *International Journal of Bilingualism, 7*(1), 71–87.

Cenoz, J., & Hoffman, C. (Eds.). (2003). The effect of bilingualism on third language acquisition [Special issue]. *International Journal of Bilingualism, 7*(1).

Cenoz, J., & Valencia, J. F. (1994). Additive trilingualism: Evidence from the Basque Country. *Applied Psycholinguistics, 15*(2), 195–207.

Center for Applied Special Technology. (2001). *Universal design for learning.* Wakefield, MA: CAST.

Chamot, A. U., Barnhardt, S., El-Dinary, P. B., & Robbins, J. (1999). *The learning strategies handbook.* White Plains, NY: Addison Wesley Longman.

Chamot, A. U., & El-Dinary, P. B. (1999). Children's learning strategies in language immersion classrooms. *The Modern Language Journal, 83*(3), 319–338.

Chappuis, J., Stiggins, R., Chappuis, S., & Arter, J. (2012). *Classroom assessment for student learning: Doing it right—using it well* (2nd ed.). Upper Saddle River, NJ: Pearson Education.

Chumak-Horbatch, R. (2012). *Linguistically appropriate practice: A guide for working with young immigrant children.* Toronto, ON: University of Toronto Press.

Clay, M. M. (1993). *An observation survey of early literacy achievement.* Auckland, NZ: Heinemann.

Clay, M. M. (2003). *Le sondage dobservation en lecture-écriture.* Montreal, QC: Chenelière/McGraw-Hill.

Coelho, E. (2004). *Adding English: A guide to teaching in multilingual classrooms* (2nd ed.). Toronto, ON: Pippin.

Coelho, E. (2012). *Language and learning in multilingual classrooms: A practical approach.* Bristol, UK: Multilingual Matters.

Coelho, E. (2016). *Adding English: A guide to teaching in multilingual classrooms* (2nd ed.). Toronto, ON: University of Toronto Press.

Coffield, F., Moseley, D., Hall, E., & Eccelstone, K. (2004). *Learning styles and pedagogy in post-16 learning: A systematic and critical review.* London, UK: Learning & Skills Research Centre. Retrieved from http://sxills.nl/lerenlerennu/bronnen/Learning%20styles%20by%20Coffield%20e.a..pdf

Colby-Kelly, C., & Turner, C. E. (2007). AFL research in the L2 classroom and evidence of usefulness: Taking formative assessment to the next level. *Canadian Modern Language Review/La revue canadienne de langues vivantes, 64*(1), 9–37.

Collier, V. P. (1987). Age and rate of acquisition of second language for academic purposes. *TESOL Quarterly, 21*(4), 617–641.

Collier, V. P. (1995). Acquiring a second language for school. *Directions in Language and Education, 1*(4). Retrieved from National Clearinghouse for Bilingual Education http://www.ncbe.gwu.edu/nchepubs/directions/O4.htm

Council of Ministers of Education, Canada. (2010). *Working with the common European framework for languages in the Canadian context: Guide for policy-makers and curriculum designers.* Toronto, ON: Author.

Coxhead, A. (2000). A new academic word List. *TESOL Quarterly, 34*(2), 213–238. Retrieved from http://www.jstor.org/stable/3587951

Culligan, K. (2010). Pente or slope? Using student voices to explore program choice and experiences in secondary French immersion mathematics. *Canadian Modern Language Review, 66*(3), 421–444.
Cummins, J. (1983). *Bilingualism and special education: Issues in assessment and pedagogy.* Bristol, UK: Multilingual Matters.
Cummins, J. (2000). *Language, power and pedagogy: Bilingual children in the crossfire.* Bristol, UK: Multilingual Matters.
Cummins, J. (2001). *Negotiating identities: Education for empowerment in a diverse society* (2nd ed.). Los Angeles, CA: California Association for Bilingual Education.
Cummins, J., & Early, M. (Eds.). (2011). *Identity texts: The collaborative creation of power in multilingual schools.* Stoke-on-Trent, UK: Trentham Books.
Cunningham, A. E. (2005). Vocabulary growth through independent reading and reading aloud to children. In E. H. Hiebert & M. Kamil (Eds.), *Teaching and learning vocabulary: Bringing research to practice* (pp. 45–68). Mahwah, NJ: Erlbaum.
Cunningham, A. E., & Stanovich, K. E. (1998). What reading does for the mind. *American Educator, 22*(1&2), 8–17.
Dagenais, D., & Berron, C. (2001). Promoting multilingualism through French immersion and language maintenance in three immigrant families. *Language, Culture, and Curriculum, 14*(2), 142–155.
Davies, A. (2007). *Making classroom assessment work* (3rd ed.). Courtenay, BC: Connections.
DeCapua, A., Smathers, W., & Tang, F. (2007). Addressing the challenges and needs of students with interrupted formal education (SIFE). *Educational Policy & Leadership, 65*, 40–46.
Delpit, L. (2006). *Other people's children: Cultural conflict in the classroom.* New York, NY: New Press.
Dicks, J. E. (1995). *A comparative study of the acquisition of French verb tense and aspect in early, middle, and late immersion.* Sainte-Foy, QC: Centre International de Recherche en Amènagement Linguistique.
Dicks, J., & Kristmanson, P. (2008). French immersion: When and why? In *The state of French-second-language education in Canada* (p. 16). Ottawa, ON: Canadian Parents for French.
Dörnyei, Z. (1994). Motivation and motivating in the foreign language classroom. *The Modern Language Journal, 78*(3), 273–284.
Dörnyei, Z. (1998). Motivation in second and foreign language learning. *Language Teaching, 31*(3), 117–135.
Dörnyei, Z. (2005). *The psychology of the language learner: Individual differences in second language acquisition.* Mahwah, NJ: Lawrence Erlbaum.
Dörnyei, Z. (2007). Creating a motivating classroom environment. In J. Cummins & C. Davison (Eds.), *International handbook of English language teaching* (Vol. 2, pp. 719–731). New York, NY: Springer.
Dörnyei, Z. (2009). *The psychology of second language acquisition.* Oxford, UK: Oxford University Press.
Dörnyei, Z., & Csizér, K. (1998). Ten commandments for motivating language learners: Results of an empirical study. *Language Teaching Research, 2*(3), 203–229.
Douglas, S. (2013). After the first 2,000: A response to Horst's "Mainstreaming second language vocabulary acquisition." *Canadian Journal of Applied Linguistics, 16*(1), 189–199.
Dunn, L., Morgan, C., O'Reilly, M., & Parry, S. (2004). *The student assessment handbook.* New York, NY: RoutledgeFalmer.
Durgunoglu, A. (2002). Cross-linguistic transfer in literacy development and implications for language learning. *Annals of Dyslexia, 52*(1), 189–204.
Eagleton, M. (2008). Universal design for learning. *EBSCO Research Starters: Academic topic overviews,* 1. Retrieved from https://www.ebscohost.com/uploads/imported/thisTopic-dbTopic-1073.pdf
Echevarria, J., Vogt, M. E., & Short, D. J. (2016). *Making content comprehensible for English learners: The SIOP model* (5th ed.). Boston, MA: Pearson.
Ellis, N. C. (2001). Memory for language. In P. Robinson (Ed.), *Cognition and second language instruction* (pp. 33–68). Cambridge, UK: Cambridge University Press.
Erlam, R. (2005). Language aptitude and its relation to instructional effectiveness in second language acquisition. *Language Teaching Research, 9*(2), 147–171.
Fadel, C. (2008). *Multimodal learning through media: What the research says.* San Jose, CA: Cisco Systems.
Fairbairn, S. B., & Jones-Vo, S. (2010). *Differentiating instruction and assessment for English learners: A guide for K–12 teachers.* Philadelphia, PA: Caslon.
Farrand, P., Hussain, F., & Hennessy, E. (2002). The efficacy of the "mind map" study technique. *Medical Education, 36*(5), 426–431.
Fisher, D., & Frey, N. (2014). Scaffolded reading instruction of content-area texts. *The Reading Teacher, 67*(5), 347–351.

Fountas, I. C., & Pinnell, G. S. (2001). *Guided readers and writers.* Portsmouth, NH: Heinemann.
Fraser, G. (2012, June). Key note address. *Proceedings of the Canadian Parents for French roundtable on academically challenged students in French-second-language programs.* Ottawa, ON: Canadian Parents for French.
Fuchs, D., & Fuchs, L. S. (2006). Introduction to response to intervention: What, why, and how valid is it? *Reading Research Quarterly, 41*(1), 93–99.
Genesee, F. (1991, avril–juin). L'immersion et l'apprenant défavorisé. *Études de linguistique appliquée, 82,* 77–93.
Genesee, F. (1992). Second/foreign language immersion and at-risk English-speaking children. *Foreign Language Annals, 25*(3), 199–213.
Genesee, F. (1998). French immersion in Canada. In J. Edwards (Ed.), *Language in Canada* (pp. 305–326). Cambridge, UK: Cambridge University Press.
Genesee, F. (2007a). French immersion and at-risk students: A review of research evidence. *Canadian Modern Language Review/La revue canadienne des langues vivantes, 63*(5), 655–687.
Genesee, F. (2007b). Literacy outcomes in French immersion. In *Encyclopedia of language and literacy development* (pp. 1–8). London, ON: Canadian Language and Literacy Research Network. Retrieved from http://literacyencyclopedia.ca/index.php?fa=items.show&topicId=27
Genesee, F. (2013). Insights into bilingual education from research on immersion programs in Canada. In C. Abello-Contesse, P. M. Chandler, M. D. López-Jiménez, & R. C. Beltrán (Eds.), *Bilingual and multilingual education in the 21st century: Building on experience* (pp. 24–41). Bristol, UK: Multilingual Matters.
Genesee, F., & Jared, D. (2008). Literacy development in early French immersion programs. *Canadian Psychology, 49*(2), 140–147.
Genesee, F., Paradis, J., & Crago, M. (2004). *Dual language development and disorders: A handbook on bilingualism and second language learning.* Baltimore, MD: Paul H. Brookes.
Giasson, J., & Theriault, J. (1983). *Apprentissage et enseignement de la lecture.* Montreal, QC: Les Éditions Ville-Marie.
Grenoble, L. A., & Whaley, L. J. (2006). *Saving languages: An introduction to language revitalization.* New York, NY: Cambridge University Press.
Harry, B., & Klingner, J. (2014). *Why are so many minority students in special education? Understanding race and disability in schools* (2nd ed.). New York, NY: Teachers College Press.
Heacox, D. (2002). *Differentiating instruction in the regular classroom: How to reach and teach all learners, grades 3–12.* Minneapolis, MN: Free Spirit.
Heacox, D. (2009). *Making differentiation a habit: How to ensure success in academically diverse classrooms.* Minneapolis, MN: Free Spirit.
Hennessey, K. (2016). *L'exploration des actions pédagogiques universelles en immersion française* (Unpublished master's thesis). University of New Brunswick, Fredericton, Canada.
Hill, J. D., & Flynn, K. (2008). Asking the right questions: Teachers' questions can build students' English skills. *Journal of Staff Development, 29*(1), 46–52. Retrieved from www.nsdc.org
Hope, S. A. (2011). Making movies: The next big thing in feedback. *Bioscience Education, 18,* 1–14. doi: 10.3108/beej.18.2SE
Horst, M. (2005). Learning L2 vocabulary through extensive reading: A measurement study. *Canadian Modern Language Review, 61*(3), 355–382.
Horst, M. (2013). Mainstreaming second language vocabulary acquisition. *Canadian Journal of Applied Linguistics, 16*(1), 171–188.
Horwitz, E. (2013). *Becoming a language teacher: A practical guide to second language learning and teaching* (2nd ed.). Toronto, ON: Pearson.
Howden, J. (1995). Talking for learning: Using cooperative learning in second language classrooms. *SPEAQ, Journal (La société pour le perfectionnement de l'enseignement de l'anglais, langue seconde, au Québec)* (spring).
Hume, K. (2009). *Start where they are: Differentiating for success with the young adolescent.* Toronto, ON: Pearson Education Canada.
Hurst, D. (1996). Teaching Spanish to children with different learning styles: Evolution of philosophy. *Hispania, 79*(1), 123–125.
Hyland, F. (2003). Focusing on form: Student engagement with teacher feedback. *System, 31*(2), 217–230.
Hyland, K., & Hyland, F. (2006). Feedback on second language students' writing. *Language Teaching, 39*(2), 83–101.
Jiang, Y. (2014). Exploring teacher questioning as a formative assessment strategy. *RELC Journal, 45,* 287–304. doi: 10.1177/0033688214546962

Jordan, A., Kircaali-Iftar, G., & Diamond, C.T. P. (1993). Who has a problem, the student or the teacher? Differences in teachers' beliefs about their work with at-risk and integrated exceptional students. *International Journal of Disability, Development and Education, 40*(1), 45–62.

Jordan, A., Lindsay, L., & Stanovich, P. (1997). Classroom teachers' instructional interactions with students who are exceptional, at-risk, and typically achieving. *Remedial and Special Education, 18*(2), 82–93.

Jordan, A., & Stanovich, P. (2001). Patterns of teacher–student interaction in inclusive elementary classrooms and correlates with student self-concept. *International Journal of Disability, Development, and Education, 48*(1), 33–52.

Joy, R., & Murphy, E. (2012). The inclusion of children with special education needs in an Intensive French as a second-language program: From theory to practice. *Canadian Journal of Education/Revue canadienne de l'éducation, 35*(1), 102–119.

Kamil, M. L., & Hiebert, E. H. (2005). The teaching and learning of vocabulary: Perspectives and persistent issues. In E. H. Hiebert & M. L. Kamil (Eds.), *Teaching and learning vocabulary: Bringing research to practice* (pp. 1–23). Mahwah, NJ: Erlbaum.

Klein, E. C. (1995). Second versus third language acquisition: Is there a difference? *Language Learning, 45*(3), 419–465.

Klein, L. (2007). Auto-évaluation: Daily self-assessment in the FSL classroom. *Canadian Modern Language Review/La revue canadienne de langues vivantes, 67*(1), 181–197.

Krashen, S. (1977). Some issues relating to the Monitor Model. In H. D. Brown, C. Yorio, & R. Crymes (Eds.), *On TESOL '77: Teaching and learning English as a second language: Trends in research and practice* (pp. 144–158). Washington, DC: TESOL.

Krashen, S. (1981). S*econd language acquisition and second language learning.* Toronto, ON: Pergamon Press Canada.

Krashen, S. (1982). *Principles and practice in second language learning and acquisition.* Elmsford, NY: Pergamon Press.

Krashen, S., & Terrell, T. (1983). *The natural approach: Language acquisition in the classroom.* Hayward, CA: Alemany Press.

Kristmanson, P., Dicks, J., LeBouthillier, J., & Bourgoin, R. (2008). L'écriture en immersion française: Les meilleurs pratiques et le rôle d'une communauté professionnelle d'apprentissage. *Canadian Journal of Applied Linguistics, 11*(1), 41–62.

Lambert, W. E., & Tucker, G. R. (1972). *Bilingual education of children: The St. Lambert experiment.* Rowley, MA: Newbury House.

Laufer, B. (1998). The development of passive and active vocabulary in a second language: Same or different? *Applied Linguistics, 12*(2), 255–271.

Laufer, B. (2006). Comparing focus on form and focus on forms in second language vocabulary learning. *Canadian Modern Language Review, 63*(1), 149–166.

LeBlanc, R. (1990). *The national Core French study—A synthesis.* Ottawa, ON: Canadian Association of Second Language Teachers.

LeBouthillier, J. (2013). The writing processes of a grade 7 French immersion student with Asperger syndrome. In K. Arnett & C. Mady (Eds.), *Minority populations in second language education: Broadening the lens from Canada.* Bristol, UK: Multilingual Matters.

LeBouthillier, J. (in press). A sociocognitive model of interventions for writing instruction. *Journal of Immersion and Content-Based Learning.*

Lee, I. (2007). Assessment for learning: Integrating assessment, teaching, and learning in the ESL/EFL writing classroom. *Canadian Modern Language Review/La revue canadienne de langues vivantes, 64*(1), 199–213.

Leung, C. (2004). Developing formative teacher assessment: Knowledge, practice, and change. *Language Assessment Quarterly, 1*, 19–41. doi: 10.1208/s15434311laq0101_3

Lightbown, P., & Spada, N. (2013). *How languages are learned* (4th ed.). Oxford, UK: Oxford University Press.

Little, D. (2005). The common European framework and the European language portfolio: Involving learners and their judgments in the assessment process. *Language Testing, 22*(3), 321–336.

Long, M. H., & Porter, P. A. (1985). Group work, interlanguage talk, and second language acquisition. *TESOL Quarterly, 19*(2), 207–228.

Long, M. H., & Sato, C. (1983). Classroom foreigner talk discourse: Forms and functions of teachers' questions. In H. W. Seliger & M. H. Long (Eds.), *Classroom oriented research in second language acquisition* (pp. 268–286). Cambridge: Newbury House.

Lyster, R. (1987). Speaking immersion. *Canadian Modern Language Review, 43*(4), 701–717.

Lyster, R. (1998). Recasts, repetition, and ambiguity in L2 classroom discourse. *Studies in Second Language Acquisition, 20*(1), 55–85.

Lyster, R. (2001). Negotiation of form, recasts, and explicit correction in relation to error types and learner repair in immersion classrooms. *Language Learning, 51*(1), 265–301.

Lyster, R., & Ranta, L. (1997). Corrective feedback and learner uptake: Negotiation of form in communicative classrooms. *Studies in Second Language Acquisition, 19*(1), 37–66.

Lyster, R., & Saito, K. (2010). Oral feedback in classroom SLA: A meta-analysis. *Studies in Second Language Acquisition, 32*, 265–302. doi:10.1017/S0272263109990520

MacCourbrey, S., Wade-Woolley, L., Klinger, D., & Kirby, J. (2004). Early identification of at-risk L2 readers. *Canadian Modern Language Review, 61*(1), 11–28.

MacIntyre, P. D. (1994). Variables underlying willingness to communicate: A causal analysis. *Communication Research Reports, 11*(2), 135–142.

MacIntyre, P. D. (1999). Language anxiety: A review of literature for language teachers. In D. J. Young (Ed.), *Affect in foreign language and second language learning* (pp. 24–43). New York, NY: McGraw Hill.

Mady, C. (2003). *Motivation to study and investment in studying Core French in secondary school: Comparing English as a second language students and Canadian-born students* (Unpublished master's thesis). Ontario Institute for Studies in Education of the University of Toronto (OISE/UT), Toronto, ON.

Mady, C. (2007a). Allophone students in second-official language programs. *Canadian Modern Language Review, 63*(5), 727–760.

Mady, C. (2007b). The suitability of Core French for recently arrived adolescent immigrants to Canada. *Canadian Journal of Applied Linguistics, 10*(2), 177–196.

Mady, C. (2013a). Adding languages, adding benefits: Immigrant students' attitudes toward and performance in FSOL programs in Canada. In K. Arnett & C. Mady (Eds.), *Minority populations in second language education: Broadening the lens from Canada* (pp. 3–21). Bristol, UK: Multilingual Matters.

Mady, C. (2013b). Learning French as a second official language in Canada: Comparing monolingual and bilingual students at grade 6. *International Journal of Bilingual Education and Bilingualism, 17*(3), 330–344. Retrieved from http://dx.doi.org/10.1080/13670050.2013.767778

Mady, C., & Arnett, K. (2009). Inclusion in French Immersion in Canada: One parent's perspective. *Exceptionality Education International, 19*(2), 37–49. Retrieved from http://ir.lib.uwo.ca/eei/vol19/iss2/4

Mady, C., & Arnett, K. (2015). French as a second language teacher candidates' conceptions of allophone students and students with learning difficulties. *Canadian Journal of Applied Linguistics, 18*(2), 78–95.

Mannavarayan, J. M. (2003). *The French immersion debate: French for all or all for French?* Calgary, AB: Detselig Enterprises.

Marzano, R. J. (2007). *The art and science of teaching: A comprehensive framework for effective instruction.* Alexandria, VA: ASCD.

Mayer, R. E., & Massa, L. J. (2003). Three facets of visual and verbal learners: Cognitive ability, cognitive style, and learning preference. *Journal of Educational Psychology, 95*(4), 833–846.

McVey, M., Bonyun, R., Dicks, J., & Dionne, L. (1990). *Early, middle, or late? Ottawa board of education students in three French Immersion programs in grade 6 and grade 8.* Ottawa, ON: Ottawa Board of Education.

Meara, P. M. (2009). *Connected words: Word associations and second language vocabulary acquisition.* Amsterdam, the Netherlands: John Benjamins.

Meara, P. M. (2014). Vocabulary research in the *Modern Language Journal*: A bibliometric analysis. *Vocabulary Learning and Instruction, 3*(1), 1–28.

Mehan, H. (1979). *Learning lessons: Social organization in the classroom.* Cambridge, MA: Harvard University Press.

Met, M. (1994). Teaching content through a second language. In F. Genesee (Ed.), *Educating second language children: The whole child, the whole curriculum, the whole community* (pp. 159–182). New York, NY: Cambridge University Press.

Moll, L. C., Amanti, C., Neff, D., & Gonzalez, N. (1992). Funds of knowledge for teaching: Using a qualitative approach to connect homes and classrooms. *Theory into Practice, 31*(2), 132–141.

Naiman, N., Frölich, M., Stern, H. H., & Todesco, A. (1996). *The good language learner.* Bristol, UK: Multilingual Matters.

Nation, P. (2001). *Learning vocabulary in another language.* Cambridge, UK: Cambridge University Press.

Nation, P. (2006). Vocabulary: Second language. In Keith Brown (Ed.), *Encyclopedia of language & linguistics* (2nd ed., pp. 448–454). Oxford, UK: Elsevier.

National Indian Brotherhood/Assembly of First Nations. (1972). *Indian control of Indian education: Policy paper.* Ottawa, ON: Author.

Netten, J., & Germain, C. (2004). Theoretical and research foundations of Intensive French. *Canadian Modern Language Review, 60*(3), 275–294.

Netten, J., & Germain, C. (2005). Pedagogy and second language learning: Lessons learned from Intensive French. *Canadian Journal of Applied Linguistics, 8*(2), 183–210.

Norton, B., & Toohey, K. (2011). Identity, language learning, and social change. *Language Teaching, 44*(4), 412–446.

Orlich, D. C., Harder, R. J., Callahan, R. C, Trevisan, M. S., & Brown, A. (2012). *Teaching strategies: A guide to effective instruction* (10th ed.). Belmont, CA: Wadsworth Cengage Learning.

Ortega, L. (2009). *Understanding second language acquisition.* London, UK: Hodder Education.

Oxford, R. (1990). *Language learning strategies: What every teacher should know.* New York, NY: Newbury House.

Oxford, R. (1992/1993). Language learning strategies in a nutshell: Update and ESL suggestions. *TESOL Journal, 2*(2), 18–22.

Paradis, J., Crago, M., Genesee, F., & Rice, M. (2003). French–English bilingual children with SLI: How do they compare with their monolingual peers? *Journal of Speech, Language, and Hearing Research, 46*(1), 113–127.

Paradis, J., Genesee, F., & Crago, M. (2011). *Dual language development and disorders: A handbook on bilingualism and second language learning* (2nd ed.). Baltimore, MD: Brookes.

Piccardo, E. (2014). *From communicative to action-oriented: A research pathway.* Retrieved from Curriculum Services Canada http://www.curriculum.org/storage/241/1408622981/TAGGED_DOCUMENT_%28CSC605_Research_Guide_English%29_01.pdf

Popham, W. J. (2016). *Classroom assessment: What teachers need to know* (8th ed.). Boston, MA: Pearson.

Rehorick, S. (1995). Principals in practice in supervising in immersion classroom. *Journal de l'Immersion, 18*(3), 21–27.

Richards, J. C., & Lockhart, C. (1994). *Reflective teaching in second language classrooms.* New York, NY: Cambridge University Press.

Richards, M., & Burnaby, B. (2008). Restoring Aboriginal languages: Immersion and intensive language program models in Canada. In T. W. Fortune & D. J. Tedick (Eds.), *Pathways to multilingualism: Evolving perspectives on immersion education* (pp. 202–221). Clevedon, UK: Multilingual Matters.

Rivard, L., Dilk, S., & Barnabé, G. (2007). Étude comparative des competences grammaticales d'élèves du secondaire en FL1 et en FL2 au Manitoba. *Canadian Modern Language Review/La Revue canadienne des langues vivantes, 63*(4), 487–516.

Rose, D. H., & Meyer, A. (2002). *Teaching every student in the digital age: Universal design for learning.* Alexandria, VA: ASCD.

Rubin, J. (1987). Learner strategies: Theoretical assumptions, research history and typology. In A. Wenden & J. Rubin (Eds.), *Learner strategies and language learning* (pp. 15–29). Englewood Cliffs, NJ: Prentice Hall.

Rubin, J., & Thompson, I. (1994). *How to be a more successful language learner* (2nd ed.). Belmont, CA: Heinle Cengage.

Séror, J. (2012). Show me! Enhanced feedback through screencasting technology. *TESL Canada Journal/Revue TESL du Canada, 30*(1), 104–116.

Skutnabb-Kangas, T. (2000). *Linguistic genocide in education—or worldwide diversity and human rights?* Mahwah, NJ: Lawrence Erlbaum.

Snow, M. A. (1989). *Negotiation of meaning in the immersion classroom.* Unpublished manuscript, Office of Instruction and Program Development, Montgomery County Public Schools, Rockville, MD.

Souers, K., & Hall, P. (2016). *Fostering resilient learners. Strategies for creating a trauma-sensitive classroom.* Alexandria, VA: ASCD.

Stanovich, P., & Jordan, A. (1998). Canadian teachers' and principals' beliefs about inclusive education as predictors of effective teaching in heterogeneous classrooms. *Elementary School Journal, 98*(3), 221–238.

Statistics Canada. (2011). *Immigration and ethnocultural diversity in Canada* (Catalogue No. 99-010-X2011001). Retrieved from https://www12.statcan.gc.ca/nhs-enm/2011/as-sa/99-010-x/99-010-x2011001-eng.cfm

Stewart, J. (2011). *Supporting refugee children: Strategies for educators.* Toronto, ON: University of Toronto Press.

Storch, N. (1998). A classroom-based study: Insights from a collaborative text reconstruction task. *ELT Journal, 52*(4), 291–300.

Storch, N. (2001). How collaborative is pair work? ESL tertiary students composing in pairs. *Language Teaching Research, 5*(1), 29–53.

Storch, N. (2002). Patterns of interaction in ESL pair work. *Language Learning, 52*(1), 119–158.

Swain, M., & Lapkin, S. (1982). *Evaluating bilingual education: A Canadian case study.* Clevedon, UK: Multilingual Matters.

Swain, M., Lapkin, S., Rowen, N., & Hart, D. (1990). The role of mother tongue literacy in third language learning. *Language, Culture and Curriculum, 3*(1), 65–81.

Thomas, J. (1988). The role played by metalinguistic awareness in second and third language learning. *Journal of Multilingual and Multicultural Development, 9*(3), 235–246.

Tierney, R. J., & Pearson, P. D. (1983). Toward a composing model of reading. *Language Arts, 60*(5), 568–580.

Ting-Toomey, S. (1999). *Communicating across cultures.* New York, NY: Guilford Press.

Tomlinson, C. A. (1999). *The differentiated classroom: Responding to the needs of all learners.* Alexandria, VA: ASCD.

Tomlinson, C. A. (2001). *How to differentiate instruction in mixed-ability classrooms* (2nd ed.). Alexandria, VA: ASCD.

Tomlinson, C. A. (2014). *The differentiated classroom* (2nd ed.). Alexandria, VA: ASCD.

Tomlinson, C. A., & Imbeau, M. B. (2010). *Leading and managing a differentiated classroom.* Alexandria, VA: ASCD.

Trites, R. L., & Price, M. A. (1976). *Learning disabilities found in association with French immersion programming.* Ottawa, ON: University of Ottawa Press.

Trites, R. L., & Price, M. A. (1977). *Learning disabilities found in association with French immersion programming: A cross-validation.* Ottawa, ON: University of Ottawa Press.

Turnbull, M., Lapkin, S., & Hart, D. (2001). Grade 3 immersion students' performance in literacy and mathematics: Province-wide results from Ontario (1998–99). *Canadian Modern Language Review, 58*(1), 9–26.

Turnbull, M., Lapkin, S., Hart, D., & Swain, M. (1998). Time on task and immersion graduates' French proficiency. In S. Lapkin (Ed.), *French second language education in Canada: Empirical studies* (pp. 31–55). Toronto, ON: University of Toronto Press.

Valle, J., & Connor, D. (2010). *Rethinking disability: A disability studies approach to inclusive practices.* New York, NY: McGraw-Hill Education.

Vandergrift, L. (1999). Facilitating second language listening comprehension: Acquiring successful strategies. *ELT Journal, 53*(3), 168–176.

VanPatten, B., & Williams, J. (2007). *Theories in second language acquisition.* Mahwah, NJ: Erlbaum.

Waterhouse, L. (2006). Multiple intelligences, the Mozart effect, and emotional intelligence: A critical review. *Educational Psychologist, 41*(4), 201–225.

Weissberg, R. (2006). *Connecting speaking & writing in second language writing instruction.* Ann Arbor, MI: University of Michigan Press.

Wesche, M. (1981). Language aptitude measures in streaming, matching students with methods, and diagnosis of learning problems. In K. Diller (Ed.), *Individual differences and universals in language learning aptitude* (pp. 119–139). Rowley, MA: Newbury House.

Wessels, S. (2012). *The importance of activating and building knowledge* (Department of Teaching, Learning and Teacher Education Faculty Publication No. 145). Retrieved from University of Nebraska—Lincoln http://digitalcommons.unl.edu/teachlearnfacpub/145

Wiggins, G., & McTighe, J. (2005). *Understanding by design.* Alexandria, VA: ASCD.

Wiliam, D., & Leahy, S. (2015). *Embedding formative assessment: Practical techniques for K–12 classrooms.* West Palm Beach, FL: Learning Sciences International.

Wise, N. (2011). Access to special education for exceptional students in French immersion programs: An equity issue. *Canadian Journal of Applied Linguistics, 14*(2), 177–193.

Wise, N., & Chen, X. (2010). At-risk readers in French immersion: Early identification and early intervention. *Canadian Journal of Applied Linguistics, 13*(2), 128–149.

Wiss, C. (1987). Issues in the assessment of learning problems in children from French immersion programs: A case study illustration in support of Cummins. *Canadian Modern Language Review, 43*(3), 302–313.

Wiss, C. (1989). Early immersion programs may not be suitable for every child. *Canadian Modern Language Review, 45*(5), 517–529.

Woolfolk, A. E. (2012). *Educational psychology* (12th ed.). Boston, MA: Allyn and Bacon.

Wright, W. E. (2015). *Foundations for teaching English language learners: Research, theory, policy, and practice* (2nd ed.). Philadelphia, PA: Caslon.

Zwiers, J. (2014). *Building academic language: Meeting Common Core Standards across disciplines, grades 5–12.* San Francisco, CA: Jossey-Bass.

Index

C

D

H

I

J

K

L

Q

R

S

T

U

V

W

X

Credits

4: Excerpt from Valle, J., & Connor, D. (2010). *Rethinking disability: A disability studies approach to inclusive practices* (p. 207). New York, NY: McGraw-Hill Education; **7:** Excerpt from Naiman, N., Frölich, M., Stern, H. H., & Todesco, A. (1996). *The good language learner* (p. ix). Bristol, UK: Multilingual Matter; **18:** Excerpts from Baker, C. (2011). *Foundations of bilingual education and bilingualism.* Bristol, UK: Multilingual Matters; **19:** Excerpt from Genesee, F. (2007). Literacy outcomes in French immersion. *Encyclopedia of language and literacy development* (pp. 1–8). London, ON: Canadian Language and Literacy Research Network; **19, 20, 21:** Excerpts from Genesee, F., Paradis, J., & Crago, M. (2004). *Dual language development and disorders: A handbook on bilingualism and second language learning.* Baltimore, MD: Paul H. Brookes; **20:** Excerpt from Dicks, J., & Kristmanson, P. (2008). French immersion: When and why? In *The state of French-second-language education in Canada* (p. 16). Ottawa, ON: Canadian Parents for French; **22:** Excerpt from Bruck, 1987, p. 65 as cited in Genesee, F. (1992). Second/foreign language immersion and at-risk English-speaking children. *Foreign Language Annals, 25*(3), p. 205; **22:** Excerpt from Paradis, J., Crago, M., Genesee, F., and Rice, M. (2003). French–English bilingual children with SLI: How do they compare with their monolingual peers? *Journal of Speech, Language, and Hearing Research 46*(1), 113–127. https://www.researchgate.net/publication/10846341_French-English_bilingual_children_with_SLI_How_do_they_compare_with_their_monolingual_peers; **24:** Excerpt from Cenoz, J. (2003). The additive effect of bilingualism on third language acquisition: A review. *International Journal of Bilingualism, 7*(1), pp. 71–87; **24:** Excerpt from Cenoz, J., & Hoffman, C. (Eds.). (2003). The effect of bilingualism on third language acquisition [Special issue]. *International Journal of Bilingualism, 7*(1), p. 6; **30–31:** Figure based on Krashen, S., & Terrell, T. (1983). *The natural approach: Language acquisition in the classroom.* Hayward, CA: Alemany Press; **33:** Figure based on Wright, W. E. (2015). *Foundations for teaching English language learners: Research, theory, policy, and practice* (2nd ed.). Philadelphia, PA: Caslon Publishing; **37:** Symbols by Julie Miryash/Shutterstock; **44:** Excerpt from Moll, L. C., Amanti, C., Neff, D., & Gonzalez, N. (1992). Funds of knowledge for teaching: Using a qualitative approach to connect homes and classrooms. *Theory into Practice, (31)*2, 132–141; **68, 75, 123 (top), 134, 149, 155, 164, 171, 174:** Illustrations by David Cheung; **74:** Photo (top) Image Source Salsa/Alamy; (bottom) Hero Images Inc./Alamy; **85:** Excerpt from Rose, D. H., & Meyer, A. (2002). *Teaching every student in the digital age: Universal design for learning.* Alexandria, VA: ASCD Press, as cited in Eagleton, M. (2008). Universal design for learning. *EBSCO Research Starters: Academic topic overviews*, p. 1. https://www.ebscohost.com/uploads/imported/thisTopic-dbTopic-1073.pdf; **95, 183:** Illustrations by Crowle Art Group; **126:** Photo by Renée Bourgoin; **160:** Photo by Bogdan Wankowicz/Fotolia; **163:** Photo by Myrleen Pearson/Alamy; **166:** Photo by Julie Beyea; **216:** Figure based on Lyster, R., & Ranta, L. (1997). Corrective feedback and learner uptake: Negotiation of form in communicative classrooms. *Studies in Second Language Acquisition, 19*(1), pp. 37–66; **226:** Excerpts from Séror, J. (2012). Show me! Enhanced feedback through screencasting technology. *TESL Canada Journal/Revue TESL du Canada, 30*(1), 104–116; **253:** Excerpt from Fraser, G. (2012, June). Key note address. *Proceedings of the Canadian Parents for French roundtable on academically challenged students in French-second-language programs.* Ottawa, ON: Canadian Parents for French.